SHEFFIELD HALLAM UNIVERSITY
LEARNING CENTRE
CITY CAMPUS, POND STREET,
SHEFFIELD, S1 1WB.

101 557 535 8

ONE WEEK LOAN

- 6 NOV 2001

19 NOV 2001

12 APR 2002

2 4 OCT 2002
31 OCT 2002
11 NOV 2002

- 5 NOV 2004

- 3 NOV 2003

- 7 JAN 2005

2 8 APR 2010

D1380351

LEARNING CENTRE
WITHDRAWN FROM STOCK

From the Earth Summit to Local Agenda 21

Working Towards Sustainable Development

Edited by William M. Lafferty and Katarina Eckerberg

Earthscan Publications Ltd, London

First published in the UK in 1998 by
Earthscan Publications Limited

Copyright © Program for Research and Documentation for a Sustainable Society
(ProSus), 1998

All rights reserved

A catalogue record for this book is available from the British Library

ISBN: 1 85383 547 1

Typesetting by PCS Mapping & DTP, Newcastle upon Tyne
Printed and bound by Biddles Ltd, Guildford and Kings Lynn
Cover design by Andrew Corbett

For a full list of publications please contact:

Earthscan Publications Limited
120 Pentonville Road
London N1 9JN
Tel: (0171) 278 0433
Fax: (0171) 278 1142
Email: earthinfo@earthscan.co.uk
http://www.earthscan.co.uk

Earthscan is an editorially independent subsidiary of Kogan Page Limited and
publishes in association with WWF-UK and the International Institute for
Environment and Development.

Contents

Notes on Contributors

Carlo Aall received a graduate degreee (cand.agric.) in 1987 from The Norwegian University of Agriculture. He has also worked as an environmental officer for the municipality of Ølen (1988-90). Employed as a researcher since 1991 at The Western Norway Research Institute in Sogndal, he is now doing a PhD on Municipal Environmental Policy at the University of Ålborg. He has recently published numerous reports in Norwegian on the 'Eco-municipality Program' and 'Environmental auditing in Norwegian municipalities'.

Christiane Beuermann is an economist by profession. Currently working at the Climate Policy Division of the Wuppertal Institute for Climate, Environment and Energy in Wuppertal, Germany, her main areas of research are international and German climate policy, institutional adjustments and social-learning processes in response to the issues of climate change and sustainable development. Recently published articles deal with the sustainability transition, its chances and impediments in Germany, as well as with the implementation of Chapter 28 of Agenda 21 in Germany.

Frans H.J.M. Coenen holds a Masters' degree in Public Administration and a PhD in Environmental Policy Planning. He is currently a Researcher at the Centre for Clean Technology and Environmental Policy (CSTM) which is an interfaculty institute for environmental studies at the University of Twente. He publishes and lectures in the fields of planning, environmental policy and evaluation research, and among his most recent publications is *The effectiveness of municipal environmental policy planning* (1996, CSTM report series).

Katarina Eckerberg is Associate Professor at the Department of Political Science, Umeå University. Her research and lecturing focus on environmental politics and policy, including comparative international studies. Her most recent publications include *Environmental Protection in Swedish Forestry* (Avebury, 1990); *Process and Policy Evaluation in Structure Planning* (Swedish Council for Building Research, 1993); and *Comparing Nordic and Baltic Countries – Environmental Problems and Policies in Agriculture and Forestry* (Nordic Council of Ministers, 1995). She also holds the Chair of the Umeå School of Environmental Studies, a collaboration between Umeå University and the Swedish University of Agricultural Sciences in Umeå.

Björn Forsberg is a doctoral student at the Department of Political Science, Umeå University. He is currently writing his dissertation on the LA21 process in Sweden, with special emphasis on emerging tendencies at local level which – given that sustainable development implies fundamental re-orientations in environmental, social and economic values — indicate a potential conflict between a traditional and a new paradigm.

William M. Lafferty is Professor of Political Science at the University of Oslo and Director of the Program for Research and Documentation for a Sustainable Society (ProSus) within the Research Council of Norway. He is currently a member of the Executive Committee of the International Political Association (IPSA), and member of the Governing Council of the Norwegian Helsinki Committee for Human Rights. His most recent publications include *Democracy and the Environment* (1996, Edward Elgar: with James Meadowcroft) and *The Pursuit of Sustainable Development* (forthcoming, Macmillan: with Oluf Langhelle).

Ger Mullally is a Research Fellow at the Centre for European Social Research (CESR), University College, Cork. He has been involved in several pan-European research projects on environmental policy and politics since 1992. These include 'Framing and Communicating Environmental Issues', 'Extended Producer Responsibility for Complex Products' and a comparative project on the politics of sustainable mobility in Europe. He is currently completing his PhD dissertation on 'A Cognitive Re-construction of Irish Environmentalism' at the Department of Sociology, University College Cork. His most recent publication is 'Relocating Protest: Environmental Social Movement Organisations in Late Twentieth Century Ireland' (in Mario Diani (ed.), *Movement Organisations in the Information Society: A Comparative Analysis of Environmental Groups in Five West European Countries*, forthcoming).

Anita Niemi-Iilahti is Associate Professor of Public Administration at the Department of Administrative Sciences, University of Vaasa, Finland, and Chair of the Finnish Association for Local-Government Studies. Her teaching and research are in the areas of comparative (Nordic) local government, including policy, organisation and reforms, and environmental policy implementation, particularly within the fields of agri-environmental policy and Agenda 21.

Otto Schütz has his graduate degree in Agronomy from the University for Agriculture, Forestry and Renewable Natural Resources (BOKU) in Vienna, and has studied at the University of Minnesota, St. Paul. He has worked in horticultural and agricultural businesses in Hungary, Austria, and the USA, and, since 1994, is a Research Fellow at the Austrian Association for Agricultural Research (OEVAF). He is currently involved in conducting and co-ordinating interdisciplinary research in the field of sustainable agricultural production and closed-cycle economies.

Per Wickenberg (BA/MA) was previously a teacher in Sweden, and is now a doctoral student and Research Fellow in the Sociology of Law at Lund University. Currently working with Professor Håkan Hydén within the national research program on 'Paths to Sustainable Development – Behavior, Organizations, Structures', his most recent publications include (in Swedish) 'Forward to the Basics. A book for Inspiration about Environment for Teachers and other Future Workers' (1994, Liber Utbildning: with Bodil Jönsson), and 'Environmental Education in Schools and Agenda 21 with the Municipality as an Arena: A Case Study'(1996, National Agency for Education: with H. Axelsson, and C. Malmberg).

Stephen Young is Senior Lecturer in the Government Department at the University of Manchester. He is joint editor of *Environmental Politics* and of the Routledge series 'Issues in Environmental Politics'. His recent publications include *Cities in the 1990s* (1993, Longman: with Gerry Stoker); *The Politics of the Environment* (1993, Baseline Books); and articles/chapters on local government, participation, wildlife and environmental issues. He has recently completed a project on the participatory aspects of Local Agenda 21 for the Economic and Social Research Council of the UK (ESRC).

List of Abbreviations and Acronyms

BBU	Federal Association of Environmental Action Groups (Germany)
BLG	Program for Reform of Local Government (Ireland)
BMBau	Federal Ministry of Urban Development (Germany)
BMF	Federal Ministry of Finances (Germany)
BMI	Federal Ministry of the Interior (Germany)
BML	Federal Ministry of Agriculture (Germany)
BMU	Federal Ministry of the Environment (Germany)
BMV	Federal Ministry of Transport (Germany)
BMWi	Federal Ministry of Economics (Germany)
BOVAG	Association of Garages (The Netherlands)
BUGM	Program for Funding of Municipal Environmental Policy (The Netherlands)
CAF	Clearing House for Applied Futures (Germany)
CCMA	City and Council Managers Association (Ireland)
CEG	Community and Enterprise Group (Ireland)
CEMR	Council of European Municipalities and Regions
CHP	Combined heat and power
COS	Regional Centres for Development Co-operation (The Netherlands)
CPG	Corporate Policy Group (Ireland)
CSD	Commission for Sustainable Development
CSERGE	Centre for Social and Economic Research on the Global Environment (UK)
CSTM	Centre for Clean Technology and Environmental Policy (The Netherlands)
CWC	Community Workers' Co-operative (Ireland)
D66	Dutch political party (Left)
DIFU	German Institute for Urban Studies
DoE	Department of the Environment
DPCSD	UN Department for Policy Co-ordination for Sustainable Development
DSt	The German Association of Cities
DSTGB	German Association for Cities and Communities
ECOSOC	United Nations Economic and Social Council
ECP	Environmental Cities Program (Norway)
EE	Environmental Education
EEC	European Economic Community

EIA	Environmental Impact Assessment
ENSI	Environment and School Initiatives
EPA	Environmental Protection Agency
EPIM	Environmental Protection in the Municipalities (Norway)
EU	European Union
FCCC	Framework Convention on Climate Change
FNCA	Finnish Nature Conservation Association
FoE-F	Friends of the Earth - Finland
FONØ	Forum for Eco-municipalities in Norway
FUN	Program for Funding of National Environmental Policy (The Netherlands)
GAP	Global Action Programme
GG	The German Constitution
ICLEI	International Council for Local Environmental Initiatives
IISD	International Institute for Sustainable Development
IKV	Inter-Church Peace Platform (The Netherlands)
IPA	Institute of Public Administration (Ireland)
IUCN	The World Conservation Union
IULA	International Union of Local Authorities
JAPL	Joint Action between Public and Local Resources (Norway)
JUP	Youth Environmental Plan (Austria)
KS	Norwegian Association for Local and Regional Authorities
LGMB	Local Government Management Board (UK)
LGO	Local Government Organisation
LOTA	Municipal 'Platform' Against Apartheid (The Netherlands)
MIK	Environmental Protection in the Municipalities (Norway)
MoE	Ministry of the Environment
N&E	Nature and Environment (Finland)
NCO	Third-world aid/solidarity organisation (The Netherlands)
NEPA	National Environmental Protection Agency (Sweden)
NEPP	National Environmental Policy Plan (The Netherlands)
NESF	National Economic and Social Forum (Ireland)
NFDA	National Forum on Development Aid (Ireland)
NIEDO	Network of Irish Environment and Development Organisations
NOVIB	Third-world aid/solidarity organisation (The Netherlands)
NRW	Government of North Rhine/Westphalia
NUP	National Environmental Plan (Austria)
OCF	Our Common Future (The Brundtland Report)
ODA	Overseas Development Aid
OECD	Organisation for Economic Co-operation and Development
ÖTV	Labour Union for Civil Services and Transport (Germany)

PDO	Dutch Program ('Platform') for Sustainable Development
ProSus	Program for Research and Documentation for a Sustainable Society
PVDA	Dutch political party (Left)
q2000	Swedish network of NGO's and activists for monitoring the Rio accords
RCEP	Royal Commission on Environmental Planning (UK)
SALA	Swedish Association of Local Authorities
SCOPE	Scientific Committee on Problems of the Environment
SFT	Norwegian Pollution Control Authority
SMI	Strategic Management Initiative (Ireland)
SPC	Strategic Policy Committee (Ireland)
SPD	The Social Democratic Party (Germany)
SRB	Single Regeneration Budget (UK)
SSCN	Swedish Society for the Conservation of Nature
UBA	Federal Environmental Protection Agency (Germany, Austria)
UDP	Unitary Development Plan
UNCED	United Nations Conference on Environment and Development
UNCSD	UN Commission for Sustainable Development
UNDP	United Nations Development Program
UNDPCSD	UN Department for Policy Co-ordination for Sustainable Development
UNESCO	United Nations Educational, Scientific and Cultural Organization
UNEP	United Nations Environment Program
UNGASS	UN General Assembly Special Session ('Earth Summit +5')
VNG	Dutch Association of Local Authorities
VOGM	Program for Further Support of Municipal Environmental Policy (The Netherlands)
VVD	Dutch political party (Right)
WCED	The World Commission on Environment and Development
WHO	World Health Organisation
WWF	Worldwide Fund For Nature

Foreword

Agenda 21 must be local if it is to be anything at all. Only by widespread citizen involvement can we hope to make the lifestyle changes which alone make sustainable development possible. Yet it cannot be *only* local. There needs to be a national and regional framework in which the local agendas can benefit from a wider view and themselves contribute to the wider pattern. It is that which makes this book so important and so interesting. It chronicles in a lively yet expert fashion the working of Agenda 21 across Europe.

As so often, the reader is struck by the similarities in European experiences and also by the diversity of response. Europe should celebrate its unity and its strength more often in this way. We can learn so much from each other. We live within a common context so that our differences are not just a matter of curiosity but instead illuminate the issues and the comparisons which lead to practical suggestions.

The shortage of resource, the difficulty of involvement, and the size of the task are all common problems. The diversity of the response to those common problems is exhilarating and enormously encouraging. The contributors' business-like approach does not prevent shafts of humour and practicality illuminating the text. This is essential reading for all those who want to see that what they do, in rising to the challenge of Rio, draws properly on the experience of others and therefore makes their contribution all the more effective.

Rt Hon John Gummer MP
April 1998

Preface

The present collection of Studies of Local Agenda 21 in Europe is the result of a research network initiated by the editors in 1995. The network began as an interchange of information on LA21 developments in Sweden and Norway, but was rapidly expanded to include other researchers in Finland, the Netherlands, Great Britain and Germany. By the end of 1996, the network had grown to include representatives from Ireland, Denmark, Italy, Austria and Spain. The representatives from Denmark, Italy and Spain were contacted too late to prepare draft chapters for this initial report, but will be working within the network in the succeeding stages of the project.

The purpose of the current volume is to present initial descriptive reports on the manner by which the idea of Local Agenda 21 has been received and subsequently pursued in the countries in question. On the basis of two preliminary meetings (Oslo in March and Lund in June of 1996), it was decided to proceed directly to descriptive reporting rather than to wait for the development of a more analytic comparative framework. This was followed up by a workshop in Twente in January of 1997, where the original draft chapters were presented and the list of countries finalized.

Our decision to proceed directly to a descriptive presentation was motivated by a felt need for more systematic documentation as a basis for further conceptual and analytic development. It was also felt that it would be a major advantage for the project to publish the studies in time for the United Nations' follow-up conference to the Rio Earth Summit in 1992 ('Earth Summit + 5', New York, June 23-27 1997). This Special Session of the UN General Assembly is specifically devoted to an assessment of Agenda 21, and the research team felt that it would be of vital importance to solicit reactions to the descriptive reports at this crucial juncture in the development of the UNCED programme. The introductory and concluding chapters are written wth this in mind; that is we have tried to keep them relatively free from academic jargon and scientific frameworks so as to generate as much feedback as possible on the country perspectives.

This does not mean, however, that the report lacks a scientific orientation. We have adopted a standardized research protocol for reporting on implementation activities; we have conducted independent surveys, pilot projects and field studies in the different countries; and we have introduced, through our network dialogues, a number of highly relevant analytic dimensions. Even though the latter are somewhat 'subliminal', they provide a foundation and point of departure for more focused data-gathering and in-depth analysis. Furthermore, we have made specific attempts to clarify the conceptual and operational distinctions related to the idea of 'Local Agenda 21', and to distinguish these from the monitoring perspectives of both national governments and international bodies. It is in this connection – that is, with reference to problems of assessment and policy evaluation – that we view the most immediate scientific cutting-edge of the project.

As to the sample of countries, it is important to stress that the selection is not based on a comparative research design but on the availability of researchers working in this general area. Seven of the eight countries are decidedly North European, and Austria only somewhat less so. The very obvious lack of cases from Southern, Central and Eastern Europe, will be compensated for in the later stages of the project (with Italy and Spain already included in the research network). Since our funding thus far has consisted only of administrative and travel resources, we have not been able to engage researchers on other than a voluntary basis. Having said this, however, we would also like to point out that there are numerous questions of comparative research interest within the sample domain. Differences between large and small democracies; between confederated and unitary political systems; between 'consociational', pluralist and corporate-pluralist systems of group integration; and between older, newer, and non-members of the European Union – all present interesting analytic opportunities.

These prospects will be further developed in the later stages of the project. For now, however, it is important to focus on what we feel has been accomplished, namely to present eight extremely interesting and different cases of LA21 implementation. More than anything, the studies document the effects of national configurations of constituional, institutional, cultural and political factors on international policy implementation. It is the relative uniqueness of each case which is the major story here; a uniqueness which stands as both hindrance and help for a more effective realisation of the UNCED program for sustainable development.

William M. Lafferty and Katarina Eckerberg

Acknowledgements

As with any project involving eight countries and eleven researchers, there are a number of people and institutions which warrant a special thanks for their efforts and support. First of all, there is the research team itself which has responded to the challenge of producing a report on very short notice. Since there was no money available for either 'buy outs' or research assistance, everyone had to contribute what they could within their normal working conditions. We are grateful to the institutions involved for the separate contributions in time and money in each case.

Extra support for the three workshops was received from the Norwegian Ministry of the Environment for the Oslo meeting; the University of Lund (Department of Sociology) and The Swedish Council for Planning and Co-ordination of Research (FRN) for the meeting in Lund; and the Centre for Clean Technology and Environmental Policy (CSTM) at the University of Twente for the Twente workshop. William M. Lafferty and Katarina Eckerberg were responsible for organising the meeting in Oslo; Håkan Hyden and Per Wickenberg for the meeting in Lund, and Hans Bressers and Frans Coenen for the workshop in Twente.

Mette Samsing of ProSus has had responsibility for the technical preparation and lay-out of the manuscript, and Mari Holmboe Ruge has proofed and commented on the entire text.

Finally, a special thanks is due to the Ministry of the Environment in Norway and to the Swedish Council for Planning and Co-ordination of Research (FRN) in Sweden, for grants in support of publication costs. Without these grants, it would not have been possible to push for publication in time for the UN General Assembly session on 'Earth Summit +5'.

1. Introduction:
The Nature and Purpose of 'Local Agenda 21'

William M. Lafferty and Katarina Eckerberg

> *Humanity stands at a defining moment in history. We are confronted with a perpetuation of disparities between and within nations, a worsening of poverty, hunger, ill health and illiteracy, and the continuing deterioration of the ecosystems on which we depend for our well-being. However, integration of environment and development concerns and greater attention to them will lead to the fulfilment of basic needs, improved living standards for all, better protected and managed ecosystems and a safer, more prosperous future. No nation can achieve this on its own; but together we can – in a global partnership for sustainable development. Agenda 21, Preamble, Section 1.1.*

One of the most characteristic features of the UNCED process is the goal of bringing together key social actors for joint co-operative efforts on vital issues of environment and development. The entire Section III of the Rio 'action plan' – Agenda 21 – is devoted to 'strengthening the role of major groups'. The action plan itself builds on the premise that the achievement of sustainable development requires new forms of social learning, whereby major collective actors seek to resolve potential conflicts on environment-and-development issues through new forms of involvement and co-operation. Chapter 28 of the Agenda is devoted to one of the most important of these actors: local political authorities. The Agenda outlines the rationale for action in this area as follows:

> *Because so many of the problems and solutions being addressed by Agenda 21 have their roots in local activities, the participation and co-operation of local authorities will be a determining factor in fulfilling its objectives. Local authorities construct, operate and maintain economic, social and environmental infrastructure, oversee planning processes, establish local environmental policies and regulations, and assist in implementing national and subnational environmental policies. As the level of governance closest to the people, they play a vital role in educating, mobilising and responding to the public to promote sustainable development. (United Nations, 1993: Agenda 21, Section 28.1)*

It is thus a key role of local authorities to take responsibility for introducing, interpreting, adapting and eventually implementing the most relevant aspects of Agenda 21 for their local communities. This clearly does not mean that local initiatives are to be 'governed' by the authorities themselves, nor does it imply that national governments do not have a responsibility for guiding and assisting local authorities in the development of effective local programs. At both the national and local levels of governance, it is assumed that the role of authorities with respect to 'major groups' is to employ the powers and resources of government in such a way as to facilitate co-operation and co-ordinated action. It is the instrumental effect of the co-operation and co-ordination itself which is the goal, and it is the intention of Chapter 28 to focus the responsibility of local authorities for pursuing the goal through dialogue and public assistance.

The underlying facilitating and mobilising intent of Chapter 28 is also manifest in its exceptional brevity. With the exception of two 'preamble' chapters (1 and 23), Chapter 28 is the shortest chapter of the entire action plan. (Reprinted in its entirety here as Appendix 1.) This brevity should not be interpreted, however, as either a lower priority or an intended lack of substance. To the contrary. Anyone familiar with the UNCED process, both prior to and at the Earth Summit itself, knows that a need for increased local activity was a major theme throughout. The lack of specifics in Chapter 28 primarily reflects the considerable variation in central-local authority domains across the member states, as well as the wide diversity in specific types of local and regional authority within the member states. The challenge facing the drafters of the chapter was thus to place it firmly on (within) the Agenda in a manner which did not seem to presuppose any one form of local government, or any one type of specific local issue.

In trying to meet this particular challenge of 'nonsubstantive instrumentality', the chapter stipulates only four specific 'objectives':

a) By 1996, most local authorities in each country should have undertaken a consultative process with their populations and achieved a
   consensus on 'a local Agenda 21' for the community;
b) By 1993, the international community should have initiated a
   consultative process aimed at increasing co-operation between local
   authorities;
c) By 1994, representatives of associations of cities and other local
   authorities should have increased levels of co-operation and co-
   ordination with the goal of enhancing the exchange of information
   and experience among local authorities;
d) All local authorities in each country should be encouraged to implement and monitor programmes which aim at ensuring that women
   and youth are represented in decision-making, planning and implementation processes. (United Nations, 1993: Agenda 21, Section
   28.2)

Here we see that, with the exception of securing the involvement of
'women and youth', the objectives of the plan are primarily procedural,
but, in contrast to many of the other chapters of the Agenda, they are quite
specifically procedural. They stipulate specific dates for specific types of
activities, providing thereby benchmarks for follow-up and assessment. It
is of key importance for the entire discussion of implementation and
assessment, however, that we note that the initial objective – calling for a
consensus on a 'local Agenda 21' – is without further specification as to
what 'a local Agenda 21' actually consists of. This can, again, be interpreted as omission by design: rather than trying to outline in detail the
content areas of a preordained plan or program, the chapter leaves this
open. The message is (as clearly indicated in the chapter's section on
'activities') that it is up to the local authorities to take responsibility for
initiating and co-ordinating the dialogue among 'citizens, local organisations and private enterprises' which is necessary to determine *the form
and content of their specific Local Agenda 21 initiative*.

At its most ambitious level, therefore, the task of implementing
Chapter 28 is one of interpreting and 'relativising' Agenda 21 to suit local
conditions and problems. The task should not be misconstrued as having
to adapt to and apply a pre-determined program or plan. As the present
collection of country reports indicates, this type of interpretation has, in
fact, served to deter a more positive and active approach to the idea of
'Local Agenda 21'. The underlying logic of the implementation problem
(what Sabatier (1986) refers to as the 'adequate causal theory') implies, in
this case, a process whereby *local authorities function as responsible
disseminators and facilitators of the Local Agenda 21 idea*. The process
requires subsequent phases of : (1) information and consciousness-raising;

(2) interpretation and relativization of Agenda 21 to local conditions and problems; (3) development of priorities and local action plans with both general and sector-specific targets; (4) determination of appropriate steering instruments, including most specifically the procurement of voluntary agreements among sector-relevant social actors ('target groups'); (5) integration of plans and priorities into public budgets and the mobilisation of other necessary resources; (6) the implementation process itself; (7) monitoring and evaluation (of both the enactment process and its effects); and (8) revision of goals, plans and initiatives.

It is important to emphasise that a list of this type (which is in any case merely suggestive) is designed to capture the general logic of the implementation task and not to express any kind of 'necessary' procedure. The 'adequacy' of the 'causal theory' in question refers to the implied instrumentality for a successful realisation of the policy intent. It is an expression of underlying general assumptions as to what is most probably necessary to achieve the policy goals in question. In the case of Chapter 28, the goals are the process itself, i.e. *the process deemed necessary to bring Agenda 21 down to the level of most immediate impact on citizens*, organisations and business. It must be assumed that local communities will vary considerably with respect to which aspects of the action plan are most relevant for moving the community towards more sustainable development. Conditions of regional location, geography, demography, and, most importantly, the nature of the local economy, will all affect interpretation and application of the plan.

CRITERIA FOR MONITORING AND REPORTING

The goal of the current effort has thus been to gather information and analyse the activities in the different countries in a manner which is both systematic and open. We wanted to lay a foundation for further conceptual and theoretical work, but we did not want to channel the process into such a narrow set of categories as to suppress important national characteristics and innovations. Building on the joint discussions in the project, the following 'protocol' of descriptive categories has been adopted as a basic monitoring framework:

1. *Baseline conditions:* What are the existing 'baseline' conditions for integrating environmental concerns at the local level of government (that is prior to Agenda 21)? What reforms, social experiments and environmental policies were in place for local government at the time of Rio, and how did these contextual conditions affect the introduction and implementation of the LA21 idea?

2. *Antecedent role in UNCED:* What role (if any) did representatives of
   the central government and/or organisations of local authorities play
   in developing the Local Agenda 21 initiative during the run-up to the
   UN Conference on Environment and Development?
3. *Government reaction:* How did central government (the legislature
   and responsible ministries/departments) initially react to and interpret the LA21 initiative? What programs, institutional changes,
   strategies, action plans, resource allocations, etc., were initiated?
4. *Local-community reaction:* Were there direct and independent
   reactions and initiatives on the part of individual local communities?
   What was the reaction of national umbrella associations for local
   authorities, and what programs or initiatives have they initiated? To
   what degree have either of these initiatives been integrated with
   central government initiatives?
5. *NGO's and the social partners:* How have leading nongovernmental
   organisations (particularly leading environmental groups, but also
   national organisations for business, labour and farming) reacted to
   and become involved in the LA21 idea? What types of major-group
   co-operation (networks, covenants, charters, negotiations) have been
   brought into play?
6. *Political impact:* Where and how have specific LA21 initiatives
   made the greatest impact? What is the short-term (5-year) prognosis
   for further development and institutionalisation of the LA21 idea?

These issues were to be addressed within a context whereby we stressed
the *essential difference of the LA21 initiative.* Recognising that the Rio
action plan would have to be relativised according to the state of existing
programs and initiatives in each country, we had to determine criteria
which focus on the particularity of the Local Agenda 21 idea. Based on
two existing overviews of the initial reactions and background conditions
for the reception of LA21 in Scandinavia, Germany and Great Britain
(Armann, Hille and Kasin, 1995 and Voisey et al., 1996), and guided by
recent conceptual work on the nature of 'sustainable development'
(Lafferty and Langhelle, 1995), we arrived at an operational set of criteria. To qualify as an initiative reflecting the intentions of Chapter 28, a
'Local Agenda 21' should reflect the following characteristics:

1. A more conscious attempt to relate environmental effects to underlying economic and political *pressures* (which in turn derive from
   political decisions, non-decisions and markets.)
2. A more active effort to relate local issues, decisions and dispositions
   to *global impacts*, both environmentally and with respect to global
   solidarity and justice.

3. A more focused policy for achieving *cross-sectoral integration* of environment-and-development concerns, values and goals in planning, decision-making and policy implementation.
4. Greater efforts to increase *community involvement*, i.e. to bring both average citizens and major stakeholder groups, particularly business and labour unions, into the planning and implementation process with respect to environment-and-development issues.
5. A commitment to define and work with local problems within: (a) a broader ecological and regional framework, as well as (b) a greatly expanded time frame (i.e. over three or more generations).
6. A specific identification with (reference to) the Rio Summit and Agenda 21.

In applying these criteria, we have tried to differentiate between three different types or levels of 'environment-and-development' activity.

The first level refers to policies and initiatives which are primarily designed to either *conserve nature or improve and redress the environment*. They are initiatives which could have been taken prior to the publication of the Brundtland Report, and which are addressed to environmental concerns in a relatively narrow, more technical and more 'natural-science' type of perspective. Such activities are simply referred to as '*environmental initiatives*', and are not presumed to reflect any of the above six characteristics.

The second level refers to policies and initiatives which *specifically refer to the concept of 'sustainable development'* as expressed in the Brundtland Report; or which *use broad concepts such as 'global ecology'* which reflect the concerns of the Brundtland Commission without using the explicit terms and categories of the report itself. Such activities should reflect most or all of criteria 1 through 5 above, and can be referred to as '*initiatives for sustainable development*'. Most of these local initiatives would have been instigated in the period following the publication and dissemination of the Brundtland Report, that is between 1987 and 1992.[1]

Finally, at the third level, are activities which make specific reference to the Rio Summit and/or Agenda 21. Only these activities qualify, in the strict sense of the term, as '*a Local Agenda 21*'. Such activities should reflect all six of the above criteria, and they should do so as a conscious attempt to implement the intentions of Chapter 28 of the Agenda.

It should be stressed that these brief 'guidelines' have been circulated as a sensitising device so as to facilitate a common approach and reporting on Local Agenda 21. The differentiations outlined have proved highly necessary if the different phenomena in question are to be treated in a systematic and meaningful way. Our preliminary analyses revealed that there was *considerable* confusion as to what 'a Local Agenda 21' signifies, particularly on the part of national governments in their reports to the Commission on Sustainable Development. If everything that has to do with either improving the environment or achieving 'sustainability' is to be categorised as a 'Local Agenda 21', there is clearly no way to meaningfully monitor and evaluate the impact of the Rio accords. The major differentiation in this regard is between the first level of more 'traditional' environmental activities, on the one hand, and the second and third levels – both anchored in the broader notion of 'sustainable development' – on the other.

The task of the project is, in other words, an extremely difficult one. We aim to shed light on the implementation of Chapter 28 of Agenda 21, but we must do so in a manner which does not exclude activities which reflect the values and goals of sustainable development, even though they may fail to refer to the Rio documents themselves. Why and how this differentiation comes into play, and the nature of its consequences for sustainable development, is an issue of central importance for the project. While we must, on the one hand, avoid being too demanding with respect to specific references to LA21, we must not, on the other, be so inclusive as to view all reports of traditional environmental activity as LA21 initiatives. The importance of this lies in the fact that, as already indicated, Agenda-21 activity is a broader category of initiative, with a 'deeper', more holistic and more globally interdependent mode of problem definition and goal prescription. Identifying with the UNCED program is in itself an important feature of the way in which the United Nations has been trying to promote a common North/South responsibility for the interconnected problems of environment and development.

DESCRIPTION, EVALUATION AND EXPLANATION

The report should thus be viewed as but the first step in a more long-term research process, where the goal is to move from description through evaluation to explanation. With respect to the current status of policy-implementation research, the project represents a unique opportunity to generate insights of both theoretical and practical relevance.

As a theoretical effort, the project focuses on the relative uniqueness of the UNCED implementation problem within this area of research. The vast majority of implementation studies focus on the national or local level of analysis, placing heavy emphasis on the 'input' as well as the 'output' aspects of the problem. The academic discourse as to different implementation models has moved through an initial stage of 'top-down' perspectives, through a counter-stage of 'bottom-up' perspectives, to the current situation where attempts at synthesis predominate (Sabatier, 1986;

Eckerberg, 1990; Goggin et al., 1990; Kjellberg and Reitan, 1995; Lafferty and Meadowcroft, 1996). The UNCED program involves, however, a process where there has been very little 'input' of a normal political nature (by either political parties or established interest groups), and where the program to be implemented is at once global in scope and comprehensive as to level-specific strategies. The introduction of LA21 initiatives provides, in this light, a unique 'laboratory' type of situation, where a novel and common 'external' stimulus produces reactions and initiatives which clearly challenge existing domain-specific paradigms.

From a more practical perspective, the project will initially highlight (and eventually systematise) specific examples of innovative implementation practices. There are already several initiatives underway for disseminating information on 'best cases' (by, for example, the International Council for Local Environmental Initiatives (ICLEI); the UN Commission for Sustainable Development (UNCSD); and within the program for 'Sustainable Cities and Towns in Europe'). These can be supplemented and developed into a more systematised data-bank for controlled inductive analysis. As the present report documents, the LA21 idea has generated a resurgence in local-community initiatives, with numerous spontaneous efforts to improve social learning and co-operation among both citizens and the 'social partners'.

Along yet another dimension, it can be pointed out that the LA21 idea also represents a highly relevant and specific challenge to the widely discussed (in Europe) 'principle of subsidiarity'. The implementation of the UNCED program must be achieved *within and across* sub-levels of political and administrative jurisdiction. While there are clearly problems of environment-and-development which require supra-national monitoring and regulation, it is the particular goal of LA21 to indicate that those issues which *can* be effectively treated at the lowest level of governance, *should* be treated at that level. It is difficult to imagine a more relevant or consequential focus for exploring the meaning and potential of subsidiarity, within and across the European Union, than through efforts to develop and implement 'Local Agenda 21's'. The current report provides insights into how seven different members of the EU (and one non-member, Norway), react to, interpret and implement a key UNCED initiative. It will be the task of future analysis to explore in greater depth how these policy efforts either complement or are in conflict with both national and EU programs for sustainable development.

Finally, there is the practical relevance of the comparative nature of the project itself. The stimulus from LA21 activities generates variation within and across several levels and domains of analysis. By studying how and why different approaches and initiatives are employed in different settings, we aim, over the longer term, to generate knowledge about the effects of tradition, culture, national and regional identity, national and EU policies, as well as the consequences of different 'mixes' of steering strategies: regulatory, economic, normative and co-operative. An initial attempt at systematising the material cross-nationally is presented in the concluding chapter (using, at this stage, more intuitive descriptive categories), but further studies will deepen the deepen the explanatory analysis along a number of different dimensions. We will be increasing the number of cases to include other European countries; we will develop more complete typologies of local communities at different stages of implementation; we will move from categorisation and evaluation to model-building and explanation; and we will seek to expand the relevance and informational content of the analysis by more specific sub-studies of (for example) local policies for and impacts on climate change and biodiversity.

FACILITATING LA21 AT THE INTERNATIONAL LEVEL

As a concluding introductory perspective, let us briefly return to the four 'objectives' set down in Chapter 28 of the Agenda. By way of initial assessment, it can be said that the reports presented here are primarily concerned with the first and the fourth objectives. We will be looking at how both national and local authorities have reacted to the general call for 'Local Agenda 21's', and we will get a first indication of how women and youth (along with other major groups) have been drawn into decision-making, planning and implementation. So as to place these findings in a broader context, however, we must look briefly at the other two objectives, both of which are to be realised at supra-national levels of co-operation and co-ordination.

The second objective of Chapter 28 stipulates that 'by 1993' (i.e. within one year of the Earth Summit), 'the international community should have initiated a consultative process aimed at increasing co-operation between local authorities'. Given the vagueness of language here, it is not clear who or what is 'the international community', but, given the fact that the third objective is specifically directed to 'representatives of associations of cities and other local authorities', we can assume that the reference is to international organisations where states are members. More specifically, it is sufficient to concentrate on the organisation which is formally responsible for UNCED and Agenda 21: the United Nations. The responsibility for following up and implementing the Earth Summit has been spread to a number of different UN bodies, committees and programs.

The most central administrative structure lies under the Economic and Social Council (ECOSOC) of the General Assembly. There are four separate bodies involved in the follow-up process: (1) the Commission on

Sustainable Development (CSD); (2) the Inter-Agency Committee on Sustainable Development; (3) the High-level Advisory Board on Sustainable Development; and the Department for Policy Co-ordination and Sustainable Development (DPCSD). It is the CSD which establishes the major policy guidelines and priorities for the follow-up, and the DPCSD which co-ordinates the different integrative, monitoring and reporting activities. LA21 activities are periodically reported in the 'CSD Update' newsletter and in the reports of the 'Ad Hoc Open-ended Inter-Sessional Working Groups' of the CSD.[2]

It is thus safe to say that the 'international community', as represented in and through the United Nations, has taken the necessary steps to integrate and co-ordinate the follow-up and implementation of Chapter 28 of Agenda 21. The documents, newsletters and bulletins emerging from and around these processes enable interested parties to monitor developments on a day-to-day basis. Reporting on overall progress vis à vis Chapter 28 is also an integral part of the preparations for the Special Session of the General Assembly devoted to a review and appraisal of Agenda 21 ('Earth Summit +5'). We will return to these reports in the concluding chapter.

As for the third 'objective' of Chapter 28, it is here prescribed that 'by 1994, representatives of associations of cities and other local authorities should have increased levels of co-operation and co-ordination with the goal of enhancing the exchange of information and experience among local authorities'. Clearly, this is an area which has been followed up to an impressive degree. If one is looking for 'best cases' of fulfilling specific tasks within Agenda 21, it is difficult to find a better example than that achieved by the International Council for Local Environmental Initiatives (ICLEI). This is, in a sense, not surprising, since ICLEI had a major responsibility for the development of Chapter 28. The nature and quality of the organisation's follow-up is, nonetheless, exceptional. ICLEI has (in direct co-operation with numerous other international bodies, including the DPCSD, UNEP, UNDP and the European Union) initiated and supported numerous programs designed to realise the intentions of the LA21 concept. Given the vital importance of the ICLEI initiative, it is worthwhile to take a brief look at the background and context for its development.[3]

ICLEI was founded during the World Congress for Local Governments for a Sustainable Future held in New York in 1990. The congress was carried out in conjunction with the UN Environment Programme (UNEP) and the International Union of Local Authorities (IULA), with representatives from more than 200 local communities from 45 countries; 25 national alliances of local authorities; as well as representatives from a number of governmental and non-governmental organisations. The overall goal of ICLEI is to exchange knowledge and experience as to how local authorities work for sustainable development. It aims to serve as an arena for expressing the views of local authorities within different international fora, most particularly those concerned with environmental negotiations.

Another important milestone in the development of the LA21 initiative was the so-called 'Oslo Declaration on Environment, Health and Lifestyle'. This was formally adopted at the 30th World Congress of the International Union of Local Authorities (IULA) in 1991. The declaration provides an overview of municipal responsibility in working for sustainable development at the local level, and has been identified (Hams, 1994) as an important source for the development of Chapter 28. To a large extent, the declaration follows the broad lines of the Brundtland Report, thus providing an important supplement to the work of the World Commission on the role of local authorities. The declaration also serves to extend the sphere of responsibility of local authorities to more global concerns, placing particular emphasis on the potential of international alliances between municipalities, both within and independent of other international agreements. At the same time, there is an acknowledgement of the decisive role of the municipalities in involving their own inhabitants in the work of promoting sustainable development.

In 1994 ICLEI was also one of the principal organisers of the European Conference on Sustainable Cities and Towns in Ålborg, Denmark, where the highly influential 'Ålborg Charter' was adopted. To date, more than 120 European cities and towns have subscribed to the Charter, thereby agreeing to a common understanding of the challenges inherent in the work for sustainable development. The Charter (which has also provided a vital stimulus for more specific LA21 initiatives) highlights the following goals:

- protection of the countryside and building up resources;
- social equality;
- sustainable-development pattern;
- sustainable mobility;
- policy measures to reduce emissions of greenhouse gases;
- prevention of toxic emissions harmful to the environment;
- local autonomy;
- popular participation.

The Ålborg Charter was followed up by the 'Lisbon Action Plan', a program of 12 principles endorsed by municipal representatives at the Second European Sustainable Cities & Towns Conference at Lisbon, Portugal in October of 1996.[4] The Plan declares that:

1. We believe that the adoption of the Charter of European Cities & Towns Towards Sustainability (Ålborg Charter) is one of the best starting points for a Local Agenda 21 process.
2. We believe that the local authority should be the main facilitator of the Local Agenda 21 process.
3. We believe that the Local Agenda 21 process requires the involvement of the entire local authority – whether city, town or rural community.
4. We shall enter into consultation and partnerships with the various sectors of our community to create synergy through cooperation.
5. We shall seek to get our own house in order by implementing the principle of negotiating outward.
6. We shall carry out systematic action planning to move from analysis to action.
7. We shall integrate environmental with social and economic development to improve health and quality of life for our citizens.
8. We shall use advanced tools for sustainability management.
9. We shall establish programmes to raise awareness among our citizens, interest groups, as well as politicians and local government officers of sustainability issues.
10. We shall gain strength through inter-authority alliances: associations, networks and campaigns.
11. We shall build North-South and West-East alliances for sustainable development.
12. We shall go ahead in concert with the European Sustainable Cities & Towns Campaign.

In addition to spreading information on these historic benchmarks, ICLEI publishes its own newsletter; co-ordinates the program for 'European Local Agenda 21'; promulgates the 'Local Agenda 21 Model Communities Programme'; and provides running documentation on case-studies of the LA21 process. It has also prepared (in co-operation with the DPCSD) a comprehensive survey of LA21 activities (also to be reviewed in the concluding chapter).

In sum, there is ample evidence that the United Nations has joined together with international associations of public authorities to follow up on their responsibilities with respect to the objectives of Chapter 28 of Agenda 21. Though there will always be room for discussion as to whether UN bodies do enough with the resources provided, we point out that, in this particular case, the role of the UN bodies is primarily facilitative, and that the institutions and procedures established seemed to function according to the intentions of the General Assembly. (This says nothing, of course, as to the objective validity of the reports and overviews provided to and by the UN bodies – a topic we will return to in the concluding chapter.) As for the role of ICLEI as a task-specific organisation for local-authority associations, we view its efforts in this area as exceptional; a prime example of how information technology can be creatively applied to the communication needs of global policy implementation.

Given the relative success of the international agents responsible for implementing Chapter 28, and considering that the tasks of these agents are designed to be primarily facilitative, the question remains as to how the responsible national and local agents have pursued their obligations within the international framework. This is, of course, the subject of the present report. As mentioned previously, the selection of countries repre-sented in the report has been determined primarily by the ability of the research network to access researchers and resources on an ad-hoc basis. We feel, however, that the countries selected provide a highly interesting – though certainly not exhaustive – basis for initial cross-national analysis and insights.

In concluding this introductory perspective, we would like to summarise the understanding of 'Local Agenda 21' which has guided the joint reporting effort. As the reader will soon discover, any dialogue of assessment requires a minimal degree of common understanding as to what is being assessed. The following four points sum up the minimal understanding which has emerged within the research team during the course of the project. We do not maintain that this understanding has been rigorously and systematically applied; merely that it has gradually emerged, and that it reflects benchmarks and standards which we feel are necessary and fruitful for a meaningful evaluation discourse. We return to the relationship between these standards and those reflected in other, more official, monitoring efforts, in the concluding chapter.

As generally applied in the present set of studies, the notion of 'Local Agenda 21' implies that:

1. Chapter 28 is specifically addressed to 'Local Authorities'. The responsibility of national governments is the general responsibility accorded to them for the *whole* of Agenda 21. By implication, this means that also national governments have primarily *a facilitative role* with respect to the LA21 process.

2. The 'consultative process' stipulated by the first 'objective' is clearly meant to be a *new* and *different* process from existing protective and remedial environmental activities. The distinguishing nature of the process is to initiate a *new* understanding of the relationship between environment and development as spelled out in the principles of the Rio Declaration and the chapters of Agenda 21. The key notion of this understanding is the concept of 'sustainable development' as put forth in the Brundtland Report.

3. The 'consultative process' identified in Chapter 28 of Agenda 21 has a clear *strategic intent*. Though the actual content of 'a Local Agenda 21' is not spelled out, there is a clear presumption of both *change* and *instrumental rationality* with respect to a realisation of the Earth-Summit goals.
4. There is an underlying presupposition that the substance of any particular 'Local Agenda 21' will be *relative to the specific nature of the local community* in question (its geography, demography, economics, society and culture), and that it will *evolve dynamically over time*.

It is the manner in which these dimensions thus far have been understood and pursued in eight European countries that constitutes the descriptive substance of our research effort. We realise that the country selection is only representative for Northern Europe, and we make no claims for generalisation beyond the sample itself. In a political-science perspective, there are obviously a number of interesting comparative dimensions for cross-national analysis within the sample, and we will want to explore these in greater depth at a later date. For now, however, we focus on only the most obvious of distinguishing characteristics within and across the cases. Our purpose can best be described as 'description with an evaluative bent'; an attempt to make a more substantive complementary contribution to the debate over what has actually been achieved since the Earth Summit.

NOTES

1   As a concept for joining developmental with environmental concerns, the term 'sustainable development' was apparently used by Barbara Ward already in the mid 1970's (Holmberg and Sandbrook, 1992: 19). Dennis Pirage contributed to spread the concept further in his anthology on *The Sustainable Society* in 1977, and the International Union for the Conservation of Nature (IUCN) made it a central idea of its *World Conservation Strategy* in 1980. (See Dahle, 1997: 197). It was not, however, until the idea was made the core concept of the Brundtland Report and the UNCED process that it gained its current prominence and legitimacy. (See Lafferty and Langhelle, 1995 and Trzyna, 1995).

2   The most effective source for gaining an overview of the UN follow-up activities is through the Internet and World Wide Web. The activities of relevance for Local Agenda 21 are widespread throughout the UN system, with programs and sub-programs under UNEP, UNDP, UNESCO (that is, in addition to the major activities focused within the CSD and DPCSD channels). Trying to gain a complete overview of these activities is only possible through the 'search' functions provided by Internet WWW-

software. Of the many possible starting points, we would recommend the web site for the so-called 'Rio Cluster' of UN Proceedings (http://www.igc.apc.org/habitat/un-proc).

3   All documents referred to in this section are available at ICLEI's web site: http://www.iclei.org/iclei/la21.htm.

4   The Action Plan was endorsed by the participants at the Second European Conference on Sustainable Cities and Towns in Lisbon, Portugal, 8 October 1996. The annotated text of the plan is available at: http://206.221.248.13/europractice/act-plan.htm.

REFERENCES

Armann, Kai, John Hille and Olav Kasin (1995) *Lokal Agenda 21: Norske kommuners miljarbeid etter Rio*, ('Local Agenda 21: Norwegian Muncipal Environemntal Policy after Rio') Oslo: Prosjekt Alternativ Framtid and Stiftelsen Idébanken.

Dahle, Kjell (1997) *Forsøk for forandring? Alternative veier til et bærekraftig samfunn* ('Experiments for Change? Alternative Paths to a Sustainable Society') Oslo: Spartacus Forlag.

Eckerberg, Katarina (1990) *Environmental Protection in Swedish Forestry*, Aldershot: Avebury.

Goggin, M.; A. O'Bowman, J. Lester and L. O'Toole Jr. (1990) *Implementation Theory and Practice: Toward a Third Generation*, Glenview, Illinois: Scott, Foresman/Little Brown.

Hams, T. (1994) 'Local Environmental Policies and Strategies after Rio'. In J. Agyeman and B. Evans (eds) *Local Environmental Policies and Strategies*, Harlows: Longman.

Holmberg, Johan and R. Sandbrook (1992) 'Sustainable Development: What Is to Be Done?'. In Johan Holmberg (ed) *Policies for a Small Planet*, London: IIED/Earthscan.

Kjellberg, F. and M. Reitan (1995) *Studiet av offentlig politikk: En innføring* ('The Study of Public Administration: An Introduction') Oslo: Tano Forlag.

Lafferty, William M. and Oluf Langhelle (eds) (1995) *Bærekraftig utvikling: Om utviklingens mål og bærekraftens betingelser* ('Sustainable Development: On the Goals of Development and the Conditions for Sustainability') Oslo: Ad Notam Gyldendal.

Lafferty, William M. and James Meadowcroft (1996) 'Implementing Sustainable Development in High-Consumption Societies: A Comparative Study of National Strategies and Initiatives'. Paper presented at the First COMPSUS Workshop, Oxford Centre for the Environment, Ethics and Society, September 5–8, 1996. (Available at http://www.prosus.nfr.no/).

Sabatier, P. (1986) 'Top-down and bottom-up approaches to implementation research: A critical analysis and suggested synthesis', *Journal of Public Policy*, 6:1, 21–48.

Trzyna, Thaddeus C. (ed) (1995) *A Sustainable World: Defining and Measuring Sustainable Development*, Sacramento and Claremont: IUCN – The World

Conservation Union and the International Center for the Environment and Public Policy.

United Nations (1993). Report of the United Nations Conference on Environment and Development, Rio de Janeiro, 3–14 June 1992, Volume I: Resolutions Adopted by the Conference. New York: United Nations.

Voisey, Heather, Christiane Beuermann, Liv Astrid Sverdrup and Timothy O'Riordan (1996) 'The Political Significance of Local Agenda 21: The Early Stages of Some European Experiences', *Local Environment*, Vol. 1, No. 1, pp. 33–50.

2.

Finland:

Working With LA21 Under Conditions of Economic Uncertainty

Anita Niemi-Iilahti

The Rio plan of action, Agenda 21, and the principle of sustainable development which underlies it, have been gradually introduced into Finland during the first half of the 1990's. At the local level, similar ideas to those expressed in Rio were initiated at an earlier date (in the so-called 'eco-municipality program'), but, in general, the idea of a Local Agenda 21 (LA21) did not catch on prior to the autumn of 1996. Since then, there has been more widespread and increasingly effective LA21 activity. The enactment of sustainable development, and specifically LA21, has nonetheless encountered problems of interpretation and has had to fight for priority.

An inventory of the views of the 41 members of the Finnish National Committee on Sustainable Development (Koskinen, 1995) shows that the aim of sustainable development may be interpreted in various ways and may lead to different recommendations on overall policies. The concept of sustainable development seems to have a plethora of possible meanings, and according to local officials and politicians the content of the concept was, in the first years after the Brundtland Report, diffuse and varying (Kestävän kehityksen käsikirja kunnille, 1994) and appears to remain so.

Economic development in Finland in the early 1990s was clearly exceptional. Instead of the relatively steady economic growth of preceding decades, Finland's GNP decreased during four successive years. The foundation of the Nordic welfare model began to crumble, and the high standard of living and preconditions for an even distribution of income declined. Unemployment was also greater than ever before. The situation led to politicians and civil servants giving priority to short-term solutions by means of which rapid economic recovery (in theory) could be achieved. Given the circumstances, not much attention was paid by decision-makers to environmental matters.

At least on the international level, the endeavour to maintain national commitments has always been characteristic of Finnish policy-making. A strong legalistic tradition still supports this general mode. Thus Finnish authorities quickly created at least the formal preconditions for making the Agenda 21 documents known to the Finnish people, or at least to the country's decision-makers and administrative machinery.

All the chapters of the UNCED Agenda plan of action, including Section 28 on local government, were translated into Finnish in 1993 at the instigation of the Ministry of the Environment and the Ministry for Foreign Affairs. It was particularly stressed that the aim of the book was to encourage discussion on sustainable development as well as to increase the opportunities of citizens, organisations and authorities to promote sustainable development. Because of their strong local autonomy, Finnish municipalities were thought to have ample possibilities of promoting the implementation of the aims mentioned in the plan of action (UNCED, 1993: 113).

In this chapter, I will attempt to describe the reception that Local Agenda 21 has met with by Finnish decision-makers and other actors. I will present the measures taken by the Finnish Government in response to Agenda 21, and discuss the role of the central government in transferring the process from the international agenda to the local level of government. I will also outline some central characteristics of post-Rio sustainable development at the local level in Finland. This part includes an overall description of the situation in Finland and a more limited study of some local cases. The chapter is based on field research and research reports, articles and government documents published in Finland.

THE FINNISH GOVERNMENT'S RESPONSE TO THE CHALLENGE OF SUSTAINABLE DEVELOPMENT

When evaluating the Finnish Government's reception of the policy of sustainable development after Rio, two factors are focused on in this paper. The administrative capacity and the political will expressed as policy measures within the environmental sector are seen as indicators of effective environmental policy-making. It must be admitted, however, that it will be a difficult task to evaluate which new measures or styles may be interpreted as direct reactions to Agenda 21, and which are due to other factors.

In Finland as well as in many other countries, an active and comprehensive modernisation process has been going on at all levels of government since the mid-80s. There has been a general change from regulatory command and control policy towards greater self-regulation. Decentralisation and integration are now advocated instead of centralisation and hierarchical sectoralisation.

With reference to the Scandinavian model of politics it is argued by Nousiainen (1996) that during the last two decades the model has been replaced by transitional arrangements that are characterised by voter de-alignment, diminishing participation, obscuring of partisan goal profiles, and mounting ungovernability of the weakening welfare state. Participation in the local election in Finland shows a clear negative trend. In the 1960s and 1970s the turnout was near 80 percent; in the 1980s it gradually came down to 70 percent; and in the election held in October 1996 it was as low as 61 percent.

Administrative capacity

In an international perspective, Finland has reacted to environmental challenges in the form of political decisions (separate statutes), more or less keeping up with the pace of other European countries. It took a long time, however, for environmental administration to become an independent administrative sector (Hermanson and Joas, 1996). The Ministry of the Environment was established in 1983, and municipal environmental boards did not become compulsory until 1986. After certain reforms carried out in the 1980s and 1990s, the administrative machinery of environmental policy seems to have achieved a clearly stronger position in the Government's administrative machinery in the mid-1990s than ever before. The state has granted municipalities environmental responsibility in specific areas, but at the same time the municipalities have been given a free hand to organise the treatment of environmental matters as they see fit.

In Finland, environmental administration was reorganised in 1995. The reasons for this were above all purely administrative. On the one hand, there was an attempt to develop the administration through decentralisation, while, on the other, previously separate operations concerned with the environment and the prevention of water pollution were merged.

Within the government organisation, the Ministry of the Environment is responsible for environmental policy and for preparing legislation. According to Statute 326/93, the Ministry's task is to promote sustainable development. This includes preparing a budget and setting of binding standards. The Ministry is responsible for ensuring that the environmental perspective is given proper consideration at all levels of government, society and international co-operation. The Ministry formulates environmental policies, does strategic planning and makes decisions within its own sphere of interest (such as the Finnish action programme for sustainable development, 'Environment Programme 2005', which is a comprehensive programme integrating environmental aspects into the other sectoral programmes). The programme forms the basis for the Ministry's co-operation with the other actors in environmental policy. It is part of the organisation of environmental administration, with an overall organisation of strategies, programmes and plans. The programme is in turn influenced by the EU environmental programme, the Nordic environmental strategy, and the recommendations of the UN. The development of the programme is a continuous process and it is revised at regular intervals.

The Finnish Environment Agency is the centre for environmental research and development. The Agency provides expert services for other environment authorities and for other customers. Its duties include the promotion of sustainable development by monitoring and assessing its implementation (e.g. CSD 1997 Country Report) and by making proposals where necessary. It is also responsible for national environmental research, monitoring the overall state of the environment in Finland (e.g. Finland's Natural Resources and the Environment, 1996), providing an environmental information service and increasing public awareness of environmental issues.

Regional environmental administration has been reorganised by establishing regional environmental centres. Previously scattered operations concerned with environmental protection have been brought together. The integration was justified on operational and economic grounds. The intention of the administrative reform is to create possibilities for a joint handling of environmental matters and a clarification of the division of labour between the authorities (Ympäristöministeriön muistio, 1994).

Regional Environment Centres are responsible for: (1) environmental protection (e.g. water pollution, soil protection, air protection, waste management, impact assessment in firms, and the prevention of environmental damage); (2) land-use and nature conservation, which includes building, the establishment and care of nature preservation areas, landscape protection and biodiversity, and protection of endangered species; (3) use and management of water resources, including water procurement and sewerage, flood control and drainage; (4) the study and follow-up study of the environment and the promotion of environmental awareness, which is the only area where sustainable development is mentioned; and (5) technical and administrative tasks. Actions and ideals og Regional Environment Centres are promoting sustainable development, but Agenda 21 and plans of action intended to implement it are not mentioned.

The Centres compile information on the status of the environment at a regional level for their own purposes and to meet the needs of nationwide monitoring, research and planning. The task of the Regional

Environment Centres in implementing LA21 has been seen as primarily informing and activating municipalities and officials but not directly the inhabitants (interviews in December 1996 and in January 1997). In Finland, the central level of the environmental administration has not, with respect to the regional and local level, gone in for a 'regulatory line', but regards it instead as a precondition for the success of the project that, conforming to the LA21 process, it should start at the local level.

The Finnish Environmental Agency and the Ministry of the Environment have, in the opinion of regional officials, provided the Regional Centres with enough data on LA21. According to the district officials, the role of the Finnish Environmental Agency has been much more decisive in other areas than in setting the LA21 process in motion. No special allocations have been granted for the task, but the advancement of the LA21 process is regarded as part of the normal duties of the regional centres nonetheless.

The Regional Environment Centres have thus far endeavoured to support municipalities in the implementation of LA21 mainly in the form of informal contacts. There are, however, plans to organise joint seminars for the regional municipalities. The most active Regional Environment Centres have taken part in organising regional sustainable development co-operation. They have, for instance, organised LA21 competitions for schools as well as other activities, and they have taken initiatives to get the regional environment programme going. According to environmental officials at the regional level, Agenda 21 has not been sufficiently discussed in Finland. Knowledge as such exists, but it has not been adequately disseminated. According to the interviews, self-regulation also needs to be encouraged. There is, however, no wish to force municipalities to adopt the LA21 process by means of rules and regulations.

Evaluating the development of organisational capacity in relation to the demands of Agenda 21, it is obvious that the greatest part of the measures leading to a strengthening of environmental organisation emanate from the general administrative development. The definition of the aims of the organisations nevertheless clearly reflects the aims of Agenda 21.

Policy measures taken by the Government to promote the implementation of Agenda 21

The Finnish Government's formal response to the challenge of sustainable development after Rio can be read in the Government report 'Charting Finland's Future Options' (Implementation of Agenda 21 in Finland, 1993), where the basic goals are presented to Parliament. It is emphasised that sustainable development is based on the idea of shared responsibility and equality within and between generations. The Government also aims at strengthening Finland's capacity to actively participate in solving global problems. According to the report, these general goals are turned into sectoral strategies and programmes. Further, information on the outcome of the UNCED and the objectives of Agenda 21 has been distributed to all sectors of society. The purpose is to encourage all sectors and all levels of society to actively participate in integrating environmental issues into their plans and activities.

The general goals have been implemented by the Government through several acts, plans, preparatory projects, etc. The Building Act amended in 1990; the Local Government Act amended in 1994; and the Nature Protection Act amended in 1996, are all examples of initiatives that now devote explicit attention to the concept of sustainable development. The Environmental Impact Assessment (EIA) has, since 1994, increased the possibilities for citizens, organisations and experts to influence policy development. The EIA regulations do not officially give citizens the right of initiative with regard to the EIA-procedure, but the guiding principle is that those whose interests may be affected by the project have the right to express their opinion concerning the sufficiency of the plans and the accounts already presented. On the basis of their experience, the authorities have organised public assemblies to which all those affected by the project have been invited. Citizens have taken active part, for instance, in order to influence many building projects.

The Finnish National Commission on Sustainable Development

The Finnish National Commission on Sustainable Development, established by the Government in 1993, is another example of the efforts taken by the Government. The Commission is chaired by the Prime Minister and provides representation for five other ministers and other high-level members of central government institutions, regional and local authorities, the scientific community, professional labour and business organisations, voluntary organisations, the media and the educational sector. The term of office of the present committee expires at the end of 1997.

The broad representation on the Commission is designed to promote and encourage discussion, information and public awareness of the aims and implementation of sustainable development. The Commission did not focus, however, on the implementation of LA21 on the local level until 1996. It has served to provide inspiration and ideas for municipalities and other quarters in society, and has drawn attention to indicators to be used on different levels and to 'best cases' of LA21 implementation. In the beginning of 1997, the Commission asked the so-called 'major actors' (e.g. the Central Commercial Union, the Central Union of Agricultural

Producers and the Union of Finnish Entrepreneurs) to prepare their own action plans for sustainable development. The local level is tied in to this effort by a similar programme on the part of the Association of Finnish Local Authorities.

In the beginning of 1997, there was established a special 'local section for sustainable development' under the Commission. The section numbers 15 members, with representation from eight cities, the Association of Finnish Local Authorities, the Ministry of the Environment, the Ministry of the Interior, the Academy of Finland, regional councils and the environmental NGO 'Nature and the Environment' *(Natur och Miljö)*. The section takes part in organising of regional seminars in collaboration with the Regional Enviornment Centres. The section also intends to draft a charter of what municipal LA21 projects should consist of, and to provide an overview of what is happening in the municipalities within the LA21 framework.

Obstacles to the implementation of LA21 are, according to the secretary of the local section of the Commission, primarily a lack of co-operation between the municipal administrative bodies and a general lack of commitment from municipal politicians (Interview in February 1997). The co-operation among Finnish NGOs has also been weak. In Finland, there is a large number of small municipalities, and their scanty resources have prevented an effective implementation of Local Agendas. The Regional Agendas thus serve as a good starting-point for implementation, particularly for the smaller municipalities. Funding for LA21 at the national level has been concentrated on producing guidelines and disseminating 'best cases'.

The Ministry of the Environment: Promoting LA21 goals through the dissemination of information

Certain aspects of Agenda 21 were initiated in Finland almost as soon as the document had been drafted. Earlier efforts at promoting sustainable development include the 1988 report on the work of the World Commission on Environment and Development (the Brundtland Commission), and the 'Recommendations on Finnish Activities to Promote Environment and Development' (1989) based on these. The Government Report to Parliament on Sustainable Development was published in 1990 (Kestävä kehitys ja Suomi, 1991), and has been followed up after the Rio Conference. The great depression of the early 1990's clearly affected environmental priorities, however. The resulting employment and economic problems clearly pushed environmental questions into the background. During 1995 and 1996, however, there was another reversal of government priorities. In the budget for 1995, the Government initiated the practice of assessing the state of the country's resources and the environment. The previously mentioned plan of action with regard to sustainable development is currently under preparation and will be made public early in 1997.

Environmental accounting and evaluation have, however, been actively developed by the Ministry of the Environment since 1985. The first comprehensive evaluation of the state of the Finnish Environment was published in 1992. The preface to the newest review, 'Finland's Natural Resources and the Environment 1996', explicitly refers to Rio and Finland's commitment to comply with the decisions approved in Rio. In the review, the principles of economic and environmental interaction are emphasised, and a working and reciprocal connection between environmental and socio-economic policy is seen as the key to attaining sustainable development.

The concluding chapter of the review is entitled 'Towards Sustainable Development' and presents a fairly positive picture. We read, for example, that: 'Environmental issues are nowadays being incorporated into all business operations, for example through voluntary environmental audit systems'. The review is signed by the Minister of the Environment, Pekka Haavisto. In another publication in 1996, 'The Future of the Finnish Environment', the Minister has expressed somewhat more critical views on the future:

> As we approach the end of the century, defending environmental values has begun to become more difficult. Finland's accession to the European Union, high unemployment triggered by the recession, and continuing uncertainty about the future, all demand the attention and energies of both politicians and ordinary people. ... The message of the United Nations Conference on Environment and Development in Rio in 1992 is in danger of being forgotten during today's political and economic crises ...

However, the statistics compiled in the book show that environmental policies in Finland have been credited with considerable achievements too (Wahlström et al., 1996).

It can thus be seen that the Ministry of the Environment, in collaboration with the Finnish Environmental Agency, has emphatically stressed the production and reporting of information on the environment, and thereby tried to increase both governmental and average citizen awareness of the importance of Agenda 21 goals. The roles of the other ministries in the Agenda 21 project vary considerably. While it is not possible in the present report to go into detail, Koskinen (1995) points out (in his inventory of the views of the members of the Finnish Committee on Sustainable Development) that the field of environmental policy is viewed as too narrowly defined. One recommendation is that the environmental responsibilities of the Ministry of Finance and the ministries responsible for trade, business and industry should more clearly delimited. In addition, the Ministry of the Interior (with responsibility for local government) should be regarded as a very important factor. This ministry seems, however, to be surprisingly passive, and has not yet managed to activate the municipalities. The conclusion on the passive role of the Ministry is based on several government documents and a number of interviews made with high officials in the Ministry of the Interior.

Regional Agenda 21 in the Arctic and Baltic Areas

The Ministry of the Environment also takes part in Agenda-21 activities at the supranational level, e.g. in the preparation of an 'Arctic Agenda 21' and a 'Baltic Area Agenda 21'. The national Commission on Sustainable Development is working on a proposal for how local administration and local Agenda work can be joined to the Baltic Regional Agenda. Finland's task here is to co-ordinate the Local Agenda activities and extend them to the whole of the Baltic area. As part of the Baltic LA21, a common project between three Finnish and three Estonian municipalities is getting underway in 1997.

The Ministers of the Environment from the Baltic-Sea Region decided to develop an Agenda 21 for the Baltic Region at their meeting in Sweden in October 1996. An Agenda 21 for the Baltic Sea Region involves governments, inter-governmental organisations, international financing institutions and non-governmental organisations, as well as the European Union, academics, and the general public of the region. An Agenda 21 for the Baltic Sea Region should be ready for consideration in the spring of 1998. An important principle here will be sectoral integration, with special emphasis on agriculture, energy, fishery, forestry, industry, tourism and transport. The ministers have indicated that the process of developing an Agenda 21 for the Baltic Sea Region must be democratic, transparent and open for participation to all actors in the region. The immediate operational goal is to prepare a Baltic Agenda 21 document which promotes a common vision of the future based on the concept of sustainable development, and then to utilise this vision to strengthen and integrate sector policy development and re-vitalise regional development and environmental co-operation.

State expenditure on environmental protection and the Agenda 21 action plan

No funds are currently allocated in the state budget for the implementation of LA21. The major policy line seems to be that special economic incentives will not be adopted by the Government to launch sustainable development locally. Of even greater interest, however, is the fact that the allocation proportion of grants to non-governmental environmental organisations is low and has remained the same from 1992 to 1997 (6.2 million FIM). Large investments in support of environmental protection are, however, made by the private sector through the 'Polluter Pays' principle.

Finland spends yearly 0.8–1.0 percent of the GNP on environmental protection. In the state budget, the share of the Ministry of the Environment is 0.5 per cent. State expenditure on environmental protection has increased remarkably in Finland during 1992–1997, from FIM 1.3 billion in 1992 to FIM 3.6 billion in 1997 (Finland's Natural Resources and the Environment 1996: 8). The main part of the increase is due to the environmental subsidy for agriculture, which followed Finland's joining the EU and the sum which, beginning in 1995, is about FIM 1.5 billion or nearly half of the whole environmental outlay.

In agriculture it is not, however, a question of the Government having purposefully tried to carry out the sustainable development idea by supporting farmers economically to make them engage in pro-environmental operations. It is mainly a question of channelling agricultural profit in a different way after Finland joined the EU. From the environmental point of view the development is nevertheless positive, for in order to qualify for basic environmental support the farmers have among other things to make an environmental plan for the farm; the nutrients from crop fertilisers and manure must not exceed the prescribed limits; protective zones at least three metres wide and covered with vegetation must be established along bodies of water and streams, and banks one metre wide along ditches (Eckerberg and Niemi-Iilahti, 1996).

The environmentally related state taxes and fees has slowly grown from 12.3 billion FIM in 1992 to 20.3 billion FIM in 1997. Many of these taxes and fees have been imposed for reasons other than environmental protection. The regulatory effect of the environmentally related taxes and fees is most marked in the surtax on alcoholic beverages and soft drinks; the environmental energy surtax; the oil waste tax; the water protection fee; the oil pollution control fee; and the waste tax.

In the Finnish Government's efforts to implement Agenda 21 at local level, it can be said that the biggest stake has been in the form of a build-up of organisational capacity and other measures designed to increase the general knowledge of environmental matters. The use of economic steering instruments has thus far been minimal. The measures in question are indirect in character and clearly in line with recent trends in public administration which stress decentralisation and self-regulation.

Knowledge on environment and development has been produced by means of research and development activities (e.g. comprehensive research programmes on sustainable development, atmospheric change and biodiversity), and there have been attempts to spread such knowledge to both political decision-makers and citizens. The influence of 'informational steering' is noticeable in the first-mentioned case, and especially in national decision-making, with the notion of sustainable development being incorporated into many laws, government programmes and sectoral policies. The degree to which such ideas have penetrated into municipal decision-making and reached the ordinary citizen is, however, another matter.

At the level of central government, it is obvious that some concern was already beginning to be felt in 1996 as to whether an operational understanding of sustainable development was being sufficiently spread to other levels of government and to the populace. The first regional sustainable development seminar was organised in the autumn of 1996, with participation from representatives of regional administration from different parts of the country. At the seminar, there was an attempt to emphasise the primary importance of local activity and to support regional governmental representatives in attempts to activate the municipalities and other major actors in their area. The Finnish Environment Centre and the National Sustainable Development Committee organised the seminar.

POST-RIO 'SUSTAINABLE DEVELOPMENT' IN FINNISH MUNICIPALITIES

According to its first reports after Rio (Implementation of Agenda 21 in Finland, 1993:31–32), the Finnish Government has aimed at informing all levels of society on the UNCED process and the implementation of Agenda 21. Local authorities have also been invited to strengthen their activities, e.g. by a pilot project launched in 1992 by the Association of Finnish Local Authorities together with the Ministry of the Environment and the Ministry of the Interior. The aim of the project was to find means of promoting sustainable development locally and to obtain information on local solutions. NGOs have also been encouraged to integrate environmental issues into their agendas, which has led to different types of sustainable development projects, seminars and the publishing of booklets. Women's organisations have focused mainly on information activities and 'consciousness-raising' campaigns. The emphasis has been on the preconditions of health, the importance of conservation, sustainable consumption and the rational management of household waste.

Changing environmental tasks and organisation at local level: The ups and downs of building local capacity

The most important environmental issues in the municipalities at the end of the 1980s and the beginning of the 1990s were those concerning waste management, air and water improvement, noise control, and nature conservation. The post-Rio period has added new problem areas to the local agenda. The measures are now focused on land-use, transport, energy, citizens' attitudes, environmental education, and conservation (Ympäristökatsaus, 1995).

Environmental protection as a local policy sector is relatively new in Finland. As a matter fact, it is the newest and also the last policy sector that was formulated and organised in a 'traditional' way in the extended period of welfare-state development from the late 1950's to the middle of the 1980s. 'Traditional' here means that the central government defined local tasks and modes of local organisation in each policy area, enacted laws with rather detailed contents, and allocated ear-marked resources to the municipalities. Since the Act on Municipal Environmental Protection Administration in 1986, the municipalities are obliged to supervise and promote environmental protection as an entirety and on a comprehensive basis, rather than relying on the different sector-related measures taken earlier. Municipalities with more than 3,000 inhabitants were according to the act obliged to have an Environmental Protection board, or at least they had to designate one board as responsible for environmental initiatives. The so-called 'free municipality' experiment (which started in 1989) and the new Local Government Act since 1995 have entailed both strong deregulation and decentralisation, with the result that there are today relatively few statutory municipal boards. The environmental board is not one of them (Niemi-Iilahti, 1995).

Prior to 1986, the environmental tasks imposed on municipal decision-making were handled by different sectors within the local government. Waste management was, for example, a function of the technical board; the quality of water and air the responsibility of the health board; planning and traffic issues often a joint function of the technical and the municipal executive board, etc. The 1986 Act created an administration explicitly labelled 'environmental'. Furthermore, it started a process of employing environmental secretaries and other environmental officials, and provided a new arena – the environmental board – for local politicians with special interest in environmental issues. Within two years about 400 environmental officials were employed by the municipalities (Hakanen, 1995), and by 1994 the total number of officials employed as municipal environmental secretaries and other officials was about 500, including both full-time and half-time officials (Joas, 1995). The increase in new employment was fairly high during the last few years of the 1980's, but has levelled off since due to economic pressure on the municipalities. Municipalities can today choose different kinds of solutions in organising their environmental administration. In 1996, 70 percent of the municipalities had established their own environmental administration within the municipality, while the rest had entered into co-operation with one or more other municipalities. In every third municipality there was a special Environmental Board, while in other municipalities environmental responsibility rested with the Technical Board, the Building Board, the Health Board, or some other administrative body. According to a report on the position and state of municipal environmental administration (Kettunen, 1996), the officials responsible for environmental protection in the municipalities feel that environmental problems are easily overshadowed by other concerns. The merging of environmental boards with other executive organs – intended as a measure to rationalise administrative operations – weakens (especially in the opinion of permanent environmental officials) the political impact of environmental protection. Sustainable development is understood by the municipalities to mean that an environmental perspective should be taken into account in all decision-making, but only the largest municipalities have been able to face this challenge. Municipalities in Finland have been divided into active and passive categories from the standpoint of environmental protection, and the trend seems to continue.

Local Agenda-21 activities: An overview

How far have Finnish municipalities come in the actual implementation of LA21 processes at the beginning of 1997? At first sight one might believe that Finland has progressed well in enacting the ideas of sustainable development at the local and regional levels. The concept of sustainable development is, at least, recognised everywhere. As mentioned before, in the Local Government Act enacted in 1995 the tasks of the municipalities were redefined, such that the two main tasks of local government now are 'to promote the welfare of citizens and sustainable development'. Even though the concept of sustainable development is widely used at the local level, the regulation of municipal law with respect to the idea has aroused criticism for both its general nature and vagueness. According to interpreters of the law the regulation is seen as devoid of legal force, and from the standpoint of local government it is often considered inconvenient as it could, in principle, reduce the discretion of local authorities. In practice, however, measures taken in the name of sustainable development vary a great deal from one municipality to another.

When the Rio conference was being prepared and immediately after it, there were a number of very active 'environmental communities' in Finland, but the actual drawing up of Local Agendas has progressed very slowly in Finland. The momentum began to shift, however, toward the end of 1996. According to information collected by the Association of Finnish Local Authorities, there now exists a strongly trend towards starting new LA21 projects in many municipalities. A typical feature of the trend is that groups of small municipalities join together in implementing LA21 projects.

The Charter of European Cities and Towns aimed at sustainability was approved by the participants in the European Conference on Sustainable Cities and Towns in Ålborg, Denmark, on 27 May 1994. The charter was signed by 20 Finnish municipalities, and most of these are today front-runners in implementing Local Agenda 21. As a proportion of the total number of municipalities in Finland, this is a relatively modest number. More importantly, however, 30 percent of the inhabitants of Finland live in these cities and towns. Representatives from these urban districts partici-pated in a 'European Sustainable Cities Dissemination Conference', which was organised by the Association of Finnish Local Authorities in February 1996. The EU Group of Experts (on urban environment and sustainable cities) presented the European Sustainable Cities project and consulted with representatives of the Finnish municipalities. Representatives of the Association of Finnish Local Authorities also took an active part in the Second European Conference on Sustainable Cities and Towns in the autumn of 1996, where the next phase of the initiative – the 'Lisbon Action Plan' was launched. The Plan was endorsed by the Finnish repre-sentatives, along with representatives from more than 1,000 local and regional authorities from all over Europe.

At the beginning of 1997, some kind of local action programme (related to LA21) was under way in 148 of Finland's 452 municipalities (Table 1). The table also reveals that approximately two-thirds of Finland's population are now affected by some kind of LA21 activity.

Table 1 *Number of Finnish municipalities and the proportion of inhabitants involved in implementing Local Agenda 21: 1995–1997*

Year	Number of municipalities	Share of inhabitants
1995	44	41%
1996	88	50%
1997	148	67%

Where is the new line of activity emerging?

As mentioned previously, activity in this area first got under way in the larger towns, whereas smaller units – often in co-operative networks – became more involved toward the end of 1996. At the beginning of 1997, the Association of Finnish Local Authorities launched a new LA21 project involving 60 municipalities. The Association operates mainly as a 'facilitator', organising training events, producing and distributing information and maintaining a telephone consultation service. In the course of 1997, six training events will be organised, for the most part regionally. The aim is to get LA21 programmes properly established in the municipalities. There will be an evaluation of the programme after the first year.

Geographically the LA21 activities are spread out over the whole country, but it is again the larger units (with more than 15,000 inhabitants) that have taken the lead. While only 21 percent of the municipalities with fewer than 6,000 inhabitants have taken measures related to Agenda 21, the figure for the larger units is 58 percent (Figure 1).

Activities related to the planning and implementation of Local Agenda 21 processes in Finnish municipalities during the last few years seem to be closely connected with the degree of general environmental awareness at the local level. This can be measured in terms of the organisational model chosen and the type of staff allocated to the municipality's environmental sector. Relatively large urban municipalities have their own environmental sector with full-time, highly educated, numerous or

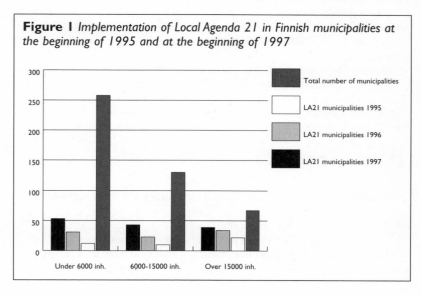

Figure 1 *Implementation of Local Agenda 21 in Finnish municipalities at the beginning of 1995 and at the beginning of 1997*

Legend:
- Total number of municipalities
- LA21 municipalities 1995
- LA21 municipalities 1996
- LA21 municipalities 1997

Categories: Under 6000 inh.   6000-15000 inh.   Over 15000 inh.

fairly numerous personnel. Small and medium-sized rural municipalities usually have, on the other hand, a more mixed type of administrative solution with part-time technical personnel with relatively low levels of education.

A significant feature of the post-Rio activities is that hardly any new economic resources have been allocated to environmental functions. Existing environmental staff has been given new responsibilities – but very few new resources. This is perhaps one of the reasons why there have emerged new modes of co-operation at the local level, with different forms of interaction and joint efforts both between administrative sectors, and between local authorities and other organisations or citizen groups. Municipalities have organised seminars and courses in order to promote new ideas, and relatively ambitious pilot projects in the spheres of land-use, traffic control and education have been developed.

The initiative in LA21 activities seems to come largely from municipal environmental officials themselves. There are, in other words, clear signs of 'top-down steering' within the municipal sphere. Given the strong legalistic tradition in Finnish public administration, it is the municipal environmental officials who apparently feel the responsibility for implementing local political decisions. The impetus for LA21 activities thus seems to depend on a political decision taken by the municipal council or executive board. Initiatives taken by voluntary organisations have been rare, though there are signs that environmentally oriented NGOs are taking up the challenge.

Governance of environmental issues at the local level in Finland is characterised by diversity. Above all the rural municipalities differ very much from each other in their attitudes to the local environment. In some municipalities, spontaneous local environmental activity can be found, while in others one finds nearly hostile attitudes towards ecological perspectives (Konttinen and Litmanen, 1996; Sairinen, 1994). Further, the larger the municipality, the greater number of measures taken. Nearly all of the cities and larger towns have initiated some kinds of new activities. But there are also some very small municipalities, such as Kumlinge, with only 445 inhabitants, which display a particular interest and activity in the environmental sphere.

Selected examples of Local Agenda-21 initiatives

Municipalities in Finland vary considerably as to basic characteristics, the most urban being Helsinki with half a million inhabitants, and the smallest the rural municipality of Sottunga with only 134 inhabitants. Each local community has different problems and different capacities for reacting to them. Six different cases will be presented in this section. The first four can be seen as pioneering LA-21 municipalities, all of them larger municipalities. The fifth case is also a relatively large municipality with only moderate LA-21 activities, but with a very innovative LA21 school experiment. The sixth case is a special regional case, with mostly very small rural municipalities.

Pori: A front-runner in integrating societal sectors and mobilising small enterprises

Pori was among the first Finnish municipalities to sign the Ålborg Charter in 1994. It is a city with 76,000 inhabitants, with 62 percent of the work force employed in the service sector and 36 percent in industry. Local Agenda 21 activity started in Pori and gradually spread to eight neighbouring municipalities to form a regional LA21 in 1995. The initiative and decision concerning LA21 were made by the municipal officials. The budget for the first year was FIM 180,000, of which the city of Pori provided half and the Regional Council half. In the years that followed, the smaller municipalities have also shared expenses. A single administrator has been engaged to co-ordinate the project. The real Agenda operations started at the beginning of 1996, when the Agenda principles were presented to the municipalities involved. After that, an 'Environmental Forum' was convened with about 100 representatives from the municipalities, the business world and civic organisations. Women and youth were also well represented. The Environmental Forum was divided into seven work groups: Industry, power generation and transport; Primary production and nature; Land-use planning and nature; Administration; Trade and consumption; Welfare, day-to-day routines and traffic; Education, instruction, information and research. The Forum has its own executive group which makes decisions concerning the funding and development of agenda activity.

The work groups meet five times a year to develop ideas for different agenda processes, and to discuss sustainable development challenges, objectives, indicators and strategies of action. Indicators are of great importance as measures of targets, standards and specific results. Among the indicators applied thus far are the amount of unsorted community waste, the number of public-transport users, the quality of the air in population centres, and the degree to which the schedules for nature conservation have been implemented. The Forum has organised seminars and training events – for example, seminars concerning business zoning and its impact on the environment – and, for farmers, there has been a seminar on the preservation of the cultural landscape. In co-operation with the Pori College of Technology, a collection of directions concerning the handling of waste water in areas of scattered settlement and holiday resorts has been produced for use in the Pori region municipalities. The initiative has also resulted in the preparation and dissemination (to all citizens) of an environmental guide for the district. It contains advice on waste management, compost techniques, and the conservation of energy and water.

A major concern in the Pori region at present is the activation of small and medium-sized enterprises. Visits are organised to inform enterprises of coming environmental regulations. Emphasis has thus far been placed on information, with leaflets distributed free of cost to participating municipalities. The leaflets contain a column containing 'ecological tips', and the Forum publishes an 'Agenda News' which appears four times a year and is distributed in the libraries. The News contains recurring updates on the progress of LA21 activity in Finland.

The Forum type of activity has been viewed as a challenging and effective way of making citizens' views known. It has also proved expedient as a means of reconciling different points of view. Although the Pori LA21 is designed to cover both Pori and its surrounding municipalities, the regional co-operation has nonetheless been less effective than expected because of the long distances between the municipalities. Integration of sectoral activity has, however, increased.

Lahti: Integrating social and economic aspects

The municipality of Lahti was also one of the first to sign the Ålborg Charter, and the Lahti Environmental Forum was established as early as 1993. The new initiative began in earnest in 1994, when the indicators currently in use were selected, among them environmental stress, the state of nature, use of natural resources, land use and environmental consciousness.

The Environmental Forum was established in Lahti partly as a result of the Agenda 21 initiative, but also as a response to ongoing environmental-protection activities and the changing state of the economy. Five neighbouring municipalities also participate in the Forum, bringing the total number of people affected to about 150,000. In addition to the municipalities, more than 90 organisations, associations and enterprises are represented on the Forum. The representatives are divided into seven groups which carry out the objectives and proposed measures of sustainable development. The propositions from the groups are brought together for extensive discussion and co-ordination, along with proposals and suggestions submitted from outside the Forum. To facilitate this, consultants have been engaged to organise information meetings and seminars for various target groups. On the basis of the aims and propositions for action approved in discussions in the various target groups, the Lahti Local Agenda 21 was established in 1996, and almost immediately set in motion thereafter.

The annual budget for the Environmental Forum in the Lahti district is FIM 200,000 – 300,000, made up of a grant from the Ministry of the Environment for research and development, a provincial developmental grant, and financial aid from the city of Lahti.

The cities of Lahti, Tampere and Riihimäki, which are geographically close to each other, have also aimed to co-operate on exchanging environmental knowledge between the authorities, expert bodies and local enterprises. The three cities have marketed this initiative under the title: 'Finland's Green Triangle' (a model adopted from Denmark). The project has, however, suffered setbacks recently due (apparently) to difficulties of communication and co-ordination.

Mikkeli: 'Eco-schools' and 'eco-teams' as boosters of LA21

The province of Mikkeli in south-east Finland has long traditions with regard to environmental matters. It has been known since 1979 as an 'eco-province', having also signed the Ålborg Charter in 1995 and taken part in the Second European Conference on Sustainable Cities and Towns in the Fall of 1996. The centre of the province is the town of Mikkeli, with approximately 33,000 inhabitants. Work on the Local Agenda was initiated almost immediately after the signing of the Ålborg agreement in 1995. Four neighbouring municipalities also participate in the Mikkeli region Agenda 21, bringing the total number of people affected to about 42,000. The Agenda, which serves as a good example of LA21 guidelines, was completed at the end of 1996.

Though there has not yet elapsed enough time to point to concrete achievements within the Agenda framework, one aspect is particularly worth noting. Twenty 'eco-schools' are involved in drawing up their own form of LA21, to be completed by the end of 1998. Also in the Mikkeli area, numerous families have become members of 'eco-teams', where the goal is to achieve sustainable development objectives in their own day-to-day routines. In addition, a large waste-paper recycling project has been implemented in the area. The idea here is to gather waste paper from households in sparsely populated areas by means of the postal delivery system. The pilot project covers an area of 1,500 households, and there are estimates which indicate that it should be possible to recover up to 80 percent of the waste paper when collected by postmen. The recoverable amount prior to the project was only 30 percent.

Tampere: NGOs take the initiative

Tampere, a city with 176,000 inhabitants, is also one of the signatories of the Ålborg Charter. Of the city work force, 69 percent are employed in the service sector and 22 percent in industry. The point of departure for Tampere's LA21 activity is the environmental policy programme approved by the city in 1994. The process leading to LA21 started on the initiative of the 'Tampere 21 Movement', made up of 18 different civic organisations and groups. The initial focus of the Tampere 21 Movement has been on air pollution. The movement has taken active initiatives, for example, in the planning of the regional traffic system, bio-waste pickup and composting, as well as in energy conservation in the municipal housing sector. The aim of the Tampere initiative is to complete the LA21 programme by the end of 1997, and a separate Forum has recently been established toward that end.

Tampere is also – along with seven other Finnish cities (Helsinki, Espoo, Oulu, Lahti, Turku, Kuopio and Kouvola) – involved in ICLEI (the International Council for Local Environmental Initiatives, founded in 1990). It has, in this connection, adopted a co-ordinator role, serving as a connecting link between the members, supplying information, and arranging training sessions on the scope and nature of LA21 activities. Tampere is also actively involved in the LA21 Model Communities Programme (co-ordinated by ICLEI), and in the LA21 community network and campaign.

Vaasa: The school as agent of LA21 processes

The city of Vaasa in Western Finland is a city with 55,000 inhabitants and workforce with roughly 69 percent engaged in the service sector and 24 percent in industry. The city participated in a regional sustainable development project between 1992 and 1994, but the Local Agenda 21 project did not get started (as an NGO initiative) until 1996. To promote the process at the outset, the city commissioned from a consultant firm a plan for Vaasa Local Agenda 21. At the beginning of 1997, the proposed plan was circulated in various municipal organs for comments and suggestions.

On the basis of the civic initiative, a training schedule was organised in the municipal course centre. Its purpose was to enhance environmental knowledge and the possibilities for increasing citizen influence on local decision-making. After completion of the training course, study circles were formed in which some 100 people took part, among them members of enterprises and civic organisations, as well as ordinary citizens. The study circles operate as discussion forums, and also adopt proposals for action and new initiatives which are then channelled into the Vaasa Agenda action plan. Areas of particular interest have been biodiversity, the improvement of the suburban environment, and environmental protection of the off-shore islands. There has also been organised a seminar for local authorities and an exhibition of LA21 in the city library.

Prior to the initiative of the NGOs and the city's LA21 activities, a school in Vaasa had started an independent LA21 process of its own. The Variska school has emphasised environmental themes and problems in its teaching for many years. The school has two teachers who are very interested in environmental issues and assiduously take part in activities concerned with the environment. They have participated in a research project called 'Children as agents for an ecological environment', the purpose of which was to find out whether children and young people can contribute to making urban life more pro-environmental. One of the school cohorts has also worked as 'eco-agents'.

In the beginning of 1996, with the help of the eco-agents, the school drafted its own Agenda 21 in line with the Rio guidelines. In addition to participating in various projects, the eco-agents visit lower school classes and kindergartens, providing information on environmental issues. They aim to make school routines more pro-environmental and, among other things, look after the school greenhouse and the garden plot close to the school. The garden contains a unique flora which, in time, will be developed into a local tourist attraction. This particular project has attracted involvement will beyond the eco-agents, bringing together other pupils of the school along with parents and teachers. In May 1996, the pupils organised an 'Environment Day' which involved a panel discussion and an eco-agent exhibition. The eco-agent activity will be considerably enhanced during the course of 1997, when it becomes upgraded to a normal school subject.

Åland: A model of zeal and regional activity

The Province of Åland constitutes a special case in Finland, with a regional Agenda-21 office financed by the Regional Council and the town of Mariehamn. All Åland's municipalities are engaged in the sustainable development programme, which also involves companies and individual citizens. The Åland section of 'Nature and Environment' (*Natur och Miljö* – established in 1994) takes an active role in producing and disseminating information on the activities of the municipalities and firms on the Island, and organises courses and meetings. Though the number of inhabitants in the municipalities is quite small (varying between about 130 and 3,130), the activities of the Agenda office in Mariehamn serve as an excellent example of NGO co-ordinating capacity. They have mobilised the local citizenry behind a 'car-free day'; have worked with local firms to improve the sorting and recycling of refuse; and have worked closely with travel agencies to promote 'sustainable tourism'.

As to other municipalities in Finland, it is safe to say that the regional perspective has not yet been significantly developed for this area. There are, however, other cases of adjacent municipalities (for instance Turku with its surroundings, the archipelago of Turku) which have recently initiated environmental co-operation. In Northern Finland, there is also the region around Oulu, and in Southern Finland the Helsinki area, both of

which are developing regional perspectives on sustainable development.
It must be stressed, however, that, even in the most active municipalities,
LA21 initiatives have only very recently been drawn up, and even in the
majority of the front-runner municipalities, implementation is still at a
very early stage.

NGO ACTIVITIES RELATED TO LA21 IN FINLAND

Finland is known for having a high level of voluntary organisational activity. The scope of interests articulated by organisations is very wide,
ranging from professional and religious associations to cultural activities,
sports clubs, and voluntary fire brigades. Some of the organisations
function in a limited local-community context, whereas others have
nation-wide coverage divided between local associations, regional district
units and a central office.

The role of the voluntary organisations in mobilizing LA21 processes
seems, however, to be very slight. At the moment no systematic data is
available on those activities, but some interpretations based on interviews
can be made. First, a striking feature is that the largest and most well-
known national conservation organisation The Finnish Nature
Conservation Association (FNCA) with roughly 200 local suborganisa-
tions didn't become involved in promoting LA21 process before 1996. In
the plans of the central organisation, there is a mention of participation in
the establishment of local agendas, but there are no programs of action or
instructions to the local organisations. The central organisation is currently
(beginning of 1997) collecting information about which local organisations do participate in LA21 work. Independently from the mother
organisation, the youth organisation of the FNCA initiated some activities
in 1996. One example is the 'environmental parliament' organised
together with the national organisation of boy-scouts and girl-scouts. The
youth groups here adopted 14 resolutions demanding that local Agenda
21 activities should be started all over the country by the end of May
1997. They also emphasized that the viewpoints of youth should be a
prominent part of such activities.

Another well-established nature conservation organisation in Finland
is the Swedish speaking Nature and the Environment (N&E). It operates
within a more limited geographical area, but has been very actively
engaged in the establishment of the Åland Agenda 21. The Finnish Friends
of the Earth (FoE-F), founded in 1996, is a newcomer among civic organisations active in the sphere of environmental protection in Finland. It has
organised a seminar on LA21 and in some areas its members operate
together in teams. Their task is to make the NGO perspective on sustain-

able development known among a broader audience. They also have published a book with criteria for ecological sustainability.

Secondly, the LA21 activities started by non-environmental NGOs are less frequent, being located for the most part in pioneering LA21 municipalities. These activities are often international in origin, such as a project conducted by the organisation for 'Environment and Development'. The project is part of the Sustainable Europe campaign (see below), where the work of the organisation of citizens and scientific research is combined. The aim is for Finland to adjust its consumption and waste levels to per-capita global tolerance limits by the year 2030.

Voluntary organisations can, of course, become important mechanisms for initiating and carrying out LA21 initiatives out in Finland. The distinction between the public and private sectors used to be fairly clear in Finland, but more recent public policy has tended to emphasize the third sector. The need to find an economically sustainable welfare model which involves all the major groups, particularly youth unemployed in societal processes, is evident. The Government (Ministry of the Interior) has now taken measures aimed at promoting participation and partnership in local communities. This can clearly lead to wider participation by NGOs in the LA21 processes.

SUMMARY AND CONCLUSIONS

The process of promoting sustainable development and implementing LA21 in Finland is currently in an interesting and very challenging phase. After a small initial 'boom' around the Rio meeting – connected mainly with random activities by environmental enthusiasts – Finland experienced a period of stagnation and decline in its efforts to implement LA21. Even though the concept of sustainable development has become relatively well embedded in legal acts, plans, programmes and declarations, work with Chapter 28 of the Agenda is not yet widely adapted by policy-makers and citizens. There can be several reasons why this is so.

Policy implementation in general is, of course, faced with numerous types of obstacles and problems. The literature is mainly filled with stories of failure (Pressman and Wildavsky, 1973; Dunsire, 1978), even though more recent studies have documented a number of more positive results (Mazmanian and Sabatier, 1990; Jänicke and Weidner, 1995). We can assume that the implementation of Agenda 21 at the local level has encountered most of the difficulties registered from previous implementation studies, and perhaps even a number of new and different ones. There are at least two features connected with the LA21 task which make implementation and evaluation in Finland very challenging.

First, there is considerable goal ambiguity connected with the task of implementing sustainable development. Although the need to move towards sustainability is generally accepted in Finland, we have learned at the same time that the concept of sustainable development has numerous meanings and is difficult to define. It can be argued, therefore, that the idea is also difficult to realise in practice. Public organisations and public policy are, however, known to have particularly vague and diverse (often contradictory) goals. At first glance, this may sound irrational, but, as pointed out by Wildavsky (1979: 215), vague and multiple objectives provide a number of advantages to those who implement the policy. The situation favours flexibility, and diverse goals can be accommodated to diverse interests. Rainey's (1993) theoretical discussion of goal ambiguity in public organisations also points out that non-routine tasks will and should lead to looser, more flexible, adaptive organisational procedures, allowing for more professional and expert judgement by those performing the tasks.

On the one hand, therefore, it would appear that the very openness of the sustainable development concept has held back the start of LA21 processes in Finland, particularly with respect to the effects from negative economic conditions. On the other hand, however, selected front-runner communities have relied on the concept to successfully develop new and more flexible local solutions.

Secondly, a successful implementation of sustainable development involves (as stipulated by the Rio accords) broad participation from, and co-operation between, all local-level actors. Thus the local authorities, individual citizens, business and labour organisations, and other NGOs should all be actively brought into the LA21 process. This aspect emphasises a need for new modes of co-operation, horizontal co-ordination and cross-sectoral integration.

This type of activity is, however, relatively undeveloped in Finland. Why?

One could argue, of course, that the Rio documents are overly ambitious on this point. The emergence of a spontaneous interest in self-governance and organisational innovation for the sake of Local Agendas is not a realistic expectation for Finland. The Nordic welfare model is well known for its strong reliance on the public sector. It is the state and the municipality which have had traditional responsibility for citizen well-being. The citizens are more used to receiving advantages and services from government than to starting their own activities and taking responsibility for local problems. A change in the direction of more active self-governance and self-implementation of policy requires stimulation and time. It thus remains to be seen whether current information and awareness-raising campaigns will result in the desired (and presumed) level of local involvement.

There would, however, seem to be lessons which can be learned from the amount of activity thus far, particularly with respect to deficits in both vertical and horizontal integration. It has taken time to transfer the knowledge from top to bottom in the system, partly because most actors have endorsed the dominant principle of self-governance, but also because of the down-grading of the goals of sustainable development in connection with the economic recession. There are also problems in horizontal integration. At the national level, the Ministry of the Environment has assumed overall responsibility, and the rest of the ministries have either been left aside, or, with good conscience, have neglected the promotion of the LA21 idea. And at the local level, transcending borders between public and private activity, and even collaborating with other municipalities, has proved difficult to achieve in practice. Networking requires both clear communication and mutual confidence, and both have been difficult to achieve in the midst of economic adversity.

In general, governments are increasingly having to tackle problems which require the combined information, abilities and actions of a variety of more or less autonomous units. Even recent political trends towards privatisation encourage this development (Alter and Hage, 1993; O'Toole ,1993; Ahrne, 1994). Some researchers claim that complicated implementation structures impede policy implementation (cf. Pressman and Wildavsky, 1973), while others believe that it is the particular character of inter-organisational relations which determines the likelihood of successful implementation (O'Toole and Montjoy, 1984). Successful and well-developed co-operation between different actors obviously leads to effective capacity-building. At the same time, however, inter-sectoral conflicts over policy goals and instruments tend to weaken that capacity. O'Toole (1993: 109) points out that co-operative 'dilemmas' can be solved in and through actual situations, and that such co-operative arrangements sometimes develop from within the community, the network, and the policy setting itself, rather than from above or outside. Such perspectives are clearly necessary if we are to maintain optimism as to the future of the LA21 program.

But what can we say more specifically as to the future prospects of successful implementation of LA21 in Finland? Signs of a new upward trend – this time extending to much wider areas of Finnish society – are now in evidence. This is visible first and foremost in the remarkable volume of information on Agenda 21 processes which environmental authorities are now making available on an increasingly user-friendly basis. Secondly, systematic processes to transfer available knowledge from the central level of government to the regional and local levels and down to the citizens themselves, have already been put into motion. Thirdly, numerous kinds of different activities are emerging in local communities. As we have seen, a majority of the municipalities have taken a decision to move ahead with LA21 processes, and NGOs are also taking an increasingly positive stance. There are even spontaneous citizen appeals for more effective LA21 implementation.

In short, we have seen that there is wide variety in the degree of involvement at the local level in Finland. We find a broad spectrum of both front-runners and non-concerned laggards, and awareness among average citizens of the UNCED program also varies widely. There is, however, a major upswing in informational and educational initiatives on both sustainable development in general and the LA21 idea in particular. There are also resolutions and proposals put forth by citizens, youth, schools, and NGOs, demanding a more serious and effective effort for Local Agenda 21. There are, in other words, a number of positive signs in the direction of more intense and consequent LA21 activity in Finland in the near future.

REFERENCES

Ahrne, Göran (1994) *Social Organizations: Interaction Inside, Outside and between Organizations*, Guildford: SAGE Publications.

Alter, C. and J. Hage (1993) *Organizations Working Together*, Newbury Park: Sage Publications.

Dunsire, Andrew (1978) *Implementation in a Bureaucracy*, Oxford: Martin Robertson & Co.

CSD Country Report (1997) *Review of progress made since UNCED, June 1992*, Helsinki: Ministry of the Environment (25.11.1996).

Eckeberg, K. and A. Niemi-Iilahti (1996) 'Implementation of agri-environmental policy in the Nordic countries: Comparing the local use of policy instruments – the issue of diffuse water pollution', Centre for Comparative Public Policy and Management, Occasional papers 2/1996, University of Vaasa, Faculty of Social Sciences.

Environment Programme 2005 (1995) Helsinki: Ministry of the Environment.

Finland's Natural Resources and the Environment (1996) Helsinki: Statistics Finland, 1996:10c.

Hakanen, Maija (1995) *Paikallisen agenda 21-ohjelman laadinta meneillään 46 kunnassa*, ('Local Agenda 21-programmes being prepared in 46 municipalities') *Kuntalehti* 21/95, Helsinki: Suomen Kuntaliitto.

Hermanson, Ann-Sofie and Marko Joas (1996) 'Finland' In *Governing the Environment: Politics, Policy and Organization in the Nordic Countries*, Århus: Nordic Council of Ministers.

Implementation of Agenda 21 in Finland (1993) Helsinki: Finnish National Commission on Sustainable Development, Ministry of the Environment.

Joas, Marko (1995) *Local environmental protection personnel: In the municipal, environmental and governmental context*, Åbo: Åbo Akademi University, Department of Public Administration.

Jänicke, Martin and Helmut Weidner (eds.) (1995) *Successful Environmental Policy: A Critical Evaluation of 24 Cases*, Berlin: Edition Sigma.

Kestävä kehitys (1995) *Lähivuosien toimenpiteitä Suomessa ja Suomen kansainvälisessä yhteistyössä* ('Sustainable Development Activity during the next few years in Finland and in connection with Finland's international cooperation') Helsinki: Ministry of the Environment.

Kestävä kehitys ja Suomi (1991) *Valtioneuvoston selonteko eduskunnalle kestävään kehitykseen tähtäävistä toimista*, ('Sustainable development and Finland') Helsinki: Valtion painatuskeskus.

Kestävän kehityksen käsikirja kunnille (1994) ('Handbook for municipalities on sustainable development') Helsinki: Suomen Kuntaliitto.

Kettunen, Aija (1996) *Kuntien ympäristöhallinnon asema ja tila, Faktaa ja käsityksiä*, ('Status and present situation of municipal environmental administration – Facts and opinions') Helsinki: Ministry of the Environment ('The Finnish Environment: 59').

Konttinen, Esa and Tapio Litmanen (1996) *Ekokuntia ja ökykuntia: Tutkimuksia ympäristöhallinnan erilaisuudesta*, ('Good and bad eco-municipalities: Studies on differences in municipal administration') Yhteiskunta, SoPhi. Yhteiskuntatieteiden, valtio-opin ja filosofian julkaisuja 6. Jyväskylän yliopisto.

Koskinen, Keijo (1995) *Kansallisen ympäristöpolitiikan toimijat*, ('Actors in Finland's National Environmental Policy') Helsinki: Ministry of the Environment, Environmental Policy Department, Report 7/1995.

Kunnat kestävää kehitystä etsimässä (1994) ('Municipalities in search of sustainable development') Helsinki: Suomen Kuntaliitto.

Mazmanian, D.A. and P.A. Sabatier (1990) *Implementation and Public Policy*, Latham, MD: University Press of America.

Niemi-Iilahti, Anita (1995) 'The Structure and Finances of Finnish Local Government in European Perspective', *Finnish Local Government Studies* 4/1995.

Nousiainen, Jaakko (1996) 'Poliittisen kulttuurin muutostendenssit' ('Recent trends in the Finnish political culture') *Aikakauskirja* 4/1996.

O'Toole, Laurence (1993) 'Applying Rational Choice Contributions To Multiorganizational Policy Implementation', In James L. Perry (ed.) *Research in Public Administration*, Vol. 2, 1993, Greenwich, CONN: JAI Press Inc.

O'Toole, L.J. and R.S. Montjoy (1984) 'Interorganizational Policy Implementation: A Theoretical Perspective', *Public Administration Review*, Vol. 44, No. 6, pp. 491–503.

Pressman, J.L. and A. Wildavsky (1973) *Implementation*. Berkeley: University of California Press.

Rainey, Hal G. (1993) 'A Theory Of Goal Ambiguity In Public Organizations'. In James L. Perry (ed.) *Research in Public Administration*, Volume 2, 1993. Greenwich, CONN: JAI Press Inc.

Sairinen, Rauno (1994) *Ympäristökonfliktit kuntien suunnittelussa ja päätöksenteossa* ('Environmental clonflicts at local level'). Helsinki: Suomen Kuntaliitto, Acta 31.

UNCED (1993) 'YK:n ympäristö- ja kehityskonferenssi Rio de Janeiro
3.–14.6.1992'. ('The UN conference on environment and development: Rio
de Janeiro 3–14.6.1992'). Helsinki: Ministry of the Environment.
Wahlström, Erik, Eeva-Liisa Hallanaro and Sanni Manninen (eds.) (1996) *The
Future of the Finnish Environment*. Helsinki: Edita Ltd.
Ympäristökatsaus (1995). ('Environmental Survey'). Helsinki: Suomen ympäristökeskus, 8:1995.
Ympäristöministeriön muistio (1994) *Ympäristöhallinnon uudistaminen*. ('Re-
forming environmental administration'). Helsinki: ympäristökeskus, 3/1994.

3. Sweden:
Setting the Pace with Pioneer Municipalities and Schools

*Katarina Eckerberg, Björn Forsberg and Per Wickenberg**

Sweden is often referred to as a forerunner in implementing Agenda 21, a reputation which the official overview of Local Agenda activities would seem to confirm. At the beginning of 1996, all 288 Swedish municipalities claimed to have started a Local Agenda 21 process.[1] The LA21 challenge has indeed implied a new and rather dynamic movement in Swedish municipalities. In this review of the Swedish experience thus far, we will analyse what sustainable development means in the practical work of local government and how the municipalities have interpreted the concept of Agenda 21. The contribution also highlights a particular aspect of Agenda 21 which we view as particularly important, namely its relevance to school education. In Sweden, Agenda 21 has been taken seriously by school authorities at both the central and local levels. An in-depth case study of LA21 activity in the schools shows how environmental consciousness can be raised among children and youth and what the results of such environmental education might imply for the community at large.

We will examine the progress in light of the issues outlined in the introductory chapter. What were the background conditions for environmental policy prior to the UNCED agreements that may affect the implementation of local Agenda 21? What has been the role of the central level in relation to the municipalities in initiating the process? Have non-governmental organisations influenced the content and scope of Agenda 21?

Our primary goal with this review of the Swedish experience, however, is to try to look into the future: Where and how will Agenda 21 make the greatest impact at the local level? What kind of obstacles, related to actors as well as structures, may appear when implementing different aspects of Agenda 21 (or implementing Agenda 21 within different areas)? In short, we want to discuss what Agenda 21 may contribute in the municipal policy perspective, including schools; generate assumptions on the mechanisms underlying local processes for sustainable development; and draw conclusions about the prospects for a more general impact on the Swedish society.

Methodologically, we use interviews with key actors at different levels of government and representatives from other organisations which are involved in the Agenda 21 process in Sweden. In particular, four municipalities (Kungsör, Sala, Trollhättan, Örebro) have been chosen to illustrate pioneer LA21 efforts.[2] In addition, we draw from various surveys[3], policy documents and reports which have been published by others, including government and non-government institutions.

The case study of LA21 and environmental education is based on interviews with students, teachers, other school employees, headmasters and parents, in addition to various types of policy documents and reports at different levels of government. In Lund, three schools in the district of Östra Torn, which are pioneers in environmental education and local Agenda 21 activities, have been followed since 1993. We also draw from a national evaluation study of Agenda 21 in Swedish schools and support of environmental education.

The chapter is divided into five parts: (1) A general background on distinguishing features of the Swedish context, including the development of local environmental policy and environmental education prior to UNCED; (2) An overview of the implementation of local Agenda 21 in Sweden, concerning the national and general local government response; (3) Case studies of four pioneer municipalities, with the purpose of drawing lessons from local governments where sustainability strategies are given high priority; (4) A study of environmental education and the Agenda 21 process within the school system, in particular from pioneer schools in implementing LA21; and (5) A concluding summary and discussion of some of the opportunities and obstacles to programming for sustainable development in a local context.

THE CONTEXT OF ENVIRONMENTAL POLICY

The political system and political culture in Sweden are, by and large, similar to those of the other Nordic countries. A characteristic feature is the strong reliance on the municipal level. Municipal autonomy includes rights to levy taxes from the citizens and to develop local policies within most sector areas. Although the private sector traditionally made up for a very limited part of the service production (education, health care, social services etc.), private business – but also labour unions and other interest groups – have influenced public policy formulation since the inception of social democratic rule (1932–76; 1982–91; 1994–). An important strategy has been to co-opt the actors on the labour market, the big companies, and different kinds of sector interests in the policy-formulation process in a corporate manner, and to build consensus 'behind closed doors'.

Whereas Sweden until the early 1990's had one of the lowest unemployment levels within the Western world (1,9 percent in 1990), it has now reached the average EU level (9 percent in January 1997). In the wake of the Swedish budget deficit and financial turbulence during most of the period 1990 to 1995, there have been considerable reductions in social welfare. These cuts in public spending have also affected the environmental sector, leading to considerable reductions in both staffing and available funds for environmental protection. In the three-year period from 1997, for example, the National Environmental Protection Agency is faced with an overall 25 percent budget cut.

Sweden became a member of the EU in January 1995 after a public referendum in which the possibilities of influencing European environmental policy were emphasised. At the international level, Sweden has been among those countries most active in raising environmental issues. The first United Nations conference on environmental issues (The UN Conference on the Human Environment) was held in Stockholm in 1972. Thereafter, Sweden has continued to play an important role, particularly in negotiations over long-range transboundary air pollution and emissions of CFCs. Sweden also promotes intensified environmental action in Central and Eastern Europe, in particular the Baltic region. Recently, the project of creating an Agenda 21 for the Baltic sea region was initiated, encompassing all countries around the Baltic Sea (Sweden's Country Profile, 1996; Baltic 21, 1996)

The National Environmental Protection Agency (NEPA) has identified 13 major threats to the environment, which are targeted through various policy goals and instruments as well as research programmes (NEPA, 1993). Many of these are to be dealt with not only at national level, but require development of local strategies for environmental protection. Having traditionally relied largely on regulative instruments in environmental policy, a breakthrough of environmental taxes occurred in the government's economic reform of 1990/91 when around 18 billion SEK (about £1,8 billion) were transferred from taxes on income and private wealth to energy and emission taxes. Since then, the most common means for achieving various environmental goals imply a combination of regulation, information and economic instruments, with increasing emphasis on the last two types of policy instruments.

Municipal environmental policy prior to LA21

Swedish municipalities are required to include environmental concerns in all their activities as a result of the government's environmental policy (Gov. Bill, 1990/91:90). A large number of different Acts and regulations determine the more precise tasks. Some matters, for example municipal responsibility for monitoring of health and pollution standards, are more precisely formulated than others, and are also nationally standardised. Most matters, however, are regulated by so called 'framework laws', leaving the municipality to interpret and translate national policy into local decisions.

The administrative decentralisation process that has taken place in Sweden over the last decade has implied a change of responsibility from national institutions to municipal government in environmental policy. Gradually, local autonomy in environmental decision-making concerning local domains has been strengthened.[4] In this respect, Agenda 21 may serve the instrumental purpose of legitimising increased local autonomy in environmental decision-making.

Since 1987, municipalities are required to maintain an updated structure plan, *översiktsplan*, containing the overall principles for development which will ensure its citizens a good environment for housing, working, communications and recreation.[5] Consultation with affected interests, with other sectoral agencies and regional authorities is compulsory before a municipal structure plan can be adopted (Gov. Bill, 1985/86:1). In addition, plans for local energy needs and the handling of waste are required by national legislation since 1990. The 1991 Municipal Act grants municipalities greater autonomy to create Boards and Inspectorates according to local priorities. Hence, environmental policy may be dispersed among several municipal boards, in addition to the Municipal Board itself or various co-ordination committees. As a result, the administrative organisation of environmental affairs varies between municipalities (SOU 1993:19, p.43).

School policy and environmental education prior to Agenda 21

In all Swedish school curricula since 1917, the importance of instruction concerning the conservation of nature and protection of wildlife has been underlined (Axelsson, 1993). In the 1969 curriculum (*Lgr 69*), and even more so in its updating (*Lgr 80*), environmental education gained importance in Swedish schools.[6] The latter was influenced by the declaration from the UNESCO and UNEP conference in Tblisi in 1977 (UNESCO,

1991). It dwells mainly on the goals which schools have to achieve, leaving generous scope for interpretations as to how teaching should actually take place. More power was allocated to the school districts for developing resources according to local priorities. Previously, the schools system was very centralised and financing of local schools was granted through the national state.

Organisation and staffing of schools are thus today in the hands of local government, as is the distribution of resources. Educational goals and the guiding principles to which schools are expected to adhere are still provided by the national government in the Education Act and in the national curriculum. Together with syllabi and detailed timetables, these central directives determine the educational content of today's schools: they apply to all schools on a national basis, both municipal and private (2 percent of pupils in the compulsory school system are in private schools).

The Act on Education was amended in 1990 stating that: 'Everyone who works within the Swedish schools system has to promote respect for the value (of each individual and) ... *for our common environment*.[7] Expectations were great, particularly among environmental teachers and activists. In February 1991, a government bill (called 'The Knowledge Bill') proposed that:

> *In the first place we have the environmental issues. Our age is characterised by population explosion, waste of natural resources, and damage to the ecosystem. To cope with welfare and growth in balance we need to acquire general knowledge on what is wrong with the system of today. Such knowledge must be given to all students.*

A new committee was appointed in September 1992 (three months after Rio) to revise the curriculum again. We return to the changes made in section (4) below.

A REVIEW OF THE GENERAL RESPONSE TO LOCAL AGENDA 21

Local Agenda 21 initiatives

Despite considerable ongoing local environmental planning, it took most local authorities until 1994 before LA21 processes were initiated.[8] By the end of 1996, however, about half of the municipalities had employed Local Agenda 21 co-ordinators, and were involved in organising seminars, courses and practical counselling for various groups, including the general public (Sweden's Country Profile, 1996).[9] Following a survey conducted by the Swedish Association of Local Authorities (SALA), two thirds of the municipalities have allocated the responsibility for developing LA21 either within the Municipal Board or within a committee directly under this board. The remainder have assigned the co-ordination to their Environment and Health Board, the Planning Board or to some other municipal committee (SALA, 1996a). Possibly, this reflects a political acceptance of the concept of sustainable development; that is a greater emphasis on integration between social, economic and environmental goals as compared with local environmental policy prior to UNCED.

Generally speaking, Swedish municipalities may be classified in two categories as to their response to LA21: the *pioneers* and the *lingerers*.[10] Most of the pioneers reacted quickly to the UNCED recommendations, since they were already heavily engaged in local environmental activities.[11] It is difficult to discern a pattern as to which type of municipality belongs to this category (according, for example, to size, industrial profile, environmental situation, degree of urbanisation, and economic growth). Instead, it seems as if the most significant criteria is a combination of power and interest within the municipal organisation. The pioneers appear to have leading politicians backed up by key bureaucrats in strategic positions who have actively introduced issues of sustainability onto the local political agenda (most often, however, the role of the politicians seems to be more modest than that of the bureaucrats) (see NEPA, 1996b). The lingerers mostly include those municipalities where political support is relatively low for environmental actions. The decision to develop LA21 among the lingerers may thus be largely symbolic (that is they are afraid that staying outside of the new trends may hurt their public relations).

National responses

In the preparations for the Rio Conference, the Swedish delegation played a very active role. Sweden belonged to the group of nations that supported more unambiguous and binding policy instruments in the negotiation process. In correspondence with its radical position on the international scene, the Government stated in October 1992: 'Agenda 21 consists of recommendations and is thus not judicially binding, but in the Government's opinion the action program is politically and morally obligating.' (Gov. Bill 1992/93:13 p.5). The municipalities are here seen as the most important level for action:

> *The municipalities will have central tasks in the implementation of Agenda 21 in Sweden ... Following the judgement of the Government, it will be an important political task and*

> *a challenge for the municipalities, in consultation with their*
> *citizens, to transform the global Agenda 21 to local action*
> *programs contributing to sustainable development.' (Ibid,*
> *p. 19)*

It took until early 1994 before Parliament adopted a national programme on 'the implementation of the decisions at the UN conference on environment and development' (Gov. Bill 1993/94:111). Later that year, the Ministry of Environment presented a guide to LA21, which outlined possible strategies for sustainability in the local context (SOU 1994:128).

In the Spring of 1995, the then recently elected Labour government set up a National Agenda 21 Committee consisting of representatives from politicians in Parliament, NGOs, the corporate sector and the scientific community. Its objective is to stimulate the implementation of Agenda 21 in Sweden, but also to collect and summarise data on Swedish Agenda 21-activities to be reported to the Special UN Session on Agenda 21 in June of 1997. Beginning in early 1996, it has published a series of reports on Agenda 21 activities in Sweden and set up a home-page on the Internet.

During 1996, the National Committee on Agenda 21 took several initiatives to sponsor round-table meetings at regional level as well as within different sectors, such as education, in order to identify implementation gaps. Furthermore, a national 'summing-up' meeting on Agenda 21 was held on 19–21 November 1996 ('Agenda 21 Forum'), drawing together public and private organisations at both national and local levels. Among others, the meeting was attended by the Swedish King, the Speaker of Parliament, the Minister of the Environment, and many prominent businessmen. Hence, this was a considerable boost for the Agenda 21 profile as a political issue on the national agenda.

The National Environmental Protection Agency, established in 1969, has been the prime motor in developing environmental policy in Sweden. From having played the role of both formulating and implementing environmental strategies, its main function from about 1990 is to formulate and evaluate policy leaving the implementation to various sector agencies and local government (NEPA, 1996a). In its environmental planning, national goals for sustainable development are developed (NEPA, 1993, Gov. Bill 1993/94:111). NEPA has reviewed the progress towards those environmental goals that so far have been adopted, and found that not only have the great majority of them not been met within the timeframe established, but probably never will be reached (Ministry of Environment, 1996). A revision of present environmental goals is, therefore, underway in order to make them more distinct and with clear implementing responsibility. Improved follow-up procedures and better information to the public are also mentioned as future needs (NEPA, 1996a).

NEPA has distributed a wealth of information to the municipal level both about Agenda 21 and about environmental goals and strategies in general over the past few years. The role of NEPA as a 'knowledge bank' is well appreciated by local administrators, although some claim that they are almost drowning in information (Granberg, 1996). Furthermore, NEPA has allocated 100 million SEK to local authorities and businesses to cover 30 percent of their costs for projects directed towards ecological development. Since 1994 there is also a special fund of 7 million SEK annually for LA21 projects carried out by local authorities and NGOs.[12] Although clearly welcomed by local authorities, this funding is viewed as meagre compared to other national projects which have effects in an opposite direction. For example, the share of the national budget devoted to environmental protection is only about 1.3 billion SEK per year as compared to roughly 25 billion SEK that go to transport and communications.[13]

In addition to the Agenda 21 work, the Government seeks ways to combine environmental goals with labour-market policy. An investment programme for sustainable development for the years 1998–2000 that amounts to a total 12.5 billion SEK (about £1 billion) was launched in the new national budget of April 1997. This includes 6 billion SEK towards projects at the local level, initiated by local governments together with other local organisations. Of this, one billion will be available already in 1998. The Governement has explicitly referred to the LA21 process as a starting point for those investments, and the selection process for which projects will be financed will be decided in collaboration between municipalities and the Government. A special committee called 'The delegation for sustainable development' was appointed by the Prime Minister in February 1997 to be responsible for the investment programme as well as for development of the Government's future policy. It consists of five young ministers: the Minister of Environment, Schools, Agriculture, Equal Opportunities and the assistant Minister of Finance. The remainder of the 12.5 billion is to stimulate recycling and energy conservation, along with renewable energy sources. Most of this will hence go to the building, transport and energy sectors on the national scale. At present, the Government is elaborating a new national strategy on environment and development to be introduced in Parliament in early 1998, along with a new and more comprehensive Environmental Code.

The role of municipal networks and NGOs

Early in 1993 the Swedish Association of Local Authorities (SALA) began to spread information about Agenda 21 among the municipalities (some material had already been provided in 1992 from the Ministry of Environment). SALA has since then conducted surveys on the influence of Agenda 21 at the local level, and also published a series of popular reports about Agenda 21 (e.g. SALA, 1995, 1996a, 1996b). Nevertheless, many LA21 co-ordinators are critical of SALA's role, especially in the initial phase.

The so called 'Eco-municipality Network' (see Aall, Chapter 4) has contributed to spreading ideas about local sustainability strategies. It stems from the early 1980's and consists mostly of small-size and rural municipalities joined in a nation-wide movement (which implies certain obligations). There has been a remarkable increase in the number of Eco municipalities since Agenda 21 was introduced and the mutual influence between the network and the Agenda 21 process can hardly be denied.14 Indeed, many of the eco-municipalities are identifiable as LA21 pioneers (NEPA, 1996b).

It is probably hard to overestimate the role of the *environmental movement* in these developments. The Swedish Society for Conservation of Nature (SSCN) has been particularly influential. Through national conferences, seminars and other prodding and co-ordinating activities (publication of newsletters, lobbying etc.), SSCN is probably the single most supporting force behind the rapid LA21 development in Sweden. An important role has also been played by the youth network 'q2000', which was established in 1992 with the challenge of continuously reminding policy-makers about their statements from Rio. q2000 has put pressure on all levels of the policy-making apparatus, and participates in a number of groups at local and national level (for example the National Agenda 21 Committee). A third NGO of importance is the Natural Step Foundation, which concentrates more on the business community.

In comparison with some other northern European countries, the existing international environmental networks between local authorities are rather marginal. In early 1997, only one Swedish municipality was a member of Cities for Climate Protection; three were in the Climate Alliance; seventeen had signed the Aalborg Charter; and four had become members of ICLEI.

The tension between the national and local level

As frequently pointed out by other analysts, the work for sustainable development in the local context cannot take place in a vacuum between local and national levels of government. Supportive policies from the national level are required for many LA21 initiatives (Voisey et al, 1996, Williams, 1996). In practice, the situation in this respect is far from satisfactory. A majority of the municipalities questioned (Granberg, 1996) claim that the national government actually inhibits LA21 work (72

Table I *Obstacles to LA21 implementation as perceived by local LA21 co-ordinators*

	Percent
Lack of time	63
Lack of economic resources	51
Lack of interest from other sectors within the municipal organisation	33
Low degree of local political support	27
Insufficient guidance from national institutions	24
Lack of local interest from the public	16

Source: SALA 1996a

percent 'yes' against 24 percent 'no'). In particular, a lack of economic resources is viewed as a serious constraint to adopting new strategies for sustainability. 73 percent of the surveyed municipalities report that the national resources provided are 'unsatisfactory' – or 'very unsatisfactory', while only 6 percent say that they are content with the economic support from the national level.

The Society for Conservation of Nature has pushed strongly for increased national support to local LA21 initiatives (SSCN, 1996). They point to a stagnation of national environmental policy as a result of state budget deficits along with EU harmonisation during the last few years. The survey carried out by SALA (Table 1) suggests that the political and financial support to LA21 from *both* national and local level are critical bottlenecks.

Scope and type of activities

Although there is no complete picture available at present to assess the status of different activities in local government policy, one of the nation-wide questionnaires on Agenda 21 gives some indication of what types of projects have been launched (Table 2). The majority of projects challenge problems which are relatively easy to grasp and which are within the power of local government to influence, such as waste handling, green purchasing, and water systems. Waste-handling projects include composting, recycling methods and reutilisation of waste products. Green purchasing projects are geared towards the internal use of products within the municipality (and in local schools, day-care centres, etc.). In addition, local campaigns directed towards citizens and local businesses are common. Water-system projects include biological methods for sewage treatment (such as wetlands) and for run-off water from urban areas.

Table 2 *Share of environmental projects within issue areas: Percentages for a sample of 115 municipalities*

	Percent
Waste	23
Consumption (green purchasing)	18
Water system	17
Energy	10
Housing	9
Conservation of nature	9
Traffic	9
Societal planning	3
Chemicals	2

Source: q2000, 1995

According to the survey by the Swedish Association of Local Authorities, many local governments have also developed their own incentives to sustainable solutions. The most common local policy instruments are differentiated garbage collection tariffs (adopted by 69 percent of the municipalities, thus encouraging recycling and composting), and a municipal policy on green purchasing (adopted by 60 percent) (SALA, 1996a).[15]

The general budget deficit of both local government and national government means that all proposed LA21 activities are weighed against other demands. 76 percent of the municipalities have allocated special local funding for LA21. The amount budgeted for this purpose is, however, quite small. The average is some 360,000 SEK per municipality, per year (equivalent to £36,000). Rural communities have allocated the largest sums per capita for LA21 (Ibid).

A growing (but still small) group of municipalities show a concern for global environmental problems expressed by more holistic perspectives in areas such as transport policy. One aspect is international co-operation carried out from the local level. In total, about 30 to 40 Swedish municipalities have given support to Eastern Europe in their efforts to combat environmental degradation. Similar co-operation with Third World countries is, however, rare, and has largely come about through initiatives of local NGOs.

Partnerships for local sustainable development

Partners for municipal collaboration include various NGOs and local businesses. Very few municipal projects are carried out together with universities or colleges (q2000, 1995). The extent to which local business is involved in LA21 varies greatly between municipalities, and some reports are less encouraging. For example, a regional follow-up on Agenda 21 found a lack of engagement among trade and industry to be a major constraint for local work on sustainable development (Lunds Miljödelegation, 1996a).

A multitude of different approaches are used to engage local citizens in the LA21 process. Compared to previous municipal environmental planning and local environmental projects, the imagination is flourishing. Projects to encourage participation by local citizens in environmental projects have been initiated in 64 percent of the municipalities. A survey by the National Environmental Protection Agency from late 1996 shows that 40 percent of the Swedish population is familiar with the concept of Agenda 21 (and what it represents). Twenty percent are aware of at least one ongoing Agenda 21 project; but only three percent are themselves actually engaged in such projects. It is, perhaps, not surprising that so few individuals among the general public are active in this field considering that it is often difficult to mobilise local citizens in political work.

Present trends

There are signs pointing towards a qualitative shift in the content of LA21 processes over time – at least in rhetoric. Lately, there has been a considerable increase in the ambitions to grasp more controversial and complex issues. For example, many municipalities are now working with radical infrastructure plans, with the goal to decrease motorism substantially. Other municipalities (Växjö, for example) plan to cease all use of fossil fuels in heating and transport.

Another tendency which has grown stronger during the mid-1990's is a more holistic view expressed by the attempt to intertwine environmental policy with issues concerning empowerment and quality-of-life. First, organising environmental projects has increasingly developed as an instrument to empower people. A justification for environmental projects today is to improve the possibilities for social interaction within the neighbourhood (for example by initiating local action/discussion groups, or developing programmes for a 'greener' and more friendly neighbourhood), but also to offer meaningful (even if temporary) 'green' work for the unemployed.

Secondly, taking environmental problems seriously indisputably necessitates dramatic reductions in material consumption within the Western world. Actions aiming at radically reducing material consumption will probably be conceived as threatening among many individual and other interests in society. During the last few years, however, there have been more and more frequent signs that a new way of looking at this type of 'conflict' is taking form. Within the LA21 movement, a growing number of people (not least among leading politicians and civil servants) now argue that environmental improvement can be successfully combined with improved human welfare.[16]

CASE STUDIES OF FOUR PIONEER MUNICIPALITIES

We have conducted case studies of LA21 in the four municipalities of Kungsör, Sala, Trollhättan and Örebro.[17] Compared to the average Swedish municipality the range of activities within different sector areas is extremely wide in the cases studied. They are also likely to have adopted more controversial issues on the political agenda (which imply conflicts between environmental goals and other sectoral goals). We assume thereby that such 'successful' municipalities constitute suitable arenas for investigating the nature of potential opportunities as well as obstacles to local sustainable development.

Motives for initiating LA21

What then are the motives behind these pioneer efforts? In three of the four cases (Kungsör, Sala and Trollhättan), concern for the environment is only one reason why the local governments have decided on radical environmental strategies. Of more direct importance, it appears as though they have been developed to solve local problems with high unemployment and structural changes within industry. Local strategies for sustainable development have thus been a way to *market* the municipalities; that is, to develop a green image and thereby attract investors etc. A related motive is the use of LA21 as a way to create new employment. To some extent, they have also been a response to the *lack of a positive local identity*. The best example of this situation is in Trollhättan, where the political leadership hopes to change the widespread perceptions of Trollhättan as a boring industrial town with deep social problems by launching a local green strategy.

Already in 1985 the local government proclaimed Örebro as an 'ecological municipality'. Consensus over local environmental policy has gradually developed among the political parties. Local politicians have played an active role from the beginning. There are numerous examples of radical environmental goals and projects stemming from the local government – sometimes questioned as being overly radical by the administrators. Whereas the development of LA21 in most Swedish municipalities relies on the initiative of local administrators, the opposite seems to be the case in Örebro.[18]

Resources

Despite the relatively high status of environmental policy in these four municipalities, the resources spent on improving the local environment are still limited. For example, the staffing is insufficient according to the LA21 co-ordinators, who report that important issues are neglected because of their shortage in time and money (Kungsör is an exception). There are many examples when even low-cost investments of major strategic or symbolic importance have been rejected by the local government, referring to the economic restrictions. Those more cost-intensive environmental projects that have come about seem to have been justified by one or several of the following reasons: (1) *There is a potential for marketing:* A good example is the Sala Eco Centre – a centre for developing and selling know-how on sustainable development to industry and others – where the municipality has invested 3,8 million SEK. (2) *It stimulates employment:* The LA21 co-ordinators relate how several projects have been realised from national governmental subsidies to combat unemployment, or through their potential for developing more long-term 'green' workplaces. This is the only way that the economic recession has stimulated LA21. (3) *There is an external financial source:* National agencies and funds have had a crucial role in most of the large investments in these municipalities.

Holism: Visions and practices

In general, today's environmental policy at the national level in Sweden shows little concern for the global environmental situation. Therefore, it may seem somewhat paradoxical that policies that support changes in life-style patterns in some instances have developed further at the local level than at the national. In one way or another, all four of the municipalities studied have attempted to integrate a concern for the global environmental situation into their local government policy. In this respect, Örebro and Kungsör are in the forefront.

In Örebro, the local government has decided to both implement concrete national environmental policy goals and to develop local reduction goals in those fields where national goals do not exist (for example the goal to reduce municipal fossil fuel consumption by 30 percent in ten years). Moreover, local strategies for how to reach the goals have been adopted where, in some cases, national strategies are lacking. Again, the strong local political support behind the LA21 process has to be mentioned as an important reason behind this radical approach.

Kungsör has approached complex environmental problems in quite a different way. Starting as a private initiative in the early 1970's, Kungsör has developed a local strategy for preserving biological diversity and recreational interests. In a Swedish context Kungsör is unique in that its primary goal with the locally adopted environmental policy is to promote a sustained biological diversity: all environmental actions are thus geared to achieving this goal.

Environmentalism versus other interests: The case of transport policy

Although LA21 co-ordinators and other local officials frequently claim that transport policy is one of the most important fields to address, there is a widespread resistance in all municipalities towards actions which limit the use of private cars. As elsewhere, the reasons can be found in the car as a symbol of individual freedom, but also in the simple fact that motorism has been the norm for infrastructural planning for decades (and still is).

All of the municipalities studied are 'victims' of large investments in road systems, decided by the Swedish parliament.[19] It is significant that local politicians who regard LA21 as the most important challenge for the future, still often choose to support transport policy goals in obvious conflict with environmental considerations. Thus, the local governments in two of the analysed municipalities plead strongly for large road investments. In addition to threatening local sustainability goals, such investments undermine the legitimacy of the LA21 process. Critical voices hold that the politicians' environmental concern is not serious, and question the purpose of individual efforts and initiatives as long as major investments are made in counter-productive projects.

There are, however, some indications that new ways to handle the problem are emerging. In Kungsör, there is an almost total consensus within political parties to resist the planned motorway through the municipality. One of the main reasons is that the planned road construction would destroy much of the improvement in biological diversity which has already been achieved. Within their LA21-processes, Trollhättan and Örebro have shown that they take the problem of motorism seriously. After the Social Democrats won the local Örebro election in 1994, they decided to stop a planned local road link for environmental reasons.

Instead they chose to transform the area where the road was to pass into a nature reserve. 130 people have been employed during the last few years for restoring old moors, enclosed pasture-lands and forests in this area. In collaboration with the Society for Conservation of Nature, Örebro is now developing an infrastructure plan aimed to reduce motorism substantially. Trollhättan decided to reduce the local prices on buses by half in 1994, and to invest in biogas fuels. Both towns supply their employees with bicycles, and in Örebro a policy decision has been made to the effect that all official travel shall normally be done by train.

Institutionalising LA21

The institutional solutions to the working with LA21 in the four municipalities vary considerably. Two innovative institutional bodies deserve special attention: *Miljöforum* (The Environmental Forum) in Kungsör and *Miljödelegationen* (The Environmental Commission) in Örebro. The Environmental Forum is a competence centre financed by the municipality of Kungsör. Its activities range from environmental auditing and provision of environmental information to the citizens (as well as the local enterprises), to eco-tourism and biodiversity issues. It is formally independent, which means that its staff is not as restricted by sector boundaries as the rest of local government administration. Örebro's environmental commission was established in 1988 and is located directly under the municipal board. It has decision-making power and operates with a goal to foster consensus-building and co-operation across sectors. The political committees (including the city executive board) and sector administrations are assigned specified goals to implement every year, and are required to report back their results to the commission in annual hearings. Failure in implementation is not readily accepted. As one administrator explains: 'At times the situation has been rather embarrassing. Some of the responsible administrators and politicians have almost tried to hide under the table during the hearings.'

Involving local organisations and business

Consultation with interest organisations is a firmly established rule in policy formulation and implementation at all levels. Within the four municipalities, various local organisations have thus been brought into the LA21 process. For instance, in Sala, there is close collaboration with the local Farmers' Union on issues related to ecological farming. In Kungsör, the staff of the Environmental Forum has as its main objective to inform different interest organisations of LA21 and to support them in developing LA21 projects.

The industrial profile varies greatly among the four municipalities. Trollhättan is the single example of a purely industrial town. SAAB and Volvo both have large plants in this small town. Their role in local employment is reported to influence the municipality's environmental ambitions in a negative way – some of our interviews indicate that pollution from the two factories tends to become non-issues on the local government's agenda (Crenson, 1971).

Despite its small size, Kungsör offers remarkable resources to encourage local enterprises to apply more sustainable production methods. A municipal environmental officer is appointed to assist private business in their marketing, while another informs them on how to avoid toxic chemicals etc. (both work within Kungsör's Environmental Forum). Certain locally adopted environmental restrictions are also applied to private firms, notably in the purchasing of products by municipal organisations.

Involving local citizens

The four municipalities use a variety of strategies to mobilise citizens as individuals or as members of neighbourhoods. Among the more ambitious strategies are the home visits which were made by municipal project workers to most households in Kungsör during 1994–95. The response from the citizens was very positive, and it inspired to further citizen-oriented actions. However, the increased contacts with citizens also raised the problem of legitimacy. Some activities within the municipality were brought up for public scrutiny and stirred up a local debate on whether Kungsör indeed was worthy of its marketing slogan 'Kungsör – the Eco-municipality'. In particular, the debate concerned the failure of a local recycling programme for household waste. The symbolic value of such failures is considerable, even though in this case the fault lies not on Kungsör but rather in the other two municipalities who share the waste-combustion plant and who would not agree to a new recycling system.

Three of the four municipalities have initiated bottom-up projects with urban and rural neighbourhoods. Such projects are particularly challenging since local authorities then actually invite their residents to a political process that may come to collide with local government policy. It looks like many local politicians, who show a strong support for bottom-up strategies in their rhetoric, may not be prepared to take the consequences when it comes to their realisation. In one of the municipalities the politicians have invested considerable prestige in bottom-up processes. In practice, however, the same politicians have repeatedly undermined the bottom-up idea by referring to economic restraints or by, in other ways, protecting their own power.[20]

A general experience from the four municipalities is that the message of sustainable development must be as operational and simple as possible. Many LA21 co-ordinators report difficulties in generating public interest concerning complex environmental problems, or overall municipal planning. (Some examples exist, however, where politicians, bureaucrats and other key individuals have formed groups to discuss local long-term strategies, such as the 'Eco Group' in Kungsör.[21]) In several cases, ambitious initial goals have gradually been watered down. It is much easier to create interest for questions related to the nearby neighbourhood than those related to, for example, the stratosphere.

It must also be emphasised that the new form of relation between the local administration and the civil society which is developing from LA21 can be described as a process of trial-and-error. It appears as though these municipalities have in some respects placed too much confidence in 'traditional' information strategies as a central tool to reach the inhabitants. Experiences from Gothenburg show that a very small share of the population actually reads the municipal environmental information (booklets, newsletters etc.). Except for the home-visit strategy, the most successful way to engage local citizens seems to be when the message has been presented in a positive and more 'fun' form. One example is the Eco Fair in Sala where various creative ideas attract the visitors' attention on how their behaviour could be changed. Another is the demonstration of the recycling system at the refuse dump in Örebro in May 1996, which was followed by a large family party (at the refuse dump!). 2000 citizens showed up, far more than expected.

THE RESPONSE TO LA21 IN THE SCHOOL SYSTEM[22]

In the new curricula from 1994, *Lpo 94* and *Lpf 94*, neither Agenda 21 nor UNCED are formally mentioned. However, many aspects central to Agenda 21, such as democracy, participation of the students, solidarity, inter-disciplinary studies, a long-term perspective and local initiatives, are emphasised. There is, indeed, strong support for environmental education and Agenda 21 initiatives in the new curriculum:

> *Through an environmental perspective, students have the possibility to both take responsibility for their immediate environment and to develop a personalized mode of conduct with respect to overarching and global environmental issues. The learning situation should illustrate how the*

functions of the society and our way of living and working together can be adopted to create sustainable development.

How have these goals been implemented in the schools? And how has environmental education been used in local Agenda 21 processes? These questions will be discussed by referring to a national evaluation as well as to a local case study of three schools in the city of Lund.

The national evaluation study[23]

At the national level, there are several co-operation projects related to Environmental Education (EE) between the National Agency for Education and the National Environmental Protection Agency, including regional conferences, in-service training for teachers, development of educational materials and an IT-network for EE. Furthermore, support for international EE networks has been significant. Environmental NGOs – particularly 'Eco-Logic!' (*NaturligtVis!*) – are also active in the field of environmental education and ecological training. By December 1996, EcoLogic! had educated some 1,400 environmental course leaders all over Sweden within pre-schools and other schools and had produced a variety of new teaching materials.

The school administrators view the local schools as an important environmental actor in the local municipality. This is new and would not have been possible 10–15 years ago. The school administrators who were interviewed spontaneously raised issues about Agenda 21 and the school's responsibility for youth and the future in this context. The newly revised local curricula have incorporated Agenda 21 issues and emphasized the LA21 process. In this way LA21 has reinforced the presence of environmental education. Our informants, both at central and local level, claim that schools and pupils are indeed part of the LA21 process in the municipality. Local environmental NGOs are clearly identified and often referred to as important actors in the LA21 process and in environmental education.

In our survey of six municipalities and 22 schools, the pupils, teachers and headmasters give a somewhat different picture of the LA21 process. Two thirds of the respondents did not know how the pupils could participate or influence the LA21 work in the municipality. They had neither heard of 'Agenda 21' nor of 'Local Agenda 21'. Only nine out of 22 headmasters had some idea as to how pupils could become involved in LA21. Furthermore, our interviews show that the schools have implemented environmental education in various school subjects – but mostly within the natural sciences. In terms of practical (ecological) actions, most of the schools have targeted the handling of waste (especially collecting paper for recycling). Two thirds of our respondents say that the pupils have taken initiatives of their own, mostly concerning paper collection, double-sided copying, and to some extent also composting. In some schools the pupils have started environmental groups. The role of dedicated individuals in the environmental work and education in schools is emphasised in the interviews. Most of them are teachers, but they may also be other kinds of professionals within the school. When such a dedicated individual leaves her/his job in the school, the process nearly always ceases. As a result of recent reforms, the role of the headmaster in environmental education has become considerably strengthened..

Another perspective in both the national curriculum and Agenda 21 is the empowerment of the pupils, their participation and influence. In 1996, this issue was evaluated in the governmental School Committee, stating that neither in the compulsory school nor in the secondary school do the students have any real influence in education. In every study where students have expressed their opinions, they emphasise the importance of an open and functional dialogue between teachers and students. But the proposals from students, if they have had the chance to express them at all, seldom lead to any change.[24]

This presents, perhaps, a relatively negative image of the situation for LA21 in Swedish schools. Let us take a closer look, however, at how students may become part of LA21 processes in a municipality which is one of the pioneers.

The case study in Lund[25]

For three years we have studied three local schools in the district of Östra Torn in Lund.[26] The initiative started in the Spring of 1993 with a working group called 'Rio-group in Östra Torn', and included parents with children in the local schools. Their aim was to have a local Agenda 21 in force by 1996.[27] The schools organised a teachers' seminar about LA21 and environmental education and applied to the local board of education for an EE project over a period of two years. 200,000 SEK was granted for the two-year project. We can identify the following achievements:

(1) Education for all and employee seminars at the schools in Östra Torn

Various educational meetings have been held in the schools. Some of them have included all personnel but mostly they have been tailored and related to specific pedagogical and environmental projects at the school.

(2) Agenda 21 in Lund and environmental education

The Environmental Delegation is a committee within the municipal executive board in Lund. Its main task, as formulated by the Municipal Council, is to ensure that: 'the Agenda 21 in Lund will become an integrated part in the local, municipal activities'. The municipality invests about 5 million SEK per year in LA21, half of which goes towards education. During 1996, and parallel to the EE project in Östra Torn, all employees in the schools in Lund were trained in environmental basics and Agenda 21. The teachers in this training come from 'The Nature School',[28] which was founded in Lund in 1986 (Nature Schools exist in about 20 percent of the Swedish municipalities). A special co-ordinator was appointed to administer and implement the additional education of all 7,000 municipal employees in Lund.

(3) The local school plan in Lund

As a result of the new decentralised school system, every municipality is required to develop its own local school plan to be adopted by the Municipal Council. The latest school plan in Lund was approved in Spring 1995 (Lunds kommun, 1995). It includes four development areas – Environment, Internationalisation, Information Technology, and Equality in Education. Regarding EE and LA21, the local school plan is quite far-reaching in that it explicitly refers to the Agenda 21 process. It has promoted environmental projects such as 'Green school yards' since 1991/92. Behind many of these projects is The Nature School.

(4) The local environmental board in the schools and the Danish 'Green Flag'

When the project had been underway for about a year, adults suddenly realised that the children were not sufficiently involved. The idea of local environmental boards, 'eco-councils', was adopted from the Danish-European environmental project 'Green School-Green Flag'.[29] The eco-councils consist of representatives from both students and employees (the students are in the majority). In 1995/96, eco-councils were elected in the three schools. They meet every second week and the students have a decisive influence on the activities. Environmental rules and an environmental action-plan were developed.

In March 1996, one of the schools was awarded the honor of hoisting the 'Green Flag'. To get the Green Flag you have to reach certain environmental goals and fulfil several obligations, including the establishment of an eco-council with students in the majority, an environmental action plan for the school, and at least 15 percent involvement among the students.

(5) Other activities of the EE project

In addition to the above, there has been the Green School Yard project, involving the growing and processing of food and thus illustrating principles of sustainability in ecological farming; recording biological and chemical changes in the river within the network 'Coast-watch Europe'; parents' participation in the Future Workshops and the water festival; eco-products in local shops; a water project with the local church collecting water from various places in the world (the Uniting Water); a newsletter which was distributed to all households in the local district supported by the Rio-group; various training and installations for 'eco-pedagogical infrastructure' in the new school building (for example, eco-toilets, use of rain water, visibility regarding all the material flows like water, electricity, waste etc.).

To sum up, it appears that the vital point in implementing environmental education in the Local Agenda 21-process is the support structure. In Östra Torn, this has included the following:

• dedicated key actors
• continuous meetings combined with in-service training
• active participation by the students
• facilitating support from the headmaster
• an 'eco-pedagogical infrastructure' and practical eco-cycle training
• participation in the local community
• co-operation by many various actors within the schools

SUMMARY AND CONCLUSIONS

By early 1996, all Swedish municipalities (288 in total) had decided to develop LA21 programmes. However, the type and scope of activities included in LA21 vary greatly. Some municipalities have more or less assigned the LA21 label to their 'normal' environmental work. A group of about 40 to 60 pioneer municipalities have initiated a wide range of activities, of which some projects and policy goals may be seen as early signs of more fundamental changes in local government policies concerning infrastructure, resource use and individual lifestyle. Environmental education within schools and day-care centres is frequently included in their interpretation of LA21.

It is worth noting that compared with several other countries investigated in this report, Sweden responded rather weakly to the Brundtland commission in 1987. Whereas *Our Common Future* played a crucial role in the domestic debates of some countries, and was subsequently followed up by significant policy changes, the shift in Sweden from existent environmental policy was less evident. From this perspective, the launching of Agenda 21 in 1992 may have filled a perceived implementation gap with respect to the notion of sustainable development in the Swedish context.

Despite the relative success in adapting and implementing Agenda 21 in Sweden, the country is far from a situation where Agenda 21 has penetrated policy-making and politics at local as well as national levels of government. In the following, the opportunities and contraints are discussed in relation to how local governments and schools can work with LA21.

Enhancing factors

Most of the LA21 activities that have been introduced so far are of an easy-to-grasp and non-controversial nature. There are, however, indications that we might go into a second phase in the development of LA21. First, a growing number of municipalities now appear to show a 'real' concern for the global environmental situation, not least by setting local environmental goals which are more stringent than the national goals (calling, for example, for the reduction of carbon dioxide emissions and the elimination of fossil fuels used for heating). A debate on how to diminish the transport flows is also developing. Second, there are signs that a shift in local environmental politics might be underway, connecting environmental actions to the quality of life, or to local culture and history, pointing thereby towards more holistic thinking.

It seems that the combination of a few dedicated individuals and the potential to market the results of LA21 processes to outside arenas are the most significant enhancing factors behind the most ambitious programmes. A somewhat remarkable conclusion is that more holistic LA21 programmes seem to originate as strategies to solve local structural problems (economic recession, unemployment, decreasing populations etc.). This is the case in three of the four municipalities studied.

The local school LA21 projects studied in Lund have evolved from a sub-municipal (administrative) level. They have become integrated in the LA21 processes at district level. In this respect, they must be regarded as genuine 'bottom-up' projects. Generally it seems that LA21 projects in Swedish schools are also co-ordinated within municipal LA21 strategies. This corresponds to the general decentralisation within the school system. However, the bottom-up organisation of LA21 in Swedish schools still seems to be an exception, when comparing the results from the pioneer schools to the general national picture.

Experiments in the schools with so called 'eco-councils', consisting of elected teachers and pupils (where the pupils are in the majority), have been very successful. This innovative institutional arrangement has fostered creative ideas among the students. Experience from the schools in Lund show that a multitude of environmental activities may develop if adequate support structures are in place – such as the existence of dedicated teachers, support from the headmaster, a democratic school culture and a good climate for co-operation within the school.

Inhibiting factors

The willingness to spend resources on LA21 projects is generally small (c.f. NEPA 1996b). Even if the LA21 processes can reach substantial results with limited resources, it is beyond doubt that more fundamental changes, for example in transport, building and sewage infrastructures, require far more investments than Swedish municipalities can come up with today. It seems that most Swedish municipalities view LA21 as not only a strategy for environmental sustainability, but also for local economic development. This is particularly articulated in those munici-palities with considerable structural problems, such as high unemployment rates.

Central government authorities are often perceived (by informants at the municipal level) as preventing the development of more effectual strategies for local sustainable development. There is wide-spread opinion among LA21 co-ordinators that there is a lack of political leadership in this respect, and that many national policies contradict the goals and values of sustainable development. Although the current Prime Minister, Mr. Göran Persson, (Social Democrat) emphasised in his inauguration speech in March 1996 that Sweden should become a forerunner in sustain-able development, the practical results of this statement are still modest.

The most common problem mentioned by virtually all municipalities with ongoing Agenda 21-processes, is the national policy within the *transport and energy sectors* (for example NEPA, 1996b). Public opinion in the 1990's increasingly holds that large investments in city road links and highways are not compatible with sustainable development. To date, the process of gradually phasing out the use of fossil fuels has been more or less counter-acted by national policy, although this might be changed after the decision in February 1997 to initiate a phase-out process for nuclear power by closing down the Barsebäck nuclear plant. In a seminar organ-ised by the Swedish Society for the Conservation of Nature in November 1996, the Minister of Transport, Ines Uusman, declared: 'We will not do anything at the national level until 30 percent of the municipalities have put up a zero-vision.'

The study of LA21 in schools provides an indication of the *real influ-ence* of Agenda 21 in the society. Although environmental education seems to be well integrated in the schools, by 1996, two-thirds of the interviewed pupils, teachers and headmasters in our national survey had not heard of Agenda 21. Even in those schools which have implemented LA21, the students have not always been involved in the development of the concept and program. Instead, a few dedicated teachers and parents have usually been the initiators of such environmental activities.

Looking forward

We have chosen to study municipalities which have taken Agenda 21 far more seriously than the average community. A common characteristic of these 'pioneers' is that their LA21 activities span over a number of areas and display holistic approaches. Nevertheless, even in these 'successful' LA21 municipalities, there is a lack of correspondence between the visions and policy goals expressed in different environmental action programmes, and the actual municipal politics in important areas. Although it looks like the political leadership in these municipalities is environmentally aware, and understands the overarching policy goals of sustainable development, when it comes to practical decisions and every-day politics, these goals are seldom prioritised. Despite the vocalised intent to integrate environmental policy into economic and employment policy, it is still subordinated and mostly treated as a separate issue.

When discussing the prospects for future development in the field of Agenda 21 and local sustainability it might be useful to first look back. Without question, there has been a considerable change in the last ten years, both in environmental attitudes and actions at the local level of government. Much of the present work in the pioneer LA21 municipalities would hardly have been supported by local governments only a few years ago. With this in mind, there are current signs of a transformation – with ethical, behavioural and material implications – in the way many people relate to the environment. A more holistic perspective on development seems to be gradually emerging at the local level. Whether the innovative LA21 programmes launched actually will result in significant change, depends largely on the extent of support from the national level. With too much resistance, there is always a danger of a political backlash, where we might see less of the traditional consensus in Swedish policy-making, and more of open conflicts between environmental activists on the one hand and politicians and business firms on the other. It remains to be seen whether the new government investment programme will suffice as a response to the Prime Minister's declaration to make Sweden a forerunner in sustainable development.

NOTES

*　　The study of LA21 in local government was conducted and authored by
　　　Katarina Eckerberg and Björn Forsberg. The research is financed by the
　　　National Environmental Protection Agency, Committee on Social Science
　　　Research.
　　　　　The study of environmental education (EE) and implementation of
　　　Agenda 21 in Swedish schools was undertaken and authored by Per
　　　Wickenberg, Lund University with research assistance from Harriet
　　　Axelsson, University of Halmstad. This research is financed by the Swedish
　　　Council for Planning and Co-ordination of Research, Committee on
　　　Environmental and Natural Resources.

1　　According to a recent survey by the Swedish Association of Local
　　　Authorities (SALA, 1996a), the 288 questioned local governments had
　　　initiated some kind of LA21 activity. This is not to say, of course, that they
　　　have developed fully-fledged LA21 plans, nor that their activities are
　　　extensive.

2　　Our field work in these four municipalities began in early 1996 and will
　　　continue throughout 1997. Therefore, the results presented here are prelimi-
　　　nary.

3　　Among these is a telephone survey in 29 pioneer municipalities carried out
　　　within our project in April 1996 (Granberg,1996). The questions concentrate
　　　on the relation between central and local initiatives in the LA21 process as
　　　well as on system constraints to local environment work in terms of legisla-
　　　tion, political support, resources etc.

4　　For example, changes in the Environmental Protection Act from 1989 has
　　　allocated more power to the municipalities in monitoring environmental
　　　protection compared to a previous emphasis on national and regional
　　　environmental authorities. Also, the Municipal Act of 1991 allows more
　　　freedom in designing the municipal organisation according to local priorities
　　　and ambitions (within certain limits). It should be noted, however, that
　　　increased decentralisation by formal powers does not necessarily lead to
　　　increased local autonomy in practice. It may as well be an efficient control
　　　strategy from central level authorities (see e.g. Mostow, 1992:143 and
　　　Hjern, 1993:15f), or a way to divert complex political issues from national
　　　to local level in symbolic policy-making (Gustafsson, 1987:46).

5　　The opportunities and limits to local environmental planning in Sweden are
　　　further discussed in Eckerberg (1995).

6　　Already at the first UN Conference on the Environment in Stockholm in
　　　1972, there was a decision to develop an international program for the field
　　　of environmental education (Recommendation 96). The international and
　　　intergovernmental conference on environmental education in Tblisi resulted
　　　in one declaration and some 40 recommendations.

7　　Act on Education 1990:1477, first chapter, second section – the so called
　　　"portal paragraph" – 2nd Dec 1990.

8　　14 municipalities started their LA21-process in 1992, followed by 45 in
　　　1993, 127 in 1994 and 74 in 1995. (SALA, 1996b)

9   The majority of LA21 co-ordinators are, however, employed on a project
    basis – i.e. on short-term contracts.
10 This classification is inspired by Young, 1995. We have used it in a previous
    analysis of LA21 in Sweden (Eckerberg and Forsberg, 1995).
11 By late 1995 we estimated the number of pioneers to be between 30 and 40.
    The Stockholm Environmental Institute's roundtable seminar on Agenda 21
    in November 1996 estimated that 60 municipalities then had "advanced
    sustainable policies and visions".
12 The demand for this fund has been great – the number of applications
    reached 500 in 1995.
13 The post for "general environmental protection" in the state budget includes
    costs for protecting biological diversity, nature conservation, water and air
    protection, waste management, car emissions, industrial pollution, environ-
    mental research, control of chemicals, radiation and nuclear safety. The
    largest single post is for running the National Environmental Protection
    Agency (356 million SEK in 1996).
14 The first eco-municipality was established in 1983, but the real take-off for
    the movement was in 1990. By January 1992 (just prior to the Rio confer-
    ence) 16 municipalities were members of the network, in 1993 it had
    increased to 30, and in early 1997 to some 40 municipalities.
15 Only 12% had introduced differentiated tariffs on water and sewage. 22%
    practice various types of environmental auditing, of which some municipali-
    ties use more than one method (e.g. internal audits of the municipal
    organisation as well as environmental accounts of activities within the entire
    municipal territory).
16 This is not to say that these ideas have been particularly influential so far.
    Whether we now see the first signs of a paradigmatic value change or not is
    too early to judge. We shall also remember that the variation between
    municipalities is great. There are still many where the action level and
    ambitions are still far below the level of the pioneer municipalities in the
    early 90's.
17 They range from a population of approx. 8,500 in Kungsör to 124,000 in
    Örebro, with Sala and Trollhättan in between (22,000 and 52,000).
18 One reason for this situation may be find in Örebro's history. Since the
    1940's, Örebro is renowned for its experimental urban planning. According
    to one of our informants, many of the leading politicians have had their
    education in natural science. It has been easy for local environmental
    officers to obtain political support to tackle environmental problems.
19 Possibly, there are recent signs of changed government policy in this
    respect. The new Minister of Communication leaves doubts whether all
    planned road investments will be implemented. Indeed, one of the most
    controversial investment projects in Stockholm (the Dennis package) has
    recently been revised due to environmental concerns.
20 For example, in a residential area that was built in the 1960's a special
    project was initiated to improve the local environment through empowering
    the local community. It was incorporated into LA21 in 1995. Although local
    politicians were publicly in favour of this project, some of the municipal
    boards effectively destroyed the possibilities for local residents to develop

an allotment-garden area by referring to that they would be too close to the housing estate. Another request from local residents was to construct a bicycle path into the town. However, the politicians claimed that this would be too costly. Not surprisingly, these incidents have influenced the bottom-up process in a negative way.

21   This Eco Group includes local politicians and representatives from the youth. A strong opinion in Kungsör forced the establishment of a local high school based on ecological education (Ekogymnasiet) in 1996. Hereafter, local politicians are reported to be more concerned about young people's attitudes.

22   Agenda 21 has a separate chapter about environmental education, chapter 36: 'Promoting education, public awareness and training'. Education, in general, is given a prominent role (the word 'education' is mentioned 486 times in the Agenda 21 document.)

23   This section builds on NAE (1996) and Wickenberg, Axelsson and Alerby (1996).

24   SOU 1996:22. See also NAE, 1996.

25   This section is based on Wickenberg and Karlsson Hertz, 1996.

26   Lund is a medium-size municipality by Swedish standards. It is a medieval town with a university, including an institute of technology. The local district Östra Torn has about 8,000 inhabitants. The three compulsory schools have about 700 students in 27 forms and some 130 employees (including those working at pupil recreation centres) of whom 45 are teachers.

27   The "Rio-group in Östra Torn" is still going strong in February 1997 and the local Agenda 21 for Lund has been adopted (Lunds Miljödelegation, 1996b).

28   See also "Nature Schools in Sweden", Appendix to Axelsson, Malmberg and Wickenberg, 1996.

29   This Eco-Schools-project is an idea within the FEEE (Foundation for European Environmental Education) involving about one million students in 15 European countries (1996). Countries in the eco-project "Green Flag" today include Denmark, France, Greece, the Netherlands, Spain, Great Britain and Germany.

REFERENCES

Axelsson, H. (1993) *Environment and School Initiatives – ENSI.* 'The Swedish report about the Environmental Education project, initiated at OECD/CERI', Report no 1993:01, Department of Education and Educational Research, University of Göteborg.

Axelsson, H., Malmberg, C. And Wickenberg, P. (1996) *Skolans miljöundervisning och Agenda 21 – med kommunen som arena. En fallstudie* ('The National Agency for Education, Environmental Education in schools and Agenda 21 – with the municipality as arena. A case study'). Forthcoming.

Baltic 21 (1996) 'Creating an Agenda 21 for the Baltic Sea Region'. Main report. Stockholm Environment Institute (SEI) Stockholm.

Crenson, M. (1971) *The Un-Politics of Air Pollution*, Baltimore: Johns Hopkins Press.

Eckerberg, K. (1995) 'Environmental planning: Dreams and reality'. In: Khakee, Elander and Sunesson (eds) *Remaking the welfare state*. *Swedish urban planning and policy-making in the 1990's*, Aldershot: Gower.

Eckerberg, K. and Forsberg, B. (1995) 'Agenda 21 i svenska kommuner – några utvecklingsvägar' (Agenda 21 in Swedish municipalities – Some developmental paths). *Alternativ Framtid*, Vol. 3: 18–27.

Government Bill (1985/86) 'The new Planning and Building Act', Parliamentary record, 1985/86: 1, Stockholm.

Government Bill (1990/91) 'En god livsmiljö' ('A good environment to live in'). Parliamentary record, 1990/91:90, Stockholm.

Government Bill (1992/93) 'The UN Conference on Environment and Development 1992 – UNCED', Ministry of the Environment, 1992/93:13, Stockholm.

Government Bill (1993/94) 'Med sikte mot hållbar utveckling'('Towards sustainable development'). Parlimentary record, 1993/94:111, Stockholm.

Granberg, A. (1996) *Lokal Agenda 21 – en studie av kommunalt handlingsutrymme* ('Local Agenda 21 – a study of municipal discretion') Department of Political Science, Umeå University, Umeå. Mimeo.

Gustafsson, A. (1988) *Kommunal självstyrelse* ('Municipal autonomy') Stockholm: Liber.

Gustafsson, G. (1987) *Decentralisering av politisk mak.* ('Decentralisation of political power') Stockholm: Carlssons.

Hjern, B. (1993) *Svenskt paradigmskifte, lokalt miljöpolitiskt ledarskap och organisering av samsyning* ('Swedish paradigm shift, local environmental political leadership and organisation for consensus') Underlagsmaterial till Utredningen om kommunernas arbete för`en god livsmiljö, SOU 1993:19, (Swedish White Paper) Stockholm.

Lunds kommun (1995) 'Skolplan för Lunds kommun 1995–98' ('School plan for the municipality of Lund': accepted by the Municipal Council 1995–04–27). Lund.

Lunds Miljödelegation (1996a) 'Bromsklossar och möjligheter – hinder för lokalt Agenda 21 arbete och visioner om framtiden'. 'Report from a regional Agenda 21 forum in Lund 26 October 1996'.

Lunds Miljödelegation (1996b) 'Med livet i behåll. Agenda 21 i Lund' ('Life Intact! Agenda 21 in Lund municipality'.). Lund.

Ministry of Environment (1996) 'Mål för miljön – Miljöstyrning på miljöområdet'. ('Goals for the environment. Goal steering in the field of environment'). The National Committee on Agenda 21, report 1996:4, Stockholm.

Mostow, J. P. (1992) *Process and Popular Sovereignty*, Philadelphia: Temple University Press.

NAE (1996) 'Bilden av skolan' ('The Image of the School'). The National Agency for Education, report no 100, Stockholm.

NEPA (1996a) "Samhällssektorernas ansvar för miljön' ('Summary of a report on NEPA's role in a more dynamic and integrated environmental work') The National Environmental Protection Agency, Report 4539, Stockholm.

NEPA (1996b) 'Agenda 21 i den offentliga sektorn – kommunerna', The National Environmental Protection Agency, Report 4681, Stockholm.

NEPA (1996c) 'Agenda 21 i den offentliga sektorn – centrala myndigheter och länsstyrelser', The National Environmental Protection Agency, Report 4680, Stockholm.

NEPA (1993) 'Ett miljöanpassat samhälle' ('An environmentally adjusted society'). The National Environmental Protection Agency. Report 4234, Stockholm.

q2000 (1995) 'Agenda 21 i praktiken' ('LA21 in practice'). A report of the survey from 1994. Published in a database, Stockholm.

SALA (1995) 'Villkor för en uthållig utveckling' ('Conditions for sustainable development'). Swedish Association for Local Authorities in collaboration with the Ministry of Environment, Stockholm.

SALA (1996a) 'Agenda 21 i Sveriges kommuner' ('LA21 in Swedish municipalities') Redovisning av enkätunders`kningen 1995. Swedish Association for Local Authorities, Stockholm.

SALA (1996b) 'Minirapport 22', Swedish Association for Local Authorities, Stockholm.

SOU (1993) 'Kommunerna och miljöarbetet' ('Municipalities and environmental work'). Ministry of Environment, SOU 1993: 19, Stockholm.

SOU (1994) 'Lokal Agenda 21 – en vägledning' ('A Guide to LA21'). Ministry of Environment, 1994:128, Stockholm.

SOU (1996) 'Inflytande på riktigt – Om elevers rätt till inflytande, delaktighet och ansvar. Delbetänkande av Skolkommittén'. ('Real Influence. Reflections of The School Committee') 1996:22, Stockholm.

SSCN (1996) 'Nationella hinder för lokala Agenda 21' ('National constraints to LA21'). Swedish Society for Conservation of Nature, Report 96/9308 in collaboration with q2000, Stockholm.

Sweden's Country Profile (1996) 'Review of progress made since UNCED June 1992. Report to CSD by the Ministry of Environment, Stockholm.

UNESCO (1991) 'Declarations and Recommendations about Education in Environmental Issues', The UNESCO Conference in Tbilisi 1977, Swedish UNESCO Council leaflet series, no 2/1991, Stockholm.

Voisey, H., C. Beuermann, L.A. Sverdrup, T. O'Riordan (1996) 'The political significance of Local Agenda 21: The early stages of some European experience'. Local Environment, Vol. 1 (No. 1): 33–50.

Wickenberg, P., H. Axelsson and E. Alerby (1996) Evaluation of the accumulated support for environmental education, The National Agency for Education, Stockholm.

Wickenberg, P. and A. Karlsson Hertz (1996) På väg mot en lokal miljöskola, Slutrapport för miljöprojektet på Östra Torns rektorsområde 1993–96 ('Towards a local eco-school. Final report about the environmental project 1993–96') Lund.

Wickenberg, P. (1995) Skolan, lagen och Agenda 21. Från styrande till stödjande strukturer – om mötet mellan de långväga processernas handlingsimpulser och underströmmens miljöaktiviteter ('Schools, the Education Act and Agenda 21. From steering to supporting structures'). A report to Swedish

Council for Planning and Coordination of Research (FRN) Sociology of Law, Department of Sociology, Lund University.

Williams, L. (1996) 'An emerging framework for Local Agenda 21', *Local Environment*, Vol. 1 (No. 1): 106–112.

World Commission on Environment and Development (1987) *Our Common Future*, Oxford: Oxford University Press.

Young, S. (1995) 'Participation – out with the old, in with the new?', *Town and Country Planning*, April 1995, pp. 110–112.

4. Norway: Confronting the Inertia of Existing Reforms

Carlo Aall

INTRODUCTION

In order to answer the question whether the present municipal practice in Norway is in accordance with the challenges of formulating a Local Agenda in a meaningful way, we take as our starting point what many people would consider self-evident, viz. that Norway is not at present experiencing sustainable development. It would be sufficient to refer to the fact that Norway is among those countries with the highest energy consumption and greenhouse-gas emissions per inhabitant. In relation to the goal of sustainable development, it would not be too far off the mark to say that Norway today satisfies those aspects of the development objective relating to the *national* distribution of welfare. Practically everybody in Norway has their basic material demands met. The sustainability problem is our welfare *level* – or rather our *consumption* level – if we accept the following understanding of the goal of a sustainable development: All people, currently living and in the future, have equal rights to have their basic demands met, and development must take place within the framework of what is ecologically justifiable in the long term.

Consequently, our introductory question must be rephrased. We must instead ask whether Norwegian local authorities seem to be about to change their course in a more sustainable direction in line with the prescriptions of Agenda 21. Our discussion will be based on four categories of assessment criteria divided according to different bodies which have formulated goals for municipal environmental policy. We distinguish between *internal* evaluation criteria formulated by municipal organisations and *external* criteria formulated by national organisations. Furthermore, we make a distinction between international and national levels (Table 1). Three types of question are at issue; First: to what degree do the national management signals imparted by the Norwegian Ministry of Environment (MoE) and the signals from the Norwegian Association of Local and Regional Authorities (KS) correlate with the recommendations in the Brundtland Report and Agenda 21? Secondly: what have Norwegian municipalities done with respect to environmental policy in general? And thirdly: to what degree have Norwegian local authorities followed up the explicit recommandations in Agenda 21 and the Brundtland Report?

Table I *Evaluation criteria for assessing the status of Local Agenda 21 related to policies in Norway*

	Internal	External
International	• The Oslo declaration • Recommendations from ICLEI • The Aalborg and Lisbon Charters on Sustainable Cities	• The Brundtland Report • Agenda 21
National	• The national ad-hoc committee on local environmental protection appointed by KS[1] • Resolutions from KS regarding the issues of Local Agenda 21	• Relevant Parliamentary White Papers • Relevant circulars • Relevant national laws

THE NORWEGIAN CONTEXT

Autonomous municipal (*kommunal*) government was established in Norway in 1837, and the independent County Councils came into existence in 1975. Prior to this, a county (*fylke*) constituted only a legal, economic and administrative union of the municipalities within that county (i.e. without its own representative council). The Local Government Act was revised in 1993 so as to strengthen and further

develop both municipal and county autonomy, while at the same time
establishing conditions which enable these subunits to become more
efficient suppliers of services to their inhabitants. An amendment to the
preamble of the New Local Government Act also introduced a more
general commitment to sustainable development:

> *The purpose of the present law is to improve the conditions*
> *for well-functioning municipal and county democracy, and*
> *to provide for a more rational and efficient management of*
> *the common interests of local and county government* within
> the framework of the national community and with a view
> towards sustainable development *(our emphasis)*.

As of January 1997, Norway is divided into 18 county and 435 municipal
units. In addition, the municipality of Oslo exercises county functions
within its boundaries. The county and the municipality both have their
separate elected councils. The counties, and particularly the municipalities, vary considerably with regard to both population and geographic
extent. The average municipal size is about 9,900 inhabitants, with one-
third of the municipalities having less than 3,000 inhabitants; one-third
between 3,000 and 7,000 inhabitants; and the remaining third with more
than 7,000 inhabitants.

There is no general act stipulating the division of authority between
the State, the county and the municipality (Table 2). The Norwegian
Parliament *(Storting)* and the Government regulate the tasks that are
delegated to the various levels. This is partly accomplished through direct
regulation by specific laws, and partly by indirect regulation through the
management of the basic economic conditions that play a decisive role in
determining the tasks that are to be dealt with. The municipalities are
responsible for the establishment and functioning of primary schools,
public day-care, primary health services, social welfare, cultural activities, performance of certain church-oriented functions, municipal roads,
water works, sewers, refuse collection and disposal, planning and
construction, local mapping and surveying, housing construction, operation of public utilities and tax collection. The municipalities and counties
are negatively restricted in their activities, i.e. they may take on any
function that the law does not forbid them to carry out, or that has not
been specifically delegated to other institutions. At the same time,
however, the municipalities are subject to general legislation and rules of
law, unless a special exception has been made.

According to the Local Government Act, all municipalities and
counties must have a Council, a Chairman of the Council, (Mayor:
ordfører) and a Chief Executive (Manager: *rådmann*). Beyond these

Table 2 *Administrative levels of competence with respect to Norwegian environmental policy*

	National authorities	Local authorities
National	• Ministry of Environment (MoE) • Directorate of Nature Management • Directorate of Pollution Control • Directorate of Cultural Heritage	• The Norwegian Association of Local and Regional Authorities (KS)
Regional	• County Governor, Division for the Environment	• County Government (*fylke*)
Local	–	• Muncipal Government (*kommune*)

requirements, the Local Government Act does not stipulate how the different local governments are to organise themselves. The Municipal/County Council is the decisive body and can specify policies, tasks and investments. The Council is elected for four years, and, within certain limits, has the right to allocate funds, set property taxes, impose user fees, and exercise authority in the form of regulations which are binding for the inhabitants. The municipality and county may establish administrative bodies as they see fit. In principle, local units have their own economic foundations and governing boards, and can act independently in many areas. The economic basis for local government is, however, primarily regulated by the central authorities. The revenue base consists of several elements, the most important of which are taxes on capital gains and income, property taxes, and municipal fees. In addition, the State provides direct transfers to municipalities and counties through a system of allocations put into effect in 1986.

Compared to Great Britain and Southern Europe, Norway and the other Scandinavian countries are characterised by a high degree of 'legal localism'. The autonomy of Norwegian municipalities should not, however, be overestimated (Bukve, 1996). There has been a long-term trend towards closer integration of national and local government policies, rooted in considerations of redistribution, equality, cost efficiency and macro economic policy needs. Even if the new Local Government Act and other recent reforms give the municipalities more freedom in procedural matters, the purpose of this freedom is not only to increase the autonomy of local governments. Rather, it has been described by some as a compromise whereby procedural freedom is considered necessary to ensure flexibility and efficiency in the implementation of defined national policy goals.

NATIONAL MANAGEMENT OF MUNICIPAL ENVIRONMENTAL POLICY

In a parliamentary White Paper on the Norwegian follow-up of the Brundtland Report (No. 46:1988-89), it is the national and international perspectives on environment and development which prevail. Out of a total of 180 pages, only five are reserved for the role of local authorities. Their task, moreover, is viewed as mainly one of implementing national environmental policy, particularly in such traditional municipal-technical areas as water works, sewers, and refuse collection and disposal. Mention is also made of local energy planning, transport planning and land-use planning, and emphasis is placed on energy conservation in municipal buildings.

In a parliamentary White Paper on 'Municipal environmental policy' (No. 46: 1988-89), the Government provides for the first time a comprehensive view of municipal environmental policy, highlighting two main groups of challenges: (1) ensuring the quality of the environment with respect to people's health, welfare, and well-being; and (2) conservation of basic life-support systems (Ministry of Environment 1991, p 28).

The Ministry of the Environment (MoE) assumes that the municipalities have the main responsibility for dealing with the former challenge, whereas the Government is alloted main responsibility for the latter group. The MoE emphasises, however, that the municipalities also have a responsibility for the second group:

> Even if the second type of challenge is mainly a national responsibility, the municipalities must also contribute to sustainable development. The environmental challenges of the 1990's shatter traditional sector boundaries. The policies of communication, land-use planning, consumption and energy, as well as the management of biological resources overlap and interlock, and the sum of municipal decisions within these sectors will have a major impact on the possibilities for sustainable development (MoE, 1991).

The MoE further points out that the municipalities are, for this reason, an arena for both local policy formulation and the implementation of national policies. The MoE lists nine central issues where municipal activity is important in reaching national environmental goals, issues which hardly seem to be in accordance with the ambitions of what the Ministry denotes as 'boundary-shattering environmental challenges' and the objectives of a sustainable development as stated in the previously mentioned White Paper. These are the more traditional areas of conservation and environmental protection, whereas the new dimensions, drawn up in the Brundtland Report under the heading of sustainable development, receive much less attention:

• management of the environment, emphasising the conservation of genetic resources and the protection of land and ocean areas with a high biological production
• management of cultural heritage
• local community initiatives
• outdoor recreation activities
• transport pollution
• energy policy and local energy planning
• municipal waste treatment
• municipal effluents
• water supply
• contingency plans for oil and chemical pollution

In yet another White Paper (No. 13: 1992-93), the MoE outlines how Norway is to follow up the commitments from the UN Conference on Environment and Development in Rio de Janeiro in 1992. Whereas Agenda 21 allocates an important role to local authorities, it is harder to trace a similar emphasis in the Norwegian White Paper. Apart from translating selected sections from Chapter 28 of Agenda 21, the White Paper devotes less than a single page to the role of local authorities. Instead, there is a reference to the earlier White Paper on 'Environmental Policy in Municipalities' (No. 46: 1988-89).

The MoE also presented in the same year a report to Parliament on Regional Planning and Land-use Policy. This document emphasizes that: 'it is a basic premise for the land-use policy to promote an ecologically justifiable use of land resources, preserving nature as a lasting source of health, well-being and industrial activity (p 7). The overriding objectives for the land-use policy presented in the White Paper are:

• ensuring an efficient use of resources and making conditions favourable for economic growth
• ensuring health, well-being, security, and good living conditions for the populace as a whole

- taking care of the natural environment and the basis for production
- securing landscapes, culture-heritage values and ensuring opportunities for recreation
- reducing polluting emissions, including noise
- developing viable and prosperous regions in all parts of the country

An important policy measure for implementing this policy was the introduction of national-political guidelines for co-ordinated transport and land-use planning in 1993. The national authorities are thus provided with the power to refuse to approve municipal land-use plans which are not consistent with the guidelines. The guidelines underline land-use economizing, co-localisation, concentration and minimisation of land-use incursions, as well as planning for reduced transportation and the preservation of arable or cultivated fields.

In the spring of 1993, the MoE followed up the parliamentary White Paper on environmental policy in the municipalities with the circular T-937: 'Think globally – act locally: Topics of national priority within municipal environmenal policy'. The MoE here highlights four principles to be applied within municipal environmental policy:

- the precautionary principle
- trans-sectoral environmental protection
- the polluter-pays principle
- popular participation in planning and decision-making

The term 'environmental protection' is still mainly used here, whereas 'sustainable development' is used only once in the introductory part of the circular. In relation to earlier signals, however, the MoE seems to go further in emphasising the role of local authorities. The circular fits with previous management signals within the traditional understanding of nature conservation and environmental protection, but with two exceptions (Table 3): Some of the challanges described under the topic of 'environment and resource-friendly urban and city development' contain elements of a distribution question linked to living conditions in cities. Besides, the ministry seeks to extend the traditional nature-conservation work in line with the UN convention on biological diversity by emphasizing a municipal responsibility for managing the remaining 'non-protected' areas.

Table 3 *Topics of national priority within municipal environmental policy*

Topics of priority	Main challenges
Environment and resource-friendly city and urban development	• Prevent environmental problems through co-ordinated land-use and transport planning • Carry out environmental measures to reduce noise and air pollution • Stimulate energy conservation in the municipality • Preserve green areas and provide people with access to recreational areas • Organise safe neighbourhoods and a good physical environment for young people • Make people feel they belong in the local community • Develop the city centre to become a natural centre of activities
Refuse and recirculation	• Introduce a system of sorting refuse • Introduce a correct pricing of the treatment of refuse • Ensure a proper collection of special types of refuse • Ensure an environmentally friendly final treatment of waste residues
Biological diversity	• Ensure biological diversity in the municipal plan • Conduct industrial and developmental activities in such a way that biological diversity is maintained and strengthened
Coastal and water environments	• Secure water quality in rivers, lakes and coastal areas • Secure a justifiable exploitation of resources in coastal and aquatic environments • Secure and organise areas linked to the rivers and coastal areas
Cultural monuments, cultural landscape, and other cultural environments	• Conserve cultural monuments, landscapes and other cultural environments of local significance • Organise the use and maintenance of cultural monuments, landscapes and other cultural environments; disseminate tradition and build up competence

Source: Ministry of the Environment (1993)

THE NORWEGIAN ASSOCIATION OF LOCAL AND REGIONAL AUTHORITIES AND MUNICIPAL ENVIRONMENTAL POLICY

In 1991, Norway hosted the 30th World Congress of the International Union of Local Authorities (IULA). The conference adopted the 'Oslo Declaration on Environment, Health, and Lifestyle', a declaration which provides an assessment of municipal responsibility in working for sustainable development. To a large extent the declaration follows the broad lines of the Brundtland Report, aiming thereby to give the notion of sustainable development greater legitimacy in relation to local authorities (despite the fact that the report actually has little to say on this matter). The declaration also extends the municipal sphere of responsibility beyond the normal perception of the role of local authorities. The declaration contains clear ambitions to the effect that municipalities should take responsibility as *international* actors through international co-operation between municipalities, independently and irrespectively of the international co-operation between national governments. At the same time, there is an acknowledgement of the decisive role of the municipalities in involving their own inhabitants in the work of promoting sustainable development.

In the spring of 1993, the KS Board of Directors appointed an ad-hoc committee for environmental protection. The mandate of the committee, was to take its point of departure in the Oslo Declaration, Agenda 21, and the objectives and projects of the ICLEI (The International Council for Local Environmental Initiatives). The Board was also invited to adopt either a *minimum* or *maximum* strategy, whereby the 'maximum' alternative would be drawn up in such a way that KS would 'play an active role as motivator' in the process, while the 'minimum' strategy would build on a more passive role for the organisation within current resource limits. The Board of Directors chose the minimum alternative.

The report from the ad-hoc committee was published and passed on to the municipalities approximately one year after the MoE circular on topics of national priority with reference to municipal environmenal policy. It seems natural to consider the committee report as a response to the MoE circular, and the report differs from the ministerial circular in three ways: (1) it devotes more space to defining and concretising the concept of sustainable development; (2) it highlights preventive and environmentally oriented health care as a topic of special priority; and (3) it points out the need to reduce the level of consumption.

Perhaps the last point is the most important. A resolution passed by the KS Congress in June 1992 elaborates on this topic. The resolution is perhaps the most radical political statement so far presented by an official

Sheffield Hallam University
Adsetts Centre (3)

Check-out receipt

16/11/07
12:39 pm

Earth Summit 2002 : a new deal.
101852828237

Due Date: 23-11-07

From the Earth Summit to Local Agenda 21
: working towards sustainable development /
edited by Will
101557535358
Due Date: 23-11-07

Green history : a reader in environmental
literature, philosophy and politics / Derek
Wall.
101429567230
Due Date: 23-11-07

First steps : local agenda 21 in practice :
municipal strategies for sustainability.
101497871284
Due Date: 23-11-07

Please retain this receipt

Don't forget to renew items online at
http://catalogue.shu.ac.uk/patroninfo
or telephone 0114 225 2116

Sheffield Hallam University
Adsetts Centre (3)

Check-out receipt

16/11/07
12:39 pm

Earth Summit 2002 : a new deal.
1018528237

Due Date: 23-11-07

From the Earth Summit to Local Agenda 21
: working towards sustainable development /
edited by Willi

1015575358
Due Date: 23-11-07

Green history : a reader in environmental   l
iterature, philosophy and politics / Derek

Wall.
1014296730
Due Date: 23-11-07

First steps : local agenda 21 in practice :

municipal strategies for sustainability.
1014971284
Due Date: 23-11-07

Please retain this receipt

Don't forget to renew items online at
http://catalogue.shu.ac.uk/patroninfo
or telephone 0114 225 2116

body in Norway, and could have direct implications for the follow-up on LA21:

> *The high consumption and economic growth in the West are incompatible with sustainable development and an equitable global distribution of the world's resources. Our pattern of consumption is an important factor in this context. Local authorities must lead the way in an active effort to promote consumption patterns which are compatible with natural resources and ecological carrying capacity. The Congress of the Norwegian Association of Local and Regional Authorities calls on each local authority to take an initiative towards translating the slogan 'Think globally – act locally' into reality. The Congress calls on local politicians to make an active contribution towards a more equitable redistribution of purchasing power and towards a pattern of consumption and lifestyle which safeguards the environment and supply of natural resources for future generations. (KS, 1993b:9)*

In the spring of 1996, the KS Congress discussed recommendations for working out a Local Agenda 21, and passed the following resolution (Bergen 18-20 March, 1996):

KS views Agenda 21 as an important tool for increasing local political involvement, and for strengthening KS's efforts to renew local democracy. KS will encourage the municipalities to carry out measures by 1996 so as to inform citizens and ensure the endorsement of Local Agenda for their own municipality ... All municipalities are called upon to carry out plans ensuring a broad popular participation in the planning, decision, and implementation processes. KS will encourage the municipalities to draw up their own climate action plans as soon as possible.

In an information booklet on Local Agenda 21 published by KS in conjunction with the MoE in the spring of 1996, the association outlines the most important differences between LA21 and more traditional municipal environmental policy:

> *After the Rio conference, it is important to highlight the significance of certain aspects of local environmental policy which an LA21 process would focus on:*

- organising broadest possible popular participation in planning
- adopting a 'multi-generational perspective' on planning

- viewing local action within a global perspective
- operating with a broad environmental concept related to the objective of improved quality of life (with due consideration to the distributional aspects of health and economic and social well-being)
- increased participation of women and young people in planning (KS, 1996, p 4).

FROM PRE- TO POST-RIO: PHASES IN MUNICIPAL POLICY DEVELOPMENT PRIOR TO LOCAL AGENDA 21

The evolution of municipal environmental policy in Norway can be divided into roughly four phases, with the final phase consisting of two parallel tracks (Table 4).

Table 4 The evolution of municipal environmental policy in Norway: four phases

1965–70	The conservation of nature and regional planning
1970–85	The 'formative period' of official environmental policy
1985–	A 'reform period' in municipal environmental policy
1990–	Interaction and tension between national steering and municipal independence

Conservation and regional planning

The emergence of an indentifiable municipal environmental policy dates back to the first national system of land-use planning of the 1940's and 1950's, but was institutionalised in earnest only in the mid 1960's (Jansen, 1991). The initial phase is introduced with the transfer of conservation issues from the Ministry of Church Affairs, Education and Research to the Ministry of Local Government and Labour, and by the adoption of the Local Planning Act in 1965. The Local Planning Act introduced mandatory master planning for all municipalities, giving the local authorities an important tool in designing their own environmental policy. Within the framework of municipal master planning, environmental policy was primarily looked upon as an issue of natural-resource management. The prevailing planning ideal was to describe the quantity and quality of natural resources and thus be able to arrive at an optimal use of resources with a balance between protection and development.

The transfer of conservation issues to the Ministry of Local Government and Labour – the ministry already in charge of regional planning – is relatively distinctive for Norwegian environmental policy. The linkage of environmental and regional policy was a deviation from the traditional perception of nature conservation as an exclusively national affair (Høyer, 1991). While the traditional perception of environmental policy was, in many cases, understood as protection of nature from any man-made incursions – the ideal of a unspoiled countryside – the linkage of conservation and regional planning represented a very different understanding. In this view, conservation becomes an issue of balancing use and protection. The general opinion was, furthermore, that this balance could best be secured through the management of the municipalities themselves. This view was linked to what eventually emerged as a particular form of Norwegian populism, with direct influence on the emergence of Norwegian eco-philosophy (see e.g. Næss, 1976).

Offical environmental policy takes form

The second phase from 1970 to the mid 1980's was a decisive period for the institutionalisation of environmental politics and policy in Norway. Christensen (1996) adopts the term 'formative period' from Rothstein (1992) to analyse the emergence of Nordic environmental organization. In this fase, existing political institutions become dysfunctional in the handling of crises and emergencies, and at a crucial moment in the process, participants manage to change the conditions for the political agenda. One of Christensen's main conlcusions is that the Nordic countries experienced a formative *period* in the late 1970s, but that the formative *moment* never materialised.

In spite of numerous initiatives (several of them quite radical), the institutionalisation of environment politics and environment policy in the Nordic countries has mainly followed existing norms for public management. The second phase was introduced with the establishment of the Ministry of Environment (MoE) in 1972, the same year as the UN's first international environmental conference in Stockholm. In the process of establishing the MoE, the question of linking environmental and regional policy within a single ministry was a central issue (Jansen, 1989). The outcome was that the MoE was given responsibility for both nature conservation and regional planning.

Throughout this period, there was an intense tug-of-war between national and local authorities as to the location of competence and responsibility for environment issues at the county level. From 1971 onwards, nature and wildlife consultants were established within the offices for development in the county governor's office. In 1977, the counties assumed responsibility for environmental competence by gaining control of the offices for development. In 1979, a parliamentary White Paper on the organisation of public environmental policy was presented, which concluded that environmental policy in principle was a national task. Then, in 1981, came a report from the parliamentary standing committee for municipal and environmental affairs (with only a small minority going against the MoE report) which stresses the significance of linking the issues of conservation to regional planning at the regional and local management levels. This turned out to be a paradoxical situation in more ways than one.

The MoE report was presented during an important period nationally of decentralisation which was characterised by a substantial development and strengthening of the counties and municipalities. In the early 1970s, the MoE had been established on the basis of the argument that linking the issues of nature conservation and regional planning would have greater validity. Towards the end of the decade, the same ministry then argues *against* linking the issues at the regional level. Then, in 1982, the county governor's environmental section is established, and environmental policy at the regional level becomes defined primarily as a national task with no formal links between nature conservation and regional planning.

Reform of environmental policy at the local level

The third phase is characterised by substantial national efforts in establishing a municipal organization for handeling environmental issues. Important distinctions between this and the previous phase are the passing by parliament of the new Local Planning Act in 1985, and the presentation of the Brundtland Report 'Our Common Future' in 1987.

The new Local Planning Act provides the municipalities with a much more flexible and effective planning tool to incorporate environmental considerations in superior master planning and land-use planning. Municipal planning will later turn out to be the most important framework for planning for environmental land-use, both as a cross-sectional and superior form of plan.

In connection with the preparation of a parliamentary White Paper on the follow-up of the Brundtland Report, a broad round of consultations was carried out where a number of organisations – including the municipalities – were invited to voice their opinions as to how they viewed their role in the follow-up. In the period between 1987 and 1989, several municipalities established so-called 'Gro Commissions' with members from non-governmental organisations, labour unions, private business etc. After the Rio conference in 1992, however, most of these were dissolved, supposedly due to a lack of local interest, as well as the extra work load on the part of the municipalities in following up the initiative (Sverdrup, 1996).

As early as 1980, suggestions were put forward to involve local and county municipalities more strongly in environmental policy. Two years before the publication of the Brundtland Report, the first pilot projects involving the establishment of municipal environmental officers were initiated, and the experiment was expanded. Neither the MoE administration nor the KS were, however, particularly interested in such projects at the start (Jansen, 1991). This situation gradually changed, however, partially due to the influence of a White Paper on 'Recreational Pursuits' (No. 40: 1986-87), where recommendations were made for the establishment of a standing committee on environmental protection in the municipalities.

In 1988, the very important programme 'Environmental Protection in the Municipalities' (the MIK programme) was introduced as a joint programme by the MoE and KS. The programme was designed to test new administrative and political models for the organisation of municipal environmental policy. The national authorities financed the appointment of a municipal environmental officer, while the pilot municipalities committed themselves in turn to the design and execution of an environment-and-natural-resource plan. 220 out of a total of 435 municipalities applied for participation in the programme, and 91 were accepted. KS feared a reform which would give the government a new channel of influence in municipal affairs, as well as increased municipal use of resources within areas which KS viewed as areas of national responsibility.

The assessment of the MIK programme showed that this fear was partly unfounded. Participation in the programme did not result in any radical departures from existing policy responsibilities (Jansen, 1991). What did materialise, however, was a growth in new and 'softer' initiatives in terms of information campaigns etc. Local state-of-the-environment reports were produced; environmental goals were debated and formulated; and several action-plans were passed. In retrospect, however, it appears as though environmental concerns only gained limited ground in the municipality's ordinary management system. This was apparently due to the fact that links between the environmental protection plans and the municipal master plans were often weak (Hovik and Johnsen, 1994).

The MIK programme was followed up by a corresponding reform through the Parliamentary White Paper on municipal environmental policy in 1991 (MoE, 1991), so that as of 1992, all municipalities with more than 3,000 inhabitants were offered state financing of an environmental officer. For smaller municipalities, the offer was limited to a half-time position. As of 1 January 1997, these ear-marked allocations will be included in the general framework grants from central government to the municipalities. At the end of 1996, about 95 percent of the municipalities had appointed an environmental officer, and roughly 80 percent of the appointments were permanent.[2]

Adaptation to national standards vs greater local independence

The fourth phase of policy development can be seen as partly a continuation of the developmental trends of the previous phase, and partly a manifestation of an alternative and parallel track. On the one hand, we can see that the national authorities have clear ambitions of continuing the MIK reform in the direction of a national strategy for 'management by objective' of environmental issues. On the other hand, however, there are some scattered signs in the municipalities towards developing a genuine municipal profile. National management of the municipalities has, through the 1980's and 1990's, moved from judicial control of specific policy areas to management of the overall framework for municipal activity (Kjellberg, 1991). Through sectoral regulation, national environmental standards are imposed upon the municipalities, and the state then supervises whether the standards are observed. In this still ongoing phase, we see the emergence of a paradigm of national-local relations whereby: (1) new national standards and guidelines are developed within a 'pre-Rio' understanding of the goals for municipal environmental policy (with reference to the parliamentary white paper on municipal environmental policy from 1991 and the circular T-937 from 1993); and (2) most of the municipalities adjust to the same national standards and guidelines – at least if placed under sufficient pressure through governmental supervision

At the same time, however, we also see a growing awareness at the national level that sustainable development should be something 'more' than what has so far emerged as the content of local – and for that matter national – environmental policy. In the autumn of 1996, circular T-937 was followed up by a so-called 'Idea handbook' published jointly by the Directorates for Nature Management, Pollution Contol, and Cultural Heritage.[3] In the introduction the three directorates states the following:

> *The ideal would be a handbook suggesting objectives, strategies and measures that cover the whole field of sustainable development (issues of health, culture, social conditions, quality of life, involvement and support on local community initiatives, business development, Local Agenda 21 etc.). The handbook is, however, a follow-up of circular*

> *T-937, and thus limited to the given topics of national prior-*
> *ity in that circular. (Directorate for Nature Management,*
> *1996: 4)*

We see the same shift from a traditional concept of 'nature conservation
and environmental protection' to the concept of sustainable development
in some of the recent national research- and development projects. One
local-community project, for example, ('Joint action between public and
local resources' – the JAPL programme) is being conducted in 11 municipalities and two counties. The major objective of the programme is to
develop and establish a meeting-place for local inhabitants and the municipal administration, where the needs of local neighbourhoods are given
priority. So-called 'dialogue forums' will be established consisting of
representatives from non-governmental organisations and the administrative leaders in the municipalities (MoE, 1994). The programme will be
carried out with the aim of presenting examples on LA21, and it is meant
to function as a model for other municipalities.

A project somewhat similar to the JAPL-program ('Sustainable
production and consumption') was launched in the winter of 1996 by the
Directorate for Pollution Control (SFT). The project is part of a major
strategic effort on the part of the directorate to put sustainable production
and consumption on the national environmental agenda. The effort is a
direct result of Norway's initiative within the United Nation's
Commission on Sustainable Development (CSD) to give Chapter 4 of
Agenda 21 greater prominence in the post-Rio follow-up. The Minister of
the Environment has hosted two international conferences in Oslo on the
subject (in 1994 and 1995), and has given the issue high priority in his
annual reports to Parliament. 56 municipalities were invited to participate
in the SFT project; 24 applied for participation; and seven municipalities
were ultimately selected. The purpose of the project is to initiate processes
involving the municipality in cooperation with non-governmental organisations, industry, citizen groups, and other representatives for the local
inhabitants (Directorate for Pollution Control, 1996). In the initial stage,
the project was criticised for insufficient knowledge of (and tie-ins with)
previous pilot projects at the community level, but attempts have now
been made to rectify this by establishing contacts with the relevant scientific experts in the MoE.

In 1992, the MoE also invited 20 major cities in Norway to participate in a project and preparatory scheme oriented towards sustainable
urban development. Five cities were selected to participate in the
'Environmental Cities Programme' (ECP) which will run until the year
2000 (the cities involved are Fredrikstad, Kristiansand, Bergen, Tromsø,
and the 'Old City' section of Oslo). The major goals of the programme
are:

Table 5 *Environmental and sustainability perspectives on the content of municipal environmental policy*

Environmental topics designated by the MIK programme (1988)	Suggested environmental goals of the Environmental Cities Programme (1995)
NATURAL RESOURCE MANAGEMENT	
• Land-use planning • Water management • Water supplies • Nature conservation • Recreational life • Freshwater fishing • Game management • Conservation of cultural monuments • Management of sand, gravel and mineral resources • Energy planning	• Reduce land-use for development and transport purposes • Reduce the energy use for transportation and heating • Ensure the natural environment and adjacent open, undeveloped areas for biological diversity and outdoor recreation, and improve accessibility to rivers, lakes and sea
POLLUTION	
• Waste-water management • Waste management • Pollution from industry • Pollution from agriculture • Pollution from traffic • Noise • Outdoor recreation	• Reduce land-use for development and transport purposes • Reduce the energy use for transportation and heating • Reduce air pollution and noise • Increase the share of environmentally friendly modes of transportation • Ensure the natural environment
QUALITY OF LIFE	
• Local community development	and adjacent open, undeveloped areas for biological diversity and outdoor recreation, and improve accessibility to rivers, lakes and sea • Ensure the inhabitants a safe environment with access to local services

continued

Table 5 *(continued)*

| | • Strengthen the inner-city as the most important meeting-place for commerce and culture |
| | • Ensure distinctive cultural-historical features, valuable buildings and the cultural landscape. Design new buildings and facilities so as to strengthen the identity of the city and contribute to a good physical environment |

LEVEL AND PATTERNS OF CONSUMPTION

| • Health and safety regulations on products | • Reduce energy use for transportation and heating |
| | • Reduce waste volume through changing patterns of consumption and modes of production, and by increased sorting of waste and recycling |

HOW THE MUNICIPALITY SHOULD HANDLE ENVIRONMENTAL ISSUES

| • Political and administrative organisation
• Environmental programmes
• Co-operation with non-governmental organisations and popular participation | • Encourage popular participation in development of the local community and a sustainable urban community |

Source: Handbooks/guidelines from the Ministry of the Environment, 1988 and 1995

- to establish 'best cases' for other cities to emulate;
- to develop specific topical examples of sustainable urban development;
- to assess new and better policy instruments for sustainable urban development;
- to develop better methods for monitoring the local state-of-the-environment;
- to illustrate the goals of Local Agenda 21 by promoting more active involvement of citizens and major groups.

The Environmental Cities Programme is perhaps the best single example thus far of central-government initiatives aimed at local and regional sustainable development. In Table 5 we have compared the topical areas designatved in the handbook prepared by the MoE and KS in connection with the MIK programme, with suggestions for environmental goals for the Environmental Cities Programme. The comparison shows a clear development over time as to what should be the considered as central to municipal environmental policy, with greater emphasis on social and economic issues. The MIK handbook clearly has a more traditional conservationist and environmental protection perspective.

The emergence of an alternative and genuinely distinct municipal sustainability-profile?

The Oslo Declaration on Environment, Health and Lifestyle from 1991 signalled the willingness on the part of the municipalities to approach the difficult task of translating the global environmental challenge to the local level – a form of *globalisation of the municipal environmental policy*. This development is clearly reflected by the establishment of the International Council for Local Environment Initiatives (ICLEI), and by subsequent international initiatives for global-local projects.[4] The trend was further strengthened through the UNCED process and the Rio conference, and in Europe through the Sustainable Cities & Towns Campaign.

What we have referred to as the 'globalisation of municipal environmental policy' may at first seem to be at odds with both 'common knowledge' in the social sciences and recent assessments of the MIK programme. Researchers have, in general, taken the position that we should not expect the local level to relate to global environmental problems. This is, for example, illustrated by Naustdalslid's (1992) typology of environmental problems in Norway along two dimensions: The generation (origin) of environmental problems and the distribution of environmental damage (Table 6).

On the basis of this typology, a hypothesis has been formulated to the effect that the local level will primarily relate to those situations in which there is a concentrated generation of problems (for example local emissions) and a concentrated distribution of environmental damage (for example pollution of a local watercourse). To a certain extent, the assessment of the MIK programme has corroborated this hypothesis. The main conclusion seems to be that municipalities only care about local environmental problems. Other research (from the same research institute) finds, however, that local authorities are showing an increased willingness to take responsibility for externally generated problems (Hovik and Harsheim, 1996: 68).

Table 6 *A typology of environmental problems*

		Generation (origin) of environmental problems	
		Concentrated	Dispersed
Distribution of environmental damage	Concentrated	Sewage from municipal purification plants and pollution of local watercourses	Acid rain generated from NO_x emissions from private transportation and acidification of local watercourses
	Dispersed	CO_2 emissions from coal-fueled power plants contributing to the greenhouse effect	CO_2 emissions from private transportation contributing to the greenhouse effect

Source: Naustdalslid, 1992

Similar views are also expressed in the first overview of how Norwegian municipalities have related to Agenda 21 (Hille et al., 1995). The report (which proved to be both highly controversial and extremely effective in placing LA21 on the political agenda in Norway) points out that, with few exceptions, municipalities seem to be most concerned with local environmental problems. Key characteristics of Agenda 21 – working with a 'century perspective'; emphasising distributive considerations between rich and poor countries and across generations; taking local responsibility for global environmental problems – seemed to have gained little policy attention in most municipalities. The report points out, however, that there are clear exceptions, particularly with respect to communities involved in the Environmental Cities and 'Eco-municipality' programmes.

The latter is of particular interest in this connection, as it is clearly the most distinct forerunner of LA21 ideas in Norway. The programme was officially launched in the Spring of 1989 with nine municipalities receiving pilot-project funding from the MoE and KS. The goal of the programme was to design strategies for sustainable development with special reference to small and medium sized peripheral municipalities

(Aall, 1992). The first Nordic eco-municipalities had already come into existence as early as 1980 (seven years prior to the Brundtland Report), with a joint commitment to the development of 'bottom-up' and 'counter expertise' competence at the local level of government.[5] The municipalities in the Norwegian programme further formalised their cooperation in 1991 through the establishment of a separate 'Forum for Norwegian Eco-municipalities' (FONØ).[6] Other municipalities wanting to join FONØ have to endorse the regulations through a formal local-council resolution, and must contribute an annual membership fee determined by the number of inhabitants. The regulations seek to define minimal standards for environmental policy by adopting the following declaration:

> *An eco-municipality commits itself to working for sustainable development. This implies, among other things:*

- the pursuit of ecological objectives in local planning
- a more widespread use of environmental impact assessment in the planning process
- mobilisation of the inhabitants to apply local knowledge and use local natural resources to create sustainable development
- protection and development of local natural and cultural heritage
- the development of local initiatives for solving global environmental problems
- solving local environmental challenges
- a strong emphasis on local management and commitment.

Local experience from the Eco-municipality Programme (EMP) indicates that several of the units involved are in the process of developing a supra-local environmental policy, and that the content of environmental policy more closely approximates UNCED objectives than that which has been developed at the national level (Aall, 1997). There are also indications that these muncipalities have managed to integrate environmental considerations more comprehensively into the overall management structure, enabling environmental issues and concerns to be put forward with weight more often than what seems to be the case at the national level. Some of the units are also in the process of integrating environment-and-development perspectives more directly into everyday politics, with respect, for example, to: social and welfare issues, environment and health issues, third-world development issues and the goal of reducing levels of consumption.[7]

There are also signs (both within the EMP and for some larger urban units), that local communities are willing to set more ambitious targets than the national government. With respect to greenhouse-gas emissions, for example, we find units which continue to pursue previously set targets (for NO_x and CO_2) after the central authorities have backed off the same goals. At the same time as Parliament, in the Winter of 1996, was abandoning the national goal of stabilising the CO_2 emissions within the year 2000 at the 1989 level, the Bergen City Council adopted a target of a 20-percent reduction. Similarly, other municipalities have – at least for the time being – decided to keep their objectives of reducing NO_x in spite of parliamentary signals that Norway will not be able to reach the target of a 30-percent reduction by 1998 with 1986 as a basis year.[8] The situation is reflected in the following observation appearing in the first LA21 plan to be adopted by a Norwegian municipality (the eco-municipality of Sogndal in West Norway, Autumn 1996): 'It is a dilemma to have to take into consideration the global climate in our local politics when the government goes in the opposite direction. Even so, we still find it necessary to apply a goal of reducing the level of local automobile transportation in Sogndal'. (Municipality of Sogndal 1996: 31)

Also in the area of pollution control, there is a growing interest for alternative municipal strategies to traditional of 'collection' and 'end-of-pipe' solutions. Several local units are thus trying to organise sorting and source-treatment of wastes and drainage. After first having been met with direct opposition from the national environment and health authorities, home-based composting has gradually become accepted as a supplement to conventional treatment of organic wastes.[9] Some municipalities are also applying the same alternative strategy to the drainage sector with local soil and wetland purification. Perhaps the most comprehensive project here is in the municipality of Tanum in Sweden, but similar tendencies are also visible in Norway.[10]

THE ROAD AHEAD: FROM ENVIRONMENTAL REFORM TO LA21

In a strictly formal sense, Norwegian municipalities have clearly done very little to comply with the recommendations of Chapter 28 in Agenda 21 to the effect that: 'By 1996 most local authorities in each country should have undertaken a consultative process with their populations and achieved a consensus on "a Local Agenda 21" for the community'. By the end of 1996 only *one* Norwegian municipality had issued a document with the title 'Local Agenda 21', and only a handful of other municipalities had started planning processes under the same heading. Even so, it is correct to say that Norwegian municipalities have – to differing degrees and within different programs – followed the *intentions* of the Brundtland Commission and the Rio accords. Practically all Norwegian municipalities have come far in establishing environmental politics as an important municipal issue, both with regard to political and administrative structures, adopting environmental objectives and implementing appropriate policy measures. Still, it is also correct to say that Norwegian municipalities – as well as the national government – have only to a limited degree adopted policies which specifically aims to satisfy the more holistic criteria of sustainable development. The prevailing mode is still characterised by an emphasis on conservation and environmental protection.

There seems to be several reasons for this. The government has, until quite recently, chosen not to relate specifically to the role of local authorities in the follow-up of Agenda 21. The MoE – partly in conjunction with KS – has apparently not been willing to place emphasis on the symbolic value of the LA21 idea, failing thereby to join more actively in what has become a world-wide process involving local authorities in a great number of countries. The MoE and KS have apparently assumed that the cost of adopting a new programmatic direction – in direct competition with existing emphases on 'Environment and resource plans' and 'Municipal master plans' – is higher than the political benefits. Furthermore, we have heard numerous expressions in our research to the effect that the prescriptions of Agenda 21 are already being fulfilled by both the existing planning system and the changes introduced by the MIK reform (MoE, 1992; Grann and Holtane, 1995).[11] Only towards the end of 1996 have we seen signals from both KS and the MoE that LA21 is intended to be something 'more' than the MIK reform, and, in January 1997, the MoE established a separate Local Agenda 21 secretariat within the ministry.

It is important, however, to understand the position of the MoE from a more structural standpoint. In the process of establishing the MoE, suggestions were made to endow the ministry with overriding responsibility in all matters regarding management of natural resources (on a par with the powers of the Ministry of Finance over economic and financial affairs). The suggestion did not gain sufficient approval, and instead a more traditional sector-oriented ministry was set up, with only marginal cross-sectoral competence in land-use planning. This combination leaves the ministry with the difficult task of giving coherent steering signals to the municipalities within the broad mandate of achieving sustainable development. In many cases, the municipalities are left with the problem of trying to resolve conflicting national goals and standards.

The Nordic countries in general are characterized by political cultures which are 'rule-deferential', that is that when rules, plans, or declarations are agreed upon, they often achieve a surprisingly strong degree of compliance (Christensen, 1996). The often very general and imprecise environmental goals have a better chance of being carried out in a political culture where authoritative rules are seen as serious and legitimate restrictions on individual behaviour. Many studies imply that national goals and standards to a large extent determine the form and content of municipal environmental policy (Hovik and Johnsen, 1994; Hille, 1995; Hovik and Harsheim, 1996; Aall, 1996). Given the hitherto rather weakly defined governmental position on the notion of sustainable development and recommendations for local action on Agenda 21, it should not come as a surprise that we find a correspondingly weak follow-up of the municipalities. For many of the issues vital to achieving sustainable development, municipalities often find themselves with only limited authority. Pollution control of industry and agriculture and transport planning are, for example, largely under central governmental authority.

Looking ahead, we can outline three alternative paths for the further development of municipal environmental policy in Norway; that is, a potential transition from MIK to LA21. The alternative paths differ with respect to both *process* and *content* (Table 7).

LA21 = MIK ('business as usual')

The first alternative is to proceed along the lines drawn up by the MIK programme without any major changes in the dominant trend. The outline of environmental policy is here viewed as primarily a task for local politicians and public administration, with the content of policy largely governed by national goals and standards in line with traditional notions of conservation and environment protection.

LA21 = popular participation (an 'empty box'?)

In this alternative current perspectives on municipal environmental problems are expanded with greater emphasis on popular participation. The assessment of the MIK programme indicates that popular participation has been focused to a small degree, with most of the activities engaging only local politicians and public-secotor employees, and with the environmental officer as the most active participant (Hovik and Johnsen, 1994). As a response to this, some of the participants in the debate regarding LA21 in Norway, have gone so far as to claim that any kind of increased popular participation – almost regardless of political content – is in line with the recommendations in Agenda 21. With such a view of LA21, there is a genuine danger of creating a more 'empty' and open-ended policy process.

Table 7 *Process and content in Norwegian municipal environmental policy*

	Process: Degree of emphasis on popular participation	
Content of policy:	Little	Large
Municipal environmental policy institutionalised to a small degree	• 1965 ➤ Early stage of mandatory municipal master planning	• 1981–91: The Local Community Projects
Conservation of nature and environmental protection	• 1988–91: The initial MIK programme • 1991 ➤ Continued MIK reform through the parliamentary White Paper 'On municipal environmental policy' • 1992: The circular T-937: 'Think globally – act locally. Topics of national priority within municipal environmenal policy' • 1993: Report from KS ad-hoc committee	• 1992 ➤ The Joint Action between Public and Local Resources programme
Sustainable development	• 1989–96: The Eco-municipality Programme • 1992 ➤ The Environment Cities Programme • 1996–97: The Sustainable Production and Consumption Project	• ➤ Local Agenda 21?

LA21 = sustainable development ('bringing in equity')

A fundamental difference between the notion of sustainable development and the traditional notion of nature conservation and environmental protection is *the distributive dimension* (Lafferty and Langhelle, 1995). This comes to bear in two ways: first, by representing new and separate policy areas related to economics and social concerns within the boundaries of environmental politics; and, second, by expanding and strengthening the level of ambition with relation to traditional conservationist and environmental perspectives. A need for reducing the *level* of consumption, rather than simply changing its *pattern*, is a clear example of the latter. The issue of greenhouse-gas emissions is another. It is hard to imagine that rich countries such as Norway will reduce CO_2 emissions unless change is integrated by distributional considerations which require all countries to take their share of emission reductions (even acknowledging that rich countries must accept the major responsibility). An on the local level, even though we have seen signs that Norwegian municipalities are willing to take up new issues in line with the notion of sustainable development, this seems mainly to be framed within the narrow political and administrative structures of the municipality, with little involvement of either local citizens or non-governmental organisations.

Assuming that there is a form of inherent 'developmentalism' in municipal policy-making, Table 7 might be interpreted as indicating a future path relying on greater popular participation and a strong emphasis on sustainable development. The question remains, however, as to whether this will in fact take place. Is it likely that local inhabitants will participate in formulating, and at the next turn give their support to, a restrictive local environmental policy which aims, for example, at reducing local mobility and the level of consumption? We fear the answer is no.

Still, one might hope that an increased focus on LA21 may bring the environmental debate a step forward in Norway – or perhaps, in a sense, *back* to what it was during the earliest days of municipal environmental policy-making in the early 1970s: linking the conservation of nature with regional planning, or, in the new terminology, linking conservation with development in a local-global framework. The head of the UN World Commission on Environment and Development, Gro Harlem Brundtland, was Prime Minister of Norway between 1986 and 1989, and again from 1990 to 1996. Her successor, Thorbjørn Jagland, has claimed that 'ecolgcially sustainable development' is the primary goal of his government, and that the Norwegian labor movement must be willing to devote as many resources to achieving a sustainable society as was previously used to achieve the welfare state.

It remains to be seen whether these signals will (also) remain in the realm of rhetoric. It seems unreasonable to expect, however, that the municipalities will develop a policy for sustainable development through LA21 processes which is, in fact, in conflict with current signals at the national level. Without strong support at the national level, any increased interest in LA21 may easily become an empty and possibly counter-productive process.

After the initial launch phase of the MIK programme in 1988 up to the parliamentary White Paper on municipal environmental policy in 1991, policy development up to the last local elections in 1995 took the shape of a four-year *establishment phase*. With the termination of the ear-marked allocations for municipal environmental officers as of January 1997, along with the belated but now active interest in LA21 on the part of the MoE, municipal environmental policy now confronts a new phase of change. This will, in the first instance, be *an adaptation phase*, where new methods and organisational models have to be developed and tested. It remains to be seen whether and how LA21 will be used as a label for integrating elements of the MIK reform with the particular demands associated with the Rio documents and UNCED program.

NOTES

1   The Norwegian Association of Local and Regional Authorities (*Kommunenes Sentralforbund*, KS).
2   The figures are derived from a survey conducted by KS in cooperation with ProSus and the Western Norway Research Institute.
3   The booklet contains a survey of 45 national environmental goals within the five national priority areas for municipal environmental policy. In addition, examples are given on how these can be concretised for use by the munici-palities with suggestions of 142 municipal goals and 281 indicators.
4   Perhaps one of the most interesting international examples is the so-called 'Climate Alliance'. 373 European municipalities and regions have signed a manifesto committing themselves to halving their CO2 emissions by the year 2010, linked with economic support to the joint organisation of the Amazon Indians in their work for preserving the Amazon rain forest (Hille, 1994)
5   The municipality of Suomussalmi in Finland (1980) and the municipality of Övertorneå in Sweden (1983).
6   By January 1997, FONØ has 10 member municipalities with an average population of 4,600, wheras the avarage for all Norwegian municipalities is 9,700.
7   Though less than in the other Nordic countries, Norwegian municipalities have established 'twin' municipalities in Eastern Europe and the third world as part of their environmental policy. In 1992, there were 481 'twinning'

agreements between Norwegian and foreign communities in 35 different countries. Six of these were in third world countries, and 42 in Central and Eastern Europe (KS, 1992).

8   The environmental movement in Norway has, throughout the 1990's, criticized the Government for abandoning earlier position as an environmental front-runner. We also find this opinion expressed in an official document presented by the Swedish Ministry of Environment on the consequences of Swedish membership in the European Union with regard to Swedish environmental policy: '... who would ever have suspected that Norway, in the beginning of the 1990's, would, in some respects, belong to the group of countries retarding change?' (The Ministry of Environment and Natural resources, 1994: 113).

9   It is primarily the eco-municipality of Tingvoll which has become renowned as a national front-runner for the introduction of home-based composting. Home-based composting was introduced in 1991, and in 1996, 50 percent of all households in Tingvoll composted their own organic waste.

10   In 1991, the local council decided to apply stronger economic policy measures in its taxation policy which in effect would make it illegal to install water toilets in new houses. Today practically all new buildings are installed with alternative drainage solutions such as bio-toilets etc. (Heiberg, 1995).

11   Grann and Holtane were, at the time of publication, the top administrative personnel within respectively KS and the MoE on the issue of municipal environmental policy.

REFERENCES

Bukve, O. (1996) 'Consensus, Majority Rule and Managerialism in Local Government: Norwegian Experiences and Prospects', *Local Government Studies*, vol. 22, no 1. pp 147–168.

Christensen, P. (ed.) (1996) *Governing the Environment: Politics, Policy, and Organization in the Nordic Countries*, Copenhagen: The Nordic Council of Ministers (Nord 1996:5).

Directorate of Nature Management et al. (1996) 'Collection of ideas for municipal environmental protection. A selection of national environment targets. Suggestions for municipal targets, strategies, measures, and indicators for five topics of national priority'. ('Idésamling for kommunalt miljøvern: Et utvalg nasjonale miljømål. Forslag til kommunale mål, strategier, tiltak og indikatorer for fem satsningsområder'.) TE 713.

Grann, O. and Einar Holtane (1995) 'Taking Rio seriously' ('Att ta Rio på alvar') *Nord Revy*, 1–1995: 14–18.

Hams, T. (1994) 'Local environmental policies and strategies after Rio', In J. Agyeman and B. Evans (eds) *Local Environmental Policies and Strategies*, Harlows: Longman.

Harsheim, J. and Sissel Hovik (1996) *Fra det globale til det lokale*. ('From the Global to the Local') Oslo: The Norwegian Institute of Urban- and Regional

Research (NIBR).

Heiberg, E. (1995) 'Vannklosettet som systemfeil' (' Water toilets as a system failure') *Plan* 6/95: 47–51.

Hille, J.; Kai Armann and Olav Kasin (1995) *Lokal Agenda 21: Norske kommuners miljøarbeid etter Rio* ('Local Agenda 21: Environmental activity in Norwegian municipalities after Rio'). Oslo: Alternativ Framtid, Rapport 5:95.

Hovik, S. and Vibeke Johnsen (1994) 'Fra forsøk til reform – evaluering av MIK-programmet' ('From experiment to reform – An evaluation of the MIK program') Oslo: The Norwegian Institute of Urban- and Regional Research (NIBR).

Høyer, K. og Tor Selstad (1991) 'Regionalpolitikkens økopolitiske grunnlag' ('The Eco-political basis of regional policy') Nord REFO, VF-rapport 19/91, Sogndal: Western Norway Research Institute.

IULA (1991) 'The Oslo Declaration on Environment, Health and Life-style'.

Jansen, A. (1989) *Makt og miljø: Om utformingen av natur- og miljøvern-politikken i Norge* ('Power and the Environment: On the emergence of conservation and environmental protection politics in Norway') Oslo: Universitetsforlaget.

Jansen, A. (1991) 'Reform og resultater: Evaluering av forsøksprogrammet Miljøvern i kommunene' ('Reform and Results: An evaluation of the pilot-project on Environment in the Municipalities') Oslo: The Norwegian Research Council.

Kjellberg, F. (1991) 'Kommunalt selvstyre og nasjonal styring: Mot nye roller for kommunene' ('Municipal self-governance and national steering'). *Norsk statsvitenskapelig tidsskrift*, 1/1991.

Kleven, T. (1993) 'Sørensens konklusjoner: Et essay om forskning og målstyring' ('Sørensens conclusions: An essay on research and management-by-objectives') Rapport 1993:1, Oslo: The Norwegian Institute of Urban- and Regional Research.

KS (1992) 'Norske kommuners vennskapssamarbeid' ('Trans-community co-operation and "twinning" by Norwegian municipalities') Oslo.

KS (1993) 'Tenke globalt – handle lokalt: Nasjonalt prioriterte satsningsområder for det kommunale miljøvernarbeidet' ('Think globally, act locally . Priorities for environmental protection at the local level') Oslo: (In coopera-tion with the Ministry of the Environment).

Lafferty, W. M. and Oluf Langhelle (eds) (1995) *Bærekraftig utvikling: Om utviklingens mål og bærekraftens betingelser.* ('Sustainable Development: On the Goals of Development and the Condition of Sustainability') Oslo: Ad Notam Gyldendal.

Ministry of The Environment /KS (1988) *Håndbok – Kommunalt miljøvern* ('Handbook in Municipal Environemntal Policy') Oslo: Kommuneforlaget.

Ministry of The Environment (1991) 'St. meld. nr. 34. Om miljøvern i kommunene' ('Government White Paper on municipal environmental policy') Oslo.

Ministry of The Environment (1993) 'Tenke globalt – handle lokalt: Nasjonalt prioriterte satsningsområder for det kommunale miljøvernarbeidet' ('Think

globally – act locally. Topics of national priority within municipal environmenal policy') T-937, Oslo.

Ministry of The Environment (1994) 'Det organiserte mangfold: Om modeller og
mennesker i nærmiljøarbeid. Erfaringer fra statlige nærmiljøforsøk
1987–1991' ('The organized variety: Experiences from state-supported
local-community projects 1987–91') T-1005.

Ministry of The Environment (1995) 'Nasjonalt program for utvikling av fem
miljøbyer' ('A national programme for developing five environmental
cities') Dokument T-1115, Oslo.

Ministry of Environment and Natural Resources (1994) 'EU, EES og miljöen',
('The European Union, the European Economic Space and the
Environment') SOU 1994:7, Stockholm.

The Municipality of Sogndal (1996) 'Kommunedelplan Miljø: Kommunen sin
del av Lokal Agenda 21. Status, målsetjingar, handlingsplan' ('Municipal
sub-masterplan on the environment: The municipality's share of Local
Agenda 21 – Status, goals and action plan') Sogndal.

Naustdalslid, J. (1992) 'Miljøproblema som styringsmessige nivåproblem'
('Environmental problems as a multi-level steering problem') Notat
1992:112, Oslo: The Norwegian Institute of Urban- and Regional Research.

Næss, A. (1976) Økologi, samfunn og livsstil, ('Ecology, society and lifestyle')
Oslo: Universitetsforlaget.

Rothstein, B. (1992) Den Kooperative Staten. ('The Co-operative State')
Stockholm: Nordstedts.

Sverdrup, L. (1996) 'Local Agenda 21 – the Norwegian response'. In Tim
O'Riordan and Heather Voisey (eds.) 'Institutional Adjustment for
Sustainable Development Strategies'. Contract EV5V-C794-0394 (DG 12
SOLS) submitted to the DG XI July 1996.

T-937: 'Think globally – act locally. National priority areas in municipal
environmental efforts'.

World Commision on Environment and Development (1987) Vår Felles Framtid,
('Our Common Future') Oslo: Tiden Norsk Forlag. Aall, C. (ed) (1996)
'Kommunal miljørevisjon. Oppsummering av forsøk med miljørevisjon i ni
kommuner i perioden 1993–96', ('Municipal Environmental Auditing. A
summing-up of pilot-projects on environmental auditing in nine Norwegian
municipalities in the period 1993–96') VF-rapport 6/96, Sogndal: Western
Norway Research Institute.

Aall, C. (1997) 'Oppsummering av økokommuneprogrammet 1989–96',
('Summary overview of the Eco-municipality Programme, 1989–96'). VF-
rapport 2/97, Sogndal: Western Norway Research Institute.

5. Germany:

Five Years After Rio and Still Uphill All the Way?

Christiane Beuermann[*]

INTRODUCTION

Chapter 28 of Agenda 21 defines the local level as one of the major stake-holders for the implementation of this legally non-binding document which was adopted at the United Nations Conference on Environment and Development (UNCED) in 1992 in Rio de Janeiro. As almost five years have gone by since UNCED, the cut-off date (end of 1996) recommended in Agenda 21 for initiating 'Local Agenda 21 (LA21)' processes by the municipalities in the signatory countries has passed. A first international evaluation of LA21 processes will be undertaken on the occasion of the UN Special Assembly in June 1997.[1] Keeping this in mind, the aim of this study is to provide an account of the current status of the development and implementation of LA21 in Germany.

From preliminary observations, it is to be concluded that almost five years after the UNCED LA21 is still a low priority issue in Germany. Exact data are not available, but it is assumed that less than 100 of the more than 16,000 German municipalities have initiated an LA21 process. A comparison of the German case to for example the UK where the LA21 process has broad support from local authorities, calls for a more detailed analysis of specific conditons and obstacles that prevent German local authorities from initiating new forms of local policy-making processes as set out in Agenda 21.

For providing an account of a country's approach towards LA21, the definition of the starting point is essential: What are the central-local government relations in the respective countries and, resulting from that, the local authorities' competence and responsibilities? And secondly, what has happened in the environmental policy sector prior and parallel to the launching of Agenda 21 in 1992? These two determinants are framework conditions on which the national Local Agenda 21 process is based and to which it will adapt. As such, they constitute important aspects of the 'national baseline' to be analysed in section two. In section three, an overview of the current status quo of the LA21 process in Germany will be provided, followed up by more specific reflections on German local transport policy in an LA21 context. In section four, attention is turned to LA21 as a new policy-making concept at the local level, with emphasis on a number of informational deficits and institutional barriers, and in section five, we conclude with perspectives on the future prospects of LA21 in Germany.

THE GERMAN 'BASELINE' FOR LA21 ACTIVITIES

The right of autonomy of the German municipalities is an important determining factor. Despite the constitutionally guaranteed rights of German local governments, there have, in recent years, been tendencies to shift power from the local to the central authorities. This gap between theoretical responsibility and practical day-to-day politics will be illustrated by giving some examples of reduced municipal room for action. In addition, a short overview of the development of environmental policy in Germany will be provided. This comparatively new policy sector was (quite successfully) added to traditional ones in a number of German municipalities. Experience with environmental policy at the local level is another fundamental condition for how local authorities will grasp and implement Agenda 21.

Central-local relations: The status of the municipalities in the federal system of Germany

Constitutionally guaranteed right of autonomy ...

The German political system has a federal structure. After the unification of former East and West Germany on October 3rd 1990, it now consists of 16 federal states (*Länder*) with a total of 16,121 municipalities. The general distribution of responsibility between the different federal levels is set out in the German constitution (*Grundgesetz* – GG). The complicated rules of responsibility are defined according to the subsidiarity principle, with the municipalities granted relative autonomy (Wehling, 1986). Art. 28 of the GG states that: 'As to the municipalities, the right is to be guaranteed to decide on all affairs of the local community under their own responsibility according to the laws (...)' (Art. 28 (2) GG).[2]

Generally, the municipalities are responsible for all tasks and decisions that have an impact at the local municipal level. The municipalities are part of the Federal States, and as such can implement laws or measures where regulatory powers normally entrusted to the Federal States have not been availed of at the state level, or where the specific task has been delegated to the municipalities (Ebert, 1994; Joseph, 1995). Municipal tasks are taken over on (1) a voluntary basis (e.g. museums, theatres, parks, town-halls); (2) a compulsory basis without directives (e.g. schools); (3) a compulsory basis with directives (where specific instruments or devices must be applied, e.g., municipal elections, social security); or (4) to fulfill state or government tasks (e.g. police) (Ebert, 1994).

The scope for municipal decision-making decreases, of course, from (1) to (4). Furthermore, the municipal autonomy with respect to administration comprises sovereign decisions with regard to personnel, organisation, planning, the right to make laws (e.g. enact municipal statutes), finances and taxes (Gisevius, 1991). As to sectoral policies, most important tasks of municipalities are in the fields of transport, education and culture, public and social security, supply services, housing, health-care, youth-care as well as state tasks (Bormann and Stietzel, 1993). Hence, German municipalities have traditionally a relatively large scope for the development of their own local policy strategies in sectors of direct relevance to LA21 such as energy, transport, waste, sewage, air quality urban planning etc. (Ebert, 1994).

Furthermore, participatory rights for citizens with differing legal characteristics exist such as constitutional rights; several forms of citizen participation in municipal decision-making processes on other legal bases; participation offered voluntarily; as well as organised participation (Gisevius, 1991). On this basis, a broadening of existing participation patterns to regular involvement of local groups (business, environment-and-development NGOs, churches etc.) in LA21 processes should be feasible.

... but a shrinking self-determination in day-to-day politics

Given the above described room for local action, the capacity of the municipalities to fulfill even their compulsory tasks is shrinking due to several alarming developments of recent years (Witte, 1992; Pohl, 1994, Karrenberg and Münstermann, 1995). Concerning municipal finances, there are three principal sources of revenue (tax revenue, financial assignments from Federation and Länder and charges for municipal services), each counting for approximately one third of the total. In the 1990's, there have been significant and increasing finance deficits, while during the 1980's a consolidation phase was achieved (Bundestagsdrucksache 12/6815). According to the Federal Ministry of Finance, the debts of German municipalities will reach 250 billion DEM in 1997. (Bundestagsdrucksache 12/213). In its 'Report on the Municipal Finances 1995 (Gemeindefinanzbericht)', the Association of German Cities (DSt, 1995) identifies declining revenue from trade taxes in combination with growing expenditure for income support and large financial transfers to former East Germany as the main reasons for the financial crisis.

In particular, tax revenue is being assessed as less than expected (both currently and in the future) primarily because of the recent recession, but will also be generally lower as a result of amendments of the tax basis by the Federal Government (Pohl, 1994; Fiedler,1994; DSt, 1995). Other authors, however, assign some responsibility for the present situation to the municipalities themselves because of excessive expenditure during the economic boom (Bonsen, 1993). Income support is expected to steadily grow in the future. An important factor is the growing number of long-term unemployed people who receive income support after having passed through a graduated system of unemployment aid. The development of unemployment is shown in Figure 1. The major implication of these tendencies is that municipal expenditure is decreasingly under the control of the municipalities themselves.

Another important process with regard to LA21 is the aim of the Federal Government to privatise state owned enterprises (for example the federal-level postal services and railway) and to transfer and promote such a process at the local level. The idea is that this will improve efficiency in those enterprises which have been municipally owned until now (utilities and services, credit institutes etc.) and reduce costs. The revenue of the 'sell off' (*Ausverkauf*) as critics call this process is supposed to consolidate the municipal finances (Handelsblatt, 1.2.1994). However, the privatisation of utilities reduces the municipalities' influence and opportunities to develop sustainable local energy policies. Another aspect of privatisation is seen to be, once again, that economic considerations are given first priority. Consequently, decision-making regarding public welfare (Gemeinwohl), traditionally a basic constituent of municipal political life, seems to be pushed aside.

These tendencies are seen to be a fundamental attempt to undermine the municipalities' right of autonomy, aiming to reshift responsibility and power from local to federal Government, and are harshly criticised by the municipalities' own umbrella association '*Deutscher Städtetag*' (Handelsblatt, 1.2.1994) but also by the labour union for civil services and transport

Figure 1 *Unemployment in Germany 1980–1994 (average)*

Source: Statistisches Bundesamt, several volumes

(ÖTV) (Handelsblatt, 14.4.1994). The Federal Government, meanwhile, denies any such attempt (Bundestagsdrucksache 12/ 6815). As a matter of fact, many municipalities are simply forced to privatise enterprises although they realise their responsibility will thereby be reduced and clearly disapprove of the change (Kommunale Briefe für Ökologie, No. 8/94).

ENVIRONMENTAL POLICY IN GERMANY

The federal level

The introduction of 'the environment' as a policy sector was a centrally steered act by the then social-liberal Federal Government in 1969.3 Stimulated by political developments abroad, above all in the USA and Japan, the upcoming 1972 Stockholm Conference on the Environment and publications attracting public attention (e.g. Carson, 1990) during the 1960s, the Social Democratic Party (SPD) took over the environment as an election issue. Motivated by the severe pollution at that time, one of the most famous election slogans of Willy Brandt was that 'the sky over the Ruhr area must once again become blue'. Once the social-liberal Federal Government came into power, much attention was paid to the environment in the official government declaration to the German Parliament. Launching a process which made Germany one of the forerunners in environmental policy, it has been maintained that '(...) in 1969, the initiators of this declaration were not as yet fully aware of the political implications and subsequent explosiveness of environmentalism' (Müller, 1986).

The five year period 1969 to 1974 was characterised by establishing the organisational, political and legal frame for the new priority issue. Already in 1969, responsibilities related to pollution control were transferred to and concentrated in the Federal Ministry of the Interior (BMI). Subsequently, with regard to the cross-sectoral character of an environmental policy focusing on affected environmental media (traditionally air, water, noise and waste) rather than on pollution generating sectors, other ministries established their own environment departments. Other organisational adjustments were stimulated by examples from the US. In 1971, the Council of Environmental Experts was established to give policy advice to the Government, and the Environment Protection Agency (UBA) was established in 1974 as a subordinate body to the BMI. Not least due to the preparation for the Stockholm Conference in 1972, the first Environmental Program was developed in 1971 and adopted by the Federal Government (Jäger et al, 1993).

Subsequently, the precautionary principle, polluter-pays principle and co-operation principle were introduced as the three basic elements of German environmental policy. Reasons why the program was both so far-reaching and received such strong support from the Federal Government were the intellectual challenge to the drafting group in the BMI and, generally, a reformist political climate with coalition-based and co-operative policy style. More specifically, the initiative was backed by the chancellor's office and prospective 'offenders' took a wait-and-see attitude. Finally, between 1971 and 1974 a number of federal laws on pollution control concerning different environmental media were quickly passed.

The period 1974 to 1978 was characterised by increasing conflicts in general and stagnation with regard to environmental policy. Different kinds of conflicts resulted in a more regressive mood, and achievements already implemented had to be defended. Most significantly, the world-wide recession following the oil crisis of 1974/75 led to a reformulation of political priorities. In one high-profile unofficial conference it was decided that economic interests should regain priority over environmental issues (Gymnich conference). Generally, the political climate was very tense because of terrorist activities (reaching a high point in 1977) and the policy style changed to imposition. Some conceptually good environmental legislation was nonetheless passed, but implementation was insufficient.

At the same time, however, there gradually occurred an opening for reinvigorating the environmental issue. As a reaction to the stagnation at the policy level, the ecological commitment at the grass-roots level was strengthened and the green movement became better organised.[4] As public environmental awareness rose steadily, the Green Party was founded at the end of the 1970s. Succeeding very quickly in the Länder elections, the Greens finally entered the Federal Parliament in 1983. As a reaction to the successes of the Greens, the established political parties started a greening of their own party programs so as to regain or capture 'green' votes. However, between 1978 and 1984, there emerged increasing public discontent with federal environmental policy, even though a strong recession resulted in sharply increased unemployment figures.

The economic crisis led to the fall of the social-liberal Government in 1982. Despite fears for further reversals, some strict air-quality regulations were pushed through at the beginning of the new electoral period in response to the issue of pollution and forestry degeneration, which for the first time focused attention strongly on international environmental problems and policies. The environmental commitment of the conservative BMI was, however, increasingly questioned. Following the Chernobyl nuclear catastrophe, criticism of the BMI's handling of the problem and of the structure of environmental policy in Germany in general sharpened. As a result, the Federal Ministry for the Environment (BMU) was established in 1987 aiming to increase the viability of environmental concerns in governmental decision-making processes and to further cross-sectoral policy approaches.

On the other hand, fears arose that the BMU would not be able to defend environmental interests against stronger ministries such as the Federal Ministry for Finances (BMF), the Federal Ministry for Economics (BMWi), the Federal Ministry for Transport (BMV) or the Federal Ministry for Agriculture (BML). The BMU is one of the comparatively small ministries with respect to staff and size of budget (Beuermann and Jäger, 1996), and was thus perceived to be comparatively weak.

In the last 25 years, German environmental policy was undoubtedly to a certain extent successful and has resulted in improved local environmental quality. However, with the emergence on the public and political agenda during the 1980's and 1990's of global environmental problems such as transboundary air pollution, ozone depletion and climate change, the limits of the policy were increasingly debated at all federal levels. Despite some promising developments in the political response to these global problems (for example the adoption of a CO2 reduction target and CO2 reduction program in 1990), the implementation gap concerning traditional end-of-the-pipe policies observed during the late 1970's, is still present in the 1990's. Moreover, the dominance of economic over environmental interests, as so forcefully stressed by the Gymnich conference, prevails 20 years later.

The influence of federalism and environmental policy at the local level[5]

As another major consequence of the growing green political movement, a shift in the response to the federal environment policy at the Länder and municipal level was induced. During the 1970s, implementation of the federal environmental laws was often insufficient. As a matter of fact, municipalities refused to take responsibility for environmental policy (Quante and Schwartz, 1996). At the time, being faced with 'constitutionally strong Länder that were little interested in or even opposed to stricter environmental policy, depending on the nature of their local problems, economic situation and environmental self-interest, federalism had played a restrictive role' (Weidner, 1995).

This response changed as public environmental awareness grew steadily at the local and regional level. Norms and expectations towards municipal environmental policies and environmental tasks of the administration were changing (Schuster and Dill, 1992; Joseph, 1995). This was particularly pressing because the environmental problems then discussed had mostly regional or even local impacts. Pollution levels in the municipalities were generally high and, therefore, the urban quality-of-life perceived to be low (Quante and Schwartz, 1996). As mentioned above, the Green Party first entered assemblies at the local and Länder level, using these arenas as political training fields. By then federalism had established 'quite effective barriers against attempts by the Federal Government to weaken local environmental policy through federal regulations' (Weidner, 1995).

In the meantime, the environmental concerns of a number of local governments have been integrated into strategic decision-making within the municipalities' existing responsibilities (Ebert, 1994) and it has been concluded that some Länder and municipal authorities seem to enjoy experimenting while applying their responsibilities to environmental policy (Weidner, 1995). However, with regard to the necessity to restructure environmental and other policies within a precautionary policy to promote sustainable development (as prescribed by Agenda 21), the majority of German municipalities are not judged to be forerunners (Mäding, 1995). They mainly implement reactive measures that do not remedy the causes of the environmental problems (Quante and Schwartz, 1996).

Despite the recent municipal crisis described above, a new push focusing attention on precautionary environmental policy was introduced when the global problem of climate change emerged on the political agenda. Clearly, climate change is an issue which transcends direct cause-and-effect relations at the local level. Surprisingly, it was enthusiastically addressed at the local level, probably supported by an immense public response (Beuermann and Jäger, 1996). At present, about 400 German municipalities are organised into the Climate Alliance of the Cities, having adopted a target of 50% CO2 reduction by the year 2010 compared to 1990 levels (Climate Alliance, 1993).

To some extent, strategies developed under these initiatives are similar to what a LA21 process could contain.[6] Climate-protection strategies cover some of the policy fields of LA21, and new participatory elements are frequently integrated. However, climate-protection strategies lack the socio-economic dimension which is particularly important in LA21. In this respect, climate-protection initiatives provide, to some extent, examples of good practice on how individual aspects of an LA21 process might work in practice. For example, in order to achieve its CO2 reduction target of minus 30% by the year 2010, Heidelberg adopted a program of measures to be implemented in the energy and transport sector (Schmidt et al, 1992). To improve the acceptance of the decisions by the public at the start of the process, the local government decided to set up 'forums' to discuss the instruments and measures (Schiller-Dickhut, 1996).

THE CURRENT STATUS OF THE LA21 PROCESS IN GERMANY

In order to investigate whether the launching of LA21 has started processes aiming to implement sustainable development at the local level, an analysis of the national baseline is helpful, particularly with regard to international comparisons (Voisey et al, 1996). However, this does not provide criteria of how to find LA21 initiatives and distinguish them from processes and initiatives which probably would have happened anyway. However, considering the structure and content of Chapter 28 of Agenda 21, it can be concluded that LA21's should have, at least, the following characteristics (see also the introductory chapter):

- introduce a process of participation of all relevant local actor groups in the LA21 development process
- introduce a global partnership perspective
- consider socio-economic dimensions of the LA21 strategy
- include a long-term perspective into the LA21 strategy by applying the precautionary principle and integrating LA21 concerns into all policy sectors

A more pragmatic criterion is to investigate whether or not a formal, legally binding decision of the local council has been adopted to develop and implement LA21. However, the remaining LA21 initiatives would have to be analysed with regard to their content and structure to exclude LA21-labelling. At the same time, however, LA21 processes would be excluded that can be undertaken without formal decision.

Ideally, a systematic analysis would demand the investigation of how many of the more than 16,000 German municipalities undertake initiatives according to the chosen criteria. However, there are no comprehensive surveys or other databases on LA21 and on municipal environmental programs in Germany in general.[7] As long as municipalities do not publish or otherwise distribute information on their initiatives, they are known only locally or regionally. Therefore, the present general description and analysis of the status quo of the German response to LA21 is based on available literature on LA21 case studies, on publicly discussed pioneering municipalities, and on our own field work.

What has happened thus far?

> *It is high time for action! There are only a few municipalities which have adopted a decision to develop a LA21 (...). The English, Danes and Dutch have impressively demonstrated to us how this process is to be implemented by administration, policy and citizens (Fiedler, 1996a)*

This statement, made by a representative of the German Association of Cities, summarises the dilemma of the German LA21 'process'. Five years after Agenda 21 has been signed, the LA21 process in Germany is judged to be only at the beginning (Unmüßig, 1996, Enquete Kommission Schutz des Menschen und der Umwelt, 1996a). At present, there is a slowly growing number of municipalities voluntarily developing or initiating an LA21 process. In November 1995, the International Council for Local Environmental Initiatives (ICLEI, 1995c) stated that no more than half a dozen German municipalities had initiated processes which have been explicitly designed as LA21.[8] By the end of 1996, this number had grown to approximately 50 initiatives. These LA21 processes have, in general, an experimental character as they vary widely in structure and content. Aiming to investigate what is possible under LA21 and, at the same time, what is adequate with respect to the specific municipal conditions, requires a more comprehensive approach than is now feasible.

In contrast to other countries, for example the Netherlands where the implementation of LA21 is financially supported by the Government (Coenen, 1996 and this volume; Kuby, 1996; Pluckel, 1996), the German Federal Government is little involved in the discussion on LA21 and provides only modest support (Ökologische Briefe, 1995). In particular, the BMU, although being responsible for the Rio follow-up, is relatively passive in the German LA21 process. This attitude has been heavily criticised by municipal authorities (as witnessed by several statements in: Enquete Kommission, 1996b).

However, this situation at the Government level may change with the UN Special Assembly approaching in June 1997, when the implementation of Agenda 21 will generally be reviewed. In addition, a further push may result from another international process: BMBau stressed the importance of municipal action to solve global problems in its report to Habitat II and in several related statements (Töpfer, 1996; BMBau, 1996). In addition, the parliamentary Enquete Commission held a public hearing in November 1996 on municipal experiences with and obstacles to LA21 in Germany, where local authorities were invited to present their LA21 initiatives and comment on the framework conditions (Enquete Kommission, 1996a and 1996b).[9] As Enquete Commissions are indicators for which issues are (controversially) discussed and may gain overall political importance, LA21 may become a more important issue in the BMU. At the moment, this is only speculation.

There have, however, emerged a number of interesting developments at the state (länder) level. The Government of North-Rhine/Westphalia (NRW) started in July 1996 to financially support a LA21 co-ordination agency (named 'Agenda-Transfer') in Bonn with the Clearing-house for Applied Futures (CAF) as the responsible body.[10] Agenda-Transfer aims to provide networking and co-ordination, as well as services for capacity building (Hoffmann, 1997). Activities are fourfold and explicitly undertaken with regard to relevance and as a service function for the municipalities in NRW: (1) research and analysis of municipal LA21 initiatives and examples of good practice at the federal level, but also internationally; (2) organisation and holding of seminars and workshops on questions related to LA21, in particular the development of strategies and the organisation of participational procedures; (3) providing advice and informational presentations; and (4) the publication of a bi-monthly newsletter on LA21.

Agenda-Transfer was also represented in the German National Committee for Habitat II. During its first nine months of operation, Agenda-Transfer has experienced an enormous municipal response and increasing demands for information and other services, indicating that an interest in LA21 is growing in Germany. Other states such as Hesse and Schleswig Holstein have shown strong interest in this project and some kind of co-operation may develop. Agenda-Transfer, together with the other non-governmental institutions at the federal level mentioned above and dealing with LA21 related issues, has a strong interest to push for co-operation between these institutions. In December 1996, a first informal meeting was organised by DST aiming at bringing together national LA21 players and representatives from environmental ministries to establish an information and co-ordination platform at the national level to increase effectiveness (ibid). In doing so, there may develop some kind of 'job sharing' between Agenda-Transfer, ICLEI and DIFU.

Information on the different existing LA21 processes is being increasingly disseminated, in particular by ICLEI, Agenda-Transfer and networks of 'model-municipalities', with examples of good practice and co-ordinating activities. In October 1995, for example, ICLEI (1995c) organised the first German seminar on LA21 for local authorities in co-operation with the district of Berlin-Köpenick. This seminar was also supported by the other municipal associations and the BMU. About the same time the established municipal associations actively started promoting LA21. Subsequently, the German Association of Cities (DSt) published an opinion poll on the LA21 activities of its member cities, showing that the majority of local authorities surveyed agreed that LA21 is their policy responsibility (Rösler, 1996). Only in 17 percent of these municipalities, however, has a formal political decision been adopted to introduce an LA21, while in 24 percent such a decision is still in preparation (Rösler, 1996). Generally, LA21 has thus far mostly been seen as a re-organisation, which means that the structures considered to be necessary are being put into place. The content of the LA21's themselves remains vague, but some common elements are nonetheless visible.

There are very different points of departure with respect to roots and motivations for the existing initiatives. These are, for example, activities in response to the issue of climate change, the involvement of churches, local environmental NGOs, as well as local third-world or development groups. Often, individual local authorities, being sensitive to the issues of environment and development and local administration, introduce the LA21 process (ICLEI, 1996). Due to the early involvement of all or at least some of the local actors in bottom-up LA21 processes, the participatory element should be strengthened. This would be a major difference between LA21 processes and the traditional local environmental policy approaches. However, approaches to introduce and organise participation processes are both varied and often nonconsequential.

Among the municipalities having adopted a political decision to start LA21, there are a number of LA21's which are often chosen as examples of good practice to clarify the general structures of how LA21 processes could be organised. At the beginning of their LA21s, these model-municipalities put considerable effort into the establishment of new participation structures. However, the allocation, assignment and implementation of responsibilities and duties between new 'participants' and the administration remains a major difficulty to be solved to increase LA21 effectiveness and acceptance. Even where such processes have been introduced, not all of the relevant groups show the same interest in participation. In contrast to the involvement of local NGOs and churches, for example, participation of local businesses and industry is rare and generally perceived as difficult (ICLEI, 1996). Other municipalities working with LA21 appear to be less interested in establishing such a consultation process. From a conceptual point of view, these LA21 processes cannot be said to be in line with the basic concept of Chapter 28, and their is evidence that local actors, other than the administration itself, are frustrated by these experiences.

In connection with a formal decision to introduce an LA21, specific focal points for co-ordination have often been established (Rösler, 1996). These co-ordination offices are integrated into or affiliated with the existing municipal (environmental) administration. In most cases, these are not additional offices and staff but result from a reorganisation of existing resources and personnel (ICLEI, 1996). Additional financial support for the LA21 process is very seldom provided (Rösler, 1996). The LA21 co-ordinators aim at strengthening the LA21 idea in the municipal policy, communicating between local authorities and other municipal actors and developing concepts for their LA21. Moreover, the LA21 co-ordinators exchange their experiences and have been increasingly successful in attracting the media's interest in the issue (AKP 2/96, Politische Ökologie 44/95). The more specific tasks of these co-ordinators depend on the individual design of responsibilities by the respective municipalities. One common element in the model-LA21's is the development of relationships and informal coalitions between groups and individual actors interested in LA21 based on individual engagement and conviction.

The strategies discussed thus far focus mainly on raising public awareness with respect to LA21, and are to a lesser extent concerned with the mobilisation of local actors as well as the institutionalisation and organisation of participation procedures. The identification of options to be implemented and of types of activities to be promoted is often based on local climate policy measures in the transport and energy sector. In doing so, LA21 activities reflect the existing priority issues in a municipality and there appears to be some kind of 'labelling'. It is very seldom that new issues are added to the political agenda (ICLEI, 1996). Therefore, and because the LA21 activities of German municipalities started comparatively late, not many measures have thus far been implemented, apart from those climate-protection measures initiated prior to or during the introduction of LA21. One of the best known examples in Germany is the LA21 process in Berlin-Köpenick (Box 1).

A short summary of the status quo is provided in Box 2.

Box 1 *Participation*

City: District Berlin-Köpenick
Name: Local Agenda 21 Berlin-Köpenick
Starting date: 1993
Initiated by: P. Wazlawik
• church background
• employee of Federal Environment Ministry

What has been achieved?
INSTITUTIONS
• 'one world' initiative
• project drop-in centre 'environment and development' in the environment department
• church forum (ecumenical)
• forum for environment and development
• decision of district government to develop a LA21
• LA21 office
• four working groups of the forum 'environment and development' on:
• transport / urban planning
• energy / resources / waste
• conservation / water / tourism
• economy / social affairs / north–south / education

STRATEGIES
• project proposal
• feasibility study
• status report: 'Development and state of the Köpenick model'
• 10-point agenda

Local sectoral policies and LA21: Transport

German municipal transport and urban planning policies of the 1950s with their philosophy of the 'Car-adjusted city' as the guiding principle, resulted in cities with restricted air and living quality, daily congestions and noise, without increased mobility (Deutscher Städtetag, 1995). Dissatisfaction of the citizens being confronted with this situation day-by-day and, generally, the emergence of the German green movement in the 1970s, caused many municipalities to rethink their transport concepts. A reorientation towards public transport, bicycling, etc., and in particular

Box 2 *Summary status of the German Local Agenda 21 process at the end of 1996*

- Active municipalities   very few
- Commitment   voluntary
- Approaches   manifold
- Co-ordination of existing LA21
  initiatives   systematically in part
- Dissemination of information
  on LA21   increasing
- Support by Federal Government   little
- Dynamics   increasing interest

The process has been characterised as the:

'EMBRYONIC STAGE'

transport reduction by improved planning processes ('city of short ways') has been successfully performed in many municipalities within their opportunities for action (Schuster and Dill, 1992).

As regards options, generally, transport policy can be divided into 3 categories (Walter, 1996): Regulation (prices, restrictions), infrastructure measures (nets, facilities) and organisational measures (operating concepts and information systems). Table 1 shows the distribution of responsibility between the municipalities and the federal level, respectively, for different kinds of measures in the transport sector (ibid). Not all of the instruments given as examples are yet applied.

Although municipalities have various options to reduce transport (see, e.g. Petersen, Schallaböck, 1995), the opportunities to apply them in order to start implementing a more environmentally sound and sustainable transport policy at the local level are judged sceptically (Kallen und Fiebig, 1994). Local authorities often argue with the long-term character of transport policy. Therefore, changes in policy direction can only seem to be introduced in the long run (Petersen and Schallaböck, 1995). In contrast to the energy sector, where numerous measures to improve energy management and efficiency have been identified and to some extent implemented in the past (e.g. Fröhner et al, 1992), the number of municipalities consequently implementing measures and programs in the transport sector is more limited. An argument for these 'delays' is different priorities. Because of municipal financial constraints, a ranking of measures takes place. Such rankings, among other aspects, depend on the acceptance of the respective project by the public (Schmidt et al, 1992).

Table I *Responsibilities in transport policy at different government levels*

Measure	Actor	Examples
Regulation	(EU/) Federal Level	Tax on fuel, vehicle tax, fines according to the road traffic regulations, road pricing on highways
	Municipality	Road pricing on city streets, speed limits, limits for standing capacity, parking fees, parking for residents, job ticket
Infrastructure	(EU/) Federal Level	Waterways, railroad net, road net (outside municipalities)
	Municipality	Municipal roads, public transport, cycle lanes, park and ride
Organisation	(EU/) Federal Level	Traffic management on long distance roads, new fuels
	Municipality	Passenger information, public relations, cleanness and security of public transport, traffic-management systems

The acceptance of new instruments for transport policy by citizens is perceived to be generally low. Lines of argument are fears of personal discomfort and loss of mobility as well as the loss of status. Participation processes can help to reduce these fears.

Other difficulties arise from the framework conditions set by the federal government (Beuermann and Jäger, 1996; Kallen and Fiebig, 1994). At the national level, the goals, principles and guidelines of the transport policy of the Federal Government are set out in the Federal transport planning (Bundesverkehrswegeplan (BVP). In the past, transport policies mainly focused on adapting the existing infrastructure to increasing transport figures (DSt, 1995). Since the beginning of the 1990s, federal transport policy concentrated on two issues, the reform of the railway system (privatisation) and priority infrastructure projects (Schallaböck, 1993). Following the German unification, priority was

Box 3 *Local Sectoral Policies: Transport (GEWOFAG, 1997)*

City: Munich
Name: Housing without cars (at Kolumbusplatz II)
Starting date: September 1993 (planning permission)
Initiated by: GEWOFAG (property developer)
Incentive: Reducing costs of either building an underground
               car park or paying a fee for parking space
               due to municipal regulation (no LA21 considerations)

Objectives: • Attracting 42 tenants who do not own a car
               • Co-operation with 'Stadt-Teil-Auto', a car-sharing
                 initiative to provide alternatives to owning a car
                 (4 spaces of the remaining smaller underground
                 car park are reserved for car sharing)
               • GEWOFAG has to ensure that 42 tenants do not
                 own a car

Framework infrastructure:
               • Central residential area
               • Access to underground (2 lines)
               • Bus stop in front of the building
               • Little access to public parking
What has been achieved?
               • Construction finished
               • Since November 1996 ready for occupation
               • Several flats rented by end of January 1997

First model of co-operation in Germany where administration
together with developer reduces parking spaces by involving an
existing car-sharing initiative.

given to extremely large infrastructure projects. Existing environmental reporting systems and procedures for citizen participation in the planning processes were restricted by federal law to speed up implementation. A reorientation of Federal transport planning with respect to a gradual reduction in transport volume, as recommended by a parliamentary commission (German Bundestag, 1991), is so far not reflected in the policy of the Federal Transport Ministry.

Given these framework conditions, the LA21 transport policy efforts so far focus mainly on the organisation of consensus finding processes

Table 2 Benefits expected from the project 'München Kolumbusplatz II' (GEWOFAG, 1997)

	Actor		
	Tenants	Property developer	Municipality
Benefit expected:	Almost the same mobility with reduced cost	Reduced construction cost	Less parking space and, therefore, reduced space coverage and occupation by settlement and by transport infra-structure. Conservation of valuable stock of trees. Less emissions (pollution) from cars.

and activities to raise citizen awareness. Consequently, a widespread first step is to organise workshops and to establish transport policy forums and round-tables (several statements in Enquete Kommission 1996 b). In connection with local climate protection policies, often specific measures to reduce or mitigate municipal traffic, to strengthen public transport and to change the modal split have already been identified (e.g. Schmidt et al. 1992). These measures are now proven to be measures under LA21. Even in these cases, there is an implementation gap as local transport policy is seen to be a very sensitive issue to citizens. Generally, however, the fundamental idea of LA21 to integrate decision-making on sectoral policies and to involve citizens at an early stage of the process remains to be implemented. There are, nonetheless, already interesting projects which are or may become connected with LA21, demonstrating how the idea of LA21 could penetrate into local sectoral policies. BOX 3 gives an example of one of those projects in Munich.[11]

Although this project has been developed in response to incentives other than LA21 (reducing construction cost), it demonstrates that an integrated policy-making concept is necessary. Local transport policy is thus closely connected to other sectors. Hence, the project described may at first sight and from a traditional sectoral understanding appear to be a classical project in the field of urban planning. Thus, a rethinking of role models and targets for municipal policy-making and, therefore, the reorganisation of local decision-making appears to be necessary at an early stage of a municipal LA21 process.[12] At the same time, the project clearly shows that a more sustainable solution for a specific project can reduce costs compared to a traditional, less sustainable one. In Munich, a triple win situation is expected. The three kinds of benefits are summarised in Table 2.

In the meantime, GEWOFAG has developed other projects in connection with Munich's LA21 process. A new residential area is planned in the district Munich-Riem (Wittmannstraße). The concept is to allow only for delivery services, not for private cars at all. Benefits are expected, in particular, in the field of noise reduction. Because these projects are not explicitly designed in order to make not owning a car more attractive, a car park will be provided outside the new residential area (GEWOFAG, 1997). Nonetheless, there might be an effect regarding the reduction of short-distance traffic (less than two km) which amounts to a high proportion of total municipal traffic. A formal decision on the implementation and the final design of these projects has been made by the City Council at the end of January 1997.

IMPEDIMENTS TO A MORE DYNAMIC AND SUCCESSFUL GERMAN RESPONSE

In general, it seems safe to say that the small number of LA21 processes initiated thus far have, to a large degree, been the result of highly devoted individuals who were the focal points for action. In trying to explain why, in contrast to other countries, the interest of the majority of German municipalities in LA21 has not been very enthusiastic until recently, our empirical observation is that the following have been the most important obstacles:[13,14]

- information deficits
- priorities and structure
- insufficient support by other actors

In the above mentioned opinion poll of the Difu, local authorities themselves identified a number of impediments to the development and implementation of LA21 as shown in Figure 2. It appears that they also focus on resources, information and interest/priority conflicts but leave structural and non-municipal aspects out of consideration.

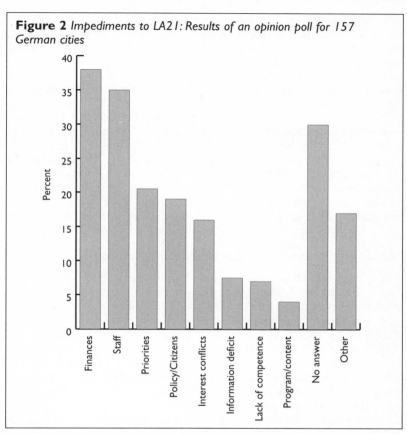

Figure 2 Impediments to LA21: Results of an opinion poll for 157 German cities

Source: Rösler 1996

Information deficits

Lack of general information on Agenda 21

Generally, the German public remembers the United Nations Conference on Environment and Development (UNCED) in Rio de Janeiro in 1992 as the 'Environment Summit' (Loske, 1996). Moreover, the first Conference of the Parties to the Framework Convention on Climate Change (FCCC) was always referred to as the 'Rio follow-up conference'. Information on the climate change issue and, in particular, on the. FCCC is good, while Agenda 21, dealing with the connection of environment and development, is practically unknown to the general public (Fiedler, 1996a). An explanation might be that, in contrast to other countries, the Brundtland Report, *Our Common Future*, was not discussed very much by the German public, so that the concept of 'sustainable development' has not been broadly disseminated (Beuermann and Burdick, 1997). One reason may be the late and inappropriate translation of the document into the German language. As a result, the discussion on sustainable development started later than in other countries.

As for the content of Agenda 21, particularly chapter 28, local authorities criticise that the federal government signed Agenda 21 but did not communicate it effectively to the actors at the different federal levels (Enquete Commission, 1996b). Therefore, knowledge of Local Agenda 21 was not widely spread. Municipal associations did not effectively compensate for this information vacuum. At present, the situation is changing and Agenda 21 seems to outstrip the issue of climate change in the public discussion due to the offensive dissemination of examples of 'good practices' by a number of municipalities.

Lack of information on potential initiatives, impacts and costs

Information deficits of local authorities who have heard about LA21 concern exact knowledge on what to do at which stage of the LA21 process. They fear experimentation in difficult times, and are convinced that they have to be provided with clear and precise guidelines and handbooks. They do not believe it is their task to develop them (ICLEI, 1995a). Though there are some good examples for guidelines and manuals (for example Hewitt 1995, but see also the introductory chapter), they have neither been translated into German nor been distributed systematically.15 In the meantime, municipal associations have, to some extent, filled this information gap, providing and distributing their own interpretation of LA21 (DSt, 1995, DSTGB, 1995). Taking a closer look at these publications shows, however, that only a limited scope of LA21 has actually been taken into consideration. Major emphasis is on the traditional local policy sectors, with very little information on the key challenge of policy integration and no specific recommendations on how to achieve this.

In addition, there is no mention of the North-South aspect of LA21, and only a short and general section on the participation aspects. Other reasons for adopting a wait-and-see policy are uncertainties as to the local economic and social impact of an LA21 process, and a general concern as to the implications of implementation for local electoral politics. Another obstacle appears to be a conviction that LA21 processes will cause additional financial burdens (Rösler, 1996). Because of the weak financial situation of many municipalities, it is felt that there is no room now for additional expenditure (Unmüßig, 1996). To a certain extent, however, this is a specious argument as there are many types of projects where it can be shown that they are most probably profitable in the long run (a general discussion of those projects can be found in Weizsäcker et al., 1995).

Priorities and structure

Focus on other issues

LA21 is seen to compete with other issues. Due to the recent municipal crisis, environmental policy is often limited to reactive measures and highest priority is given to other issues (Fiedler, 1996a). This view demonstrates that the integration aspect of LA21 has often not been recognised or is not perceived to be feasible. In a survey on the actual problems of urban development and municipal policy, local authorities perceive the following three issues as most important (DIFU, 1995):

- consolidation of municipal finances
- economic development, employment, economic structural change
- transport

Moreover, the response to LA21 is to a large extent dependent on the local policy traditions. Municipalities with a stronger environmental consciousness do not see the necessity of developing an LA21 as they are convinced that they have already implemented a 'sustainability' policy with a long-term orientation (ICLEI, 1995a). Furthermore, municipalities interested in the UNCED follow-up are often members of climate protection initiatives (ICLEI, 1993; Climate Alliance of the Cities, 1992). In both cases, characteristic elements of LA21 have already been introduced by conscious local authorities, and, in at least some of these units, the authorities seem to be less interested in going further and applying a new concept. Doing so is considered to be a simple 'renaming' of activities which already been in place for a number of years ('old wine in new bottles').[16]

Organisation of environmental administration

A major structural obstacle to the acceptance and implementation of LA21 by local authorities would appear to be the structure of municipal administration (ICLEI, 1995a).17 With the emergence of environmental issues on the political agenda generally, the administrative structures have been adjusted (Müller, 1986). Because the traditional administrative sectors were judged to be stronger or more dominant compared to the new environmental issues, the environmental sector has been established as a sector of its own (environmental agencies/agents and departments) instead of being integrated into other administrative sectors.

From a political-economic point of view, this was a logical development as environmental concerns need an independent lobby when competing with other issues. However, this structure opposes the integration aspects of LA21. Implementing an LA21 means, for example, applying a precautionary policy and involving the local community. This restructuring of policy- and decision-making processes requires cross-sectoral co-operation between the existing structures, but also the establishment of completely new structures (for public participation etc.). Many local authorities are simply not interested in such a development at this time, and want to continue their policies in a business-as-usual way. Because of its relative success in applying a more limited form of reactive environmental policy, and a 'natural' tendency of administrations to resist changing priorities, municipal environmental administrations are opposed to, or only slightly open for, policy integration and changing concepts. There is underway, however, an ongoing discussion on the restructuring of local administration (Verwaltungsstrukturreform) with respect to economic performance, and it is clear that the future of LA21 will, in many cases, be dependent on linkages to this debate.

Insufficient support by other actors

In Germany, everyone waits for a higher level to start, For instance, an initiative of the BMU (Fiedler, 1996a)

In order to investigate why such early information deficits should become so dominant in delaying the German LA21 process compared with other European countries, we must ask who should, could or is expected to provide the information needed, and why this has not happened. Agenda 21 was the result of an international negotiation process. Though municipalities, mainly through their associations, participated in the German National Committee which was the preparatory committee prior to UNCED, the outcome of the Earth Summit does not seem to have been sufficiently communicated to the subordinate federal levels (Wieser, 1996). Such a 'translation' is, however, probably essential for the ultimate success of the implementation. Let us briefly look at four actors who should be instrumental in this regard:

- the Federal Ministry for the Environment (BMU)
- the Federal Ministry for Urban Development (BMBau)
- NGOs
- other interest associations

Federal Government: The Federal Ministry for the Environment (BMU)

Together with the Ministry for Foreign Affairs, the Ministry for the Environment is responsible for the organisation and co-ordination of the UNCED follow-up. As such, it is supposed to be the contact for the municipalities with respect to LA21. The responsible authorities rhetorically acknowledge the importance of LA21 – but there is, in fact, very little support visible. This partially justified by reference to the municipalities' right of autonomy (BMU, 1994). Consequently, there is no development of a general guiding, steering or funding mechanism at the federal level. Significantly, in only one LA21 initiative (Berlin-Köpenick), is there a relationship between a municipality and the BMU, primarily as a result of personal contacts (CAF, 1995; Schiller-Dickhut, 1996). Involvement of the BMU is nonetheless seen to be very important by other LA21 players at the federal level. BMU representatives have, therefore, been invited to co-ordination meetings. Because of the limited number of and experience with such meetings thus far, it is not possible to predict whether this will result in stronger support. However, it might be a starting point for the future engagement of the BMU. In addition, there is some funding of research activities on LA21. The Federal Environment Agency (UBA), which is a subordinate body to the BMU, recently commissioned a study on the 'environmental effectiveness of municipal Agenda 21 plans for sustainable development' (ICLEI, 1996). The project is co-ordinated by ICLEI and will be finished in June 1998.

Federal Government: Federal Ministry for Urban Development (BMBau)

Though the responsibility for the Agenda 21 follow-up process lies with the BMU, another important actor could be the BMBau which is responsible for all affairs related to urban development. In the German communication to Habitat II, BMBau states that with regard to the central aims of Habitat II, the promotion of urban development with due regard for natural resources and the environment is of major importance in Germany. Investigating how this aim could be achieved by municipalities, it is stated that the principles of sustainable development should be implemented. In doing so: 'the Charter of the European Cities towards sustainability (the Aalborg Charter) referring to municipal day-to-day policies can be considered as a helpful guideline' (BMBau, 1996). The report refers otherwise, in several chapters, to the importance of LA21 but still remains very vague. At the moment it is not foreseeable whether or not the BMBau will engage further in the LA21 process.

Non-Governmental Organisations

There are several NGOs dealing with LA21 related questions at the federal level. Most prominent is the Forum for Environment and Development which is an umbrella organisation for NGOs dealing with UNCED-related issues. One of its standing working groups deals with urban development. However, this working group was first established in the Autumn of 1994 and has not been very effective in influencing the discussion or providing support. The long-term goal is to strengthen the co-operation of German NGOs on LA21 (Sibum, 1995; Dodds, 1995). Moreover, they see themselves mainly as a counterpart to the Federal Government, and have, in this capacity, participated in the preparation of the National Report of the Federal Government to Habitat II.

Associations

In contrast to the UK, where the Local Government Management Board focused very early on LA21, the German associations did not respond to the initiative for a long time (Hoffmann, 1996). Given this lack of response, the information problems mentioned above proved to a key obstacle for the majority of municipalities. Information was only provided by new organisations such as ICLEI (Hewitt, 1995). However, these networks are mainly accessed by municipalities already interested in LA21, climate protection or global issues in general. If other municipalities are to be brought into the initiative and convinced of the benefits of LA21, the idea must be promoted by the established traditional municipal associations. And, in fact, LA21 has, since mid 1995, become an issue. For example, the German Association of Cities (DSt) has adopted a resolution which establishes LA21 as a priority issue on its agenda. As discussed above, DSt developed guidelines identifying 19 sectors for projects under LA21 (DSt, 1995). In addition, DSt urged its approx. 6400 member cities to develop and implement the concept.

In a survey commissioned by the DSt, the implementation of LA21 in 157 of its member cities is reviewed. This study was published in July 1996 (Fiedler, 1996b; Rösler, 1996) and will be repeated in early 1997. Other associations have started similar LA21 initiatives (e.g. DStGb, 1995). Though it is not clear what effect these types of survey will have on LA21, it is clear that they will at least spread awareness of the idea. On the other hand, since the materials in question are very vague as to what a Local Agenda 21 might consist of, the wider diffusion of this information may in fact hinder LA21 processes in those cases where local authorities do not have access to additional sources of information. If a practice is established whereby local authorities are led to believe that existing, more traditional, environmental initiatives are, in fact, equivalent to LA21, there may develop a 'backlash' to the whole idea when they later discover that this is not the case. It is urgently necessary, therefore, to improve and supplement the informational materials being provided, a task which must be carried out at higher levels of co-ordination.

CONCLUDING REMARKS

Implementation of Agenda 21 at the local level in Germany has thus far been characterised by the initiatives of a few 'pioneer' municipalities. It is clearly not yet a broad movement. The overwhelming majority of the 16,121 German municipalities have not yet discovered LA21 as a policy concept suited to their specific municipal conditions; a concept designed to expand environment-and-development capacity within the existing bounds of municipal responsibility. Five years after Agenda 21 was signed in Rio de Janeiro, this observation is somewhat surprising in light of the response in other West European countries with similar environmental-policy profiles as Germany. Given the constitutionally guaranteed municipal responsibilities, together with high citizen awareness and a relatively strong policy tradition in this area, one would have expected that LA21 would attract more interest and response by local actors. Comparatively large successes in reducing pollution, particularly at the local level, should have provided good preconditions for receiving and enacting the LA21 idea.

The margin for the development of individual local policies has, however, been shrinking in recent years due to a worsening of municipal finances; an increase in compulsory tasks; and a general tendency to weaken local government. As shown by the establishment of German environmental policy in the early 1970's, there is no built-in procedure in local decision-making processes to adopt new issues automatically. Only subsequent to the emerging strong environmental consciousness in the public at large, spearheaded by a more active vanguard of citizens, has local government demonstrated its ability to flexibly integrate new issues. Apart from a minority of municipalities, however, sufficient integration of environmental concerns into day-to-day politics has not taken place. Municipal environmental policy remains dominated by reactive measures. And even though Germany is still a front-runner for this type of policy mode, the persistence of the reactive approach reflects in a sense an imple-mentation gap with respect to the precautionary principle adopted as the general basis of German environmental policy in 1971.

The recent broad municipal response to the issue of climate change may be seen as a decisive push to establish a common understanding at the local level to re-organise environmental policy in order to promote sustainable development. Hence, from the observations concerning the

German 'baseline', it becomes clear that LA21 would not be automatically assimilated and implemented by the majority of German municipalities, despite its potential for strengthening the role of local governments in the federal system. In addition, it can be argued that it is exactly the longer experience with municipal environmental policy which is a hindering factor for a more active LA21 profile. The differences between traditional environmental policy and the Local Agenda 21 concept have not been made sufficiently clear, so that municipalities can both see the practical possibilities for integrating new efforts into existing programs and understand the potential 'value-added' aspect of the UNCED initiative.

The relatively few LA21 processes which have been initiated are largely due to the personal commitment and enthusiasm of local authorities, or to other interested persons who recognised the potential of LA21 for implementing an integrated environmentally conscious long-term policy according to the precautionary principle. Success in initiating and developing LA21s has to a large extent depended on new coalitions which have been formed on different levels:

- Among interested individuals in the respective municipalities forming a network to establish LA21 on the local agenda (*first-mover coalitions*).
- Among interested individuals in the local government and administration across departmental borders forming networks to promote local government commitment to LA21 and to make way for integration across policy sectors (*local-authority coalitions*);
- Among different local actor groups to further acceptance and to establish structures for participation (*local-actor coalitions*);
- Among municipalities developing LA21's to exchange information via membership in 'umbrella' networks; to undertake more effective lobbying and public relations; but also to increase and secure motivation by some kind of creative competition (*LA21 coalitions*).

These coalitions have been effective in so far as a number of formal decisions have been made by local governments to develop and implement LA21. Several of these municipalities have also established participation procedures according to 'bottom-up' principles. Furthermore, these participation structures have been shown to work by initiating LA21 and focusing the local public attention on the issue of LA21. However, there is no universally applicable methodology of how such a process should be organised. Initiatives, so far, operate on a basis of trial and error. As no single municipality has yet completed a Local Agenda 21 plan (with adequate documentation and official recognition), it is an open question how effective these coalitions will be in the LA21 implementation phase. In particular, the effectiveness of 'local-authority coalitions' will be a decisive factor as it is the starting point for integrating LA21 into the normal business of municipal policy implementation. It is suggested that this type of coalition will have to be broadened and that this will be a crucial point in LA21 processes causing much resistance by other interests.

Generally, it is the North-South dimension of LA21 which appears to have received least attention thus far. Regarding information exchange, pioneering municipalities have been increasingly successful in attracting public and media attention. This diffusion of knowledge on examples of good practice is expected to push the issue of LA21. At present, there are tendencies to further promote LA21 by the establishment of new networking institutions to develop databases on LA21 in Germany. Moreover, an increasing number of research activities focus on LA21, financed in part by the Federal Government. This may be an initial sign of a more active engagement by the Federal Government in the LA21 process. There can be no doubt, at any rate, that the establishment of a central focal point at the federal level would help close the information gap and would be a sign of federal interest in both Agenda 21 and LA21.

The brief analysis of obstacles to LA21 pointed towards two types of factor inhibiting a more active implementation. For many local authorities, LA21 is only a new description of what they feel they already have been doing for years. They have developed structures and procedures for local environmental policies and do not agree on the necessity to apply a new concept. Others need more information on what to do when initiating and developing an LA21. Co-ordination and support has thus far been insufficiently provided by existing municipal associations or institutions at the federal level. The Federal Government in particular should have a strong interest in the initiative, since LA21 could be a significant instrument at the local level to achieve national environmental goals such as the reduction target for CO_2 emissions by the year 2005. The official reluctance of the Federal Government appears to be conditioned, however, by the principle of federalism and local municipal autonomy.

From these observations, it is concluded that the German LA21 process is still underdeveloped, but that recent signs point towards greater movement and initiative. Local Agenda 21 has the potential to become a priority issue in the public and municipal discussion on sustainable development. Stronger federal support and involvement could create political momentum for the idea of 'thinking globally – acting locally'. It could generate pressure to act at the municipal level, and encourage and legitimise existing initiatives. However, the difficulty of balancing the governmental support needed and organising a municipal bottom-up process remains.

NOTES

*   Parts of this paper were carried out for a project on behalf of the EU
     Commission, DG XII on 'Institutional Adjustments for Sustainable
     Development Strategies' coordinated by Prof Timothy O'Riordan, CSERGE,
     UK. The author acknowledges the comments by Georg Wilke, Wuppertal
     Institute, William M. Lafferty, Prosus, and Katarina Eckerberg, University
     of Umeå, as well as the discussions with the colleagues of the LA21
     research network initiated by ProSus on earlier drafts of this chapter.
     Responsibility remains with the author. The author is also grateful to Mrs.
     Jackie Sairawan who did the language check. Information on the LA21
     research network can be found on the Internet at http://prosus.nfr.no/
1   Information on the 'Special Session of the General Assembly to Review and
     Appraise the Implementation of Agenda 21' ('Earth summit + 5') to be held
     in New York, 23–27 June 1997 can be found on the Internet at
     http://www.un.org/ dpcsd/earthsummit/
2   Translations from German sources are unauthorized.
3   When not otherwise mentioned, the description of the German environmen-
     tal policy refers to Müller (1986), Simonis (1991) and Weidner (1995).
4   The mass movement against nuclear energy and deployment of nuclear
     missiles in Germany resulted in a new peace movement and strengthened
     environmentalist groups. By 1978, the umbrella organisation Federal
     Association of Environment Action Groups (BBU) listed 1,000 member
     groups with more than 1.5 million members.
5   Apart from the environmental policy tradition at the local level, the tradition
     of citizen participation in decision-making processes at the local level could
     have been reviewed as a decisive element of the 'baseline' conditions.
6   Criticism sometimes focuses, however, on the 'theoretical nature' of these
     reduction targets and on some of the studies investigating how to achieve
     them. A judgement as to how robust these quantified targets and studies are
     can only be made in retrospect after an appropriate period of implementation.
7   The German Association of Cities (DSt) has commissioned a survey on the
     present state of the implementation of LA21 among 157 of its member cities
     (Fiedler 1996b, Rösler 1996). The underlying opinion poll was carried out
     by the German Institute of Urban Studies (Difu) and will be regularly
     repeated. The results for the second one are to be expected for April/May
     1997.
8   Funded in 1990, ICLEI initially was a Canadian initiative promoting infor-
     mation exchange and capacity building among local authorities worldwide
     to strengthen their efforts towards sustainable local development.
9   Enquete Commissions are advisory bodies to the German parliament. Both
     politicians and experts are represented. The experts are appointed by the
     political parties according to the respective party's faction in parliament.
     Enquete Commissions are established to work on specific, crucial tasks that
     appear to become priority issues for policy-making. Ordinarily, they work
     for one legislative period.

10 This project appears to be an effective completion for two other state initiatives in NRW addressing the local level, the state act to improve municipal finances and the program for promoters.

11 However, depending on the starting point, the project can easily be understood as an urban planning project. This underlines the need for integrated municipal planning as implied by LA21 in order to optimise environmental, economic and social needs at the same time at the local level.

12 A general discussion of new 'sustainable' role models and targets can be found in Bund and Misereor (1995) which will be published in English in 1997.

13 For example, the UK, the Netherlands and Sweden.

14 A more general argument from political economy theory is that LA21 and sustainable development are strategic long-term issues. As such they contradict fundamentally the short- to mid-term orientation of policy makers as regards voting cycles etc. Moreover 'controllable' politics based on quantified targets are not seen to be suitable for policy. As this refers to any kind of long-term issues, it is not reviewed further here.

15 A German translation of ICLEI's LA21 guidelines is in preparation.

16 This interpretation is somewhat ambiguous and probably only true for an early stage of LA21. It might later serve as an argument for some municipal authorities to start an LA21. Observations made with regard to climate policy at the local level show that as soon as an issue has gained some public attention and priority, renaming is suggested as being useful for giving the policies a new push that would otherwise not sell any longer.

17 Lack of personnel is one of the more simple arguments of local authorities against the establishment of an LA21 coordination office or a comparable institution (Rösler 1996).

REFERENCES

Alternative Kommunalpolitik (AKP) Heft 2/1996.

Beuermann, Christiane and Bernhard Burdick (1997) 'The Sustainability Transition in Germany'. *Environmental Politics*, 1/1997.

Beuermann, Christiane and Jill Jäger (1996) 'Climate Change Politics in Germany: How long will any double dividend last?', in Timothy O'Riordan and Jill Jäger (eds.) *Politics of Climate Change. A European Perspective*, London: Routledge, pp.186-227.

BMBau – Federal Ministry for Regional Development, Housing and Urban Development (ed.) (1996) *Siedlungsentwicklung und Siedlungspolitik. Nationalbericht Deutschland (Habitat II)* Bonn: BMBau.

BMU (ed.) (1994) 'Umwelt 1994. Politik für eine Nachhaltige Umweltgerechte Entwicklung', Bundestagsdrucksache 12/8451, Bonn: BMU.

Bonsen, Elmar zur (1993) 'Die Klagen der Städte', *Süddeutsche Zeitung*, 17.12.1993.

Bormann, Manfred and Stietzel, Cornelia, (1993) *Stadt und Gemeinde. Kommunalpolitik in den Neuen Ländern*, Bonn: Bundeszentrale für politische Bildung.

BUND/Misereor (eds.) (1995) *Zukunftsfähiges Deutschland. Ein Beitrag zu einer global nachhaltigen Entwicklung*, Basel: Birkhäuser.

Bundestagsdrucksache 12/213 (3.3.1994).

Bundestagsdrucksache 12/6815 (9.2.1994).

Carson, Rachel L. (1990) *Der Stumme Frühling*, München: Beck.

Clearing-house for Applied Futures (CAF) (1995) 'Kommunale Strategien für eine Zukunftsfähige Entwicklung. Eine Analyse der Einflußfaktoren der Strategie-Entwicklung und Umsetzung am Beispiel von Berlin-Köpenick und Güstrow', unpublished.

Coenen, Frans (1996) 'Local Agenda 21 in the Netherlands', (unpublished).

DIFU – Deutsches Institut für Urbanistik (ed) (1995) *Aktuelle Probleme der Stadtentwicklung und der Kommunalpolitik. Umfrageergebnisse 1995*. Berlin: Difu

Dodds, Felix (1995) 'Habitat II. Der Nationale Vorbereitungsprozeß', *Rundbrief* 4/1995, (Bonn: Forum Umwelt und Entwicklung).

DSt – Deutscher Städtetag (1993) 'Rede des Präsidenten des Deutschen Städtetages Anläßlich der Außerordentlichen Hauptversammlung "Städte in Not" des Deutschen Städtetages am 18. Oktober 1993 in Bonn', unpublished.

DSt – Deutscher Städtetag (ed.) (1995) 'Städte für eine Umweltgerechte Entwicklung. Materialien für eine "Lokale Agenda 21", DST-Beiträge zur Stadtentwicklung und zum Umweltschutz', Reihe E Heft 24, Köln: DST.

DSTGB – Deutscher Städte- und Gemeindebund, Kommunale Umwelt-AktioN (U.A.N.) (ed.) (1995) *Rathaus und Klimaschutz. Hinweise für die Kommunale Praxis* (Lokale Agenda 21) Hannover: DStGb.

Ebert, Thorsten (1994) *Möglichkeiten Kommunaler Umweltpolitik. Umweltpolitische Kompetenzen im Föderalen System der Bundesrepublik Deutschland*, Diplomarbeit, Kassel: GHK.

Enquete Kommission Schutz des Menschen und der Umwelt (1996 a) 'Fragen- und Sachverständigenkatalog für die Öffentliche Anhörung zum Thema 'Kommunen und Nachhaltige Entwicklung. Beiträge zur Umsetzung der Agenda 21", *Kommissionsdrucksache* 13/3, Bonn: Enquete Kommission Schutz des Menschen und der Umwelt.

Enquete Kommission Schutz des Menschen und der Umwelt (1996 b) 'Statements der Sachverständigen im Rahmen der Öffentlichen Anhörung zum Thema "Kommunen und Nachhaltige Entwicklung"', unpublished.

Fiedler, Jobst (1994) 'Die Aktuelle Finanzkrise der Großstädte. Neue Finanzierungsquellen oder Leistungsabbau?', Mäding, Heinrich (ed.) *Stadtperspektiven. Difu Symposium 1993*, Berlin: Difu, p. 131-154.

Fiedler, Klaus (1996 a) 'Eine "Lokale Agenda 21" für Deutschland', *dh-Info* 1/96.

Fiedler, Klaus (1996 b) *Vorbericht für die Sitzung des Nationalen Komitees für Nachhaltige Entwicklung am 19.06.1996 in Bonn. Umsetzung der 'Agenda 21' auf Kommunaler Ebene in Deutschland*, unpublished.

Fröhner et al (1992) *Klimaschutz in Städten und Gemeinden. 41 Vorbildliche Kommunale Energieprojekte*, Bonn: BUND.

German Bundestag (ed) (1991) *Protecting the Earth. Third Report of the Enquete Commission of the 11th German Bundestag 'Preventive Measures to Protect the Earth's Atmosphere'*, Bonn: Economica.

GEWOFAG (Gemeinnützige Wohnungsfürsorge AG, München) (1997) Information provided by GEWOFAG, *Personal Communication*, March 1997.

Gisevius, Wolfgang (1991) *Leitfaden durch die Kommunalpolitik*, Bonn: Dietz. Handelsblatt, 1.2.1994 und 14.4.1994.

Hewitt, Nicola (1995) *European Local Agenda 21 Planning Guide. How to Engage in Long-term Environmental Action Planning Towards Sustainability*, Brussels: European Sustainable Cities and Towns Campaign.

Hoffmann, Albrecht (1996) Clearing-house for Applied Futures (*personal communication*) 13.3.1996.

Hoffmann, Albrecht (1997) Agenda-Transfer and Clearing-house for Applied Futures (*personal communication*) March 1997.

International Council for Local Environmental Initiatives (ICLEI) (ed.) (1993) *Klima Schützen heißt Städte schützen*, Freiburg: ICLEI.

International Council for Local Environmental Initiatives (ICLEI) (1995a) 'Erläuterungen zu Recherche: Kommunen auf dem Weg zu "Nachhaltiger Entwicklung"', unpublished.

International Council for Local Environmental Initiatives (ICLEI) (1995b) *Local Initiatives. ICLEI Members in Action 1993–1995*, Freiburg: ICLEI.

International Council for Local Environmental Initiatives (ICLEI) (1995c) *Initiatives*. Vol. 1 No. 1, Toronto: ICLEI.

International Council for Local Environmental Initiatives (ICLEI) (1996) *Statement*, in: Enquete Kommission Schutz des Menschen und der Umwelt (1996 b)

Jäger, Jill, Cavender Bares Jeannine, Ell, Renate (1994) 'Vom Treibhauseffekt zur Klimakatastrophe: Eine Chronologie der Klimadebatte in Deutschland.' *Jahrbuch Ökologie 1994*, München: Beck.

Joseph, Matthias (1995) *Die Analyse Kommunaler Umweltpolitik aus Sicht der Neuen Politischen Ökonomie*, Frankfurt u.a.: Lang.

Kallen, Carlo und Karl-Heinz Fiebig (1994) 'Kommunale Klimaschutzprogramme – Programmentwicklung und Maßnahmenumsetzung'. *Difu-Berichte* 2/1994, Berlin: Difu, pp. 24–27.

Karrenberg, Hanns und Münstermann, Engelbert (1995) 'Gemeindefinanzbericht 1995. Städtische Finanzen '95 – unter Staatlichem Druck', *Der Städtetag*, 3/1995.

Klimabündnis, Allianza del Clima e.V. (eds.) (1993) *Klima – lokal geschützt. Aktivitäten europäischer Kommunen*, München: Raben-Verlag.

Kommunale Briefe (1996) 'Zukunftsfähiges Deutschland Bedeutet "Sustainable Cities"', *Kommunale Briefe* Nr 1/2, 17.1.1996, pp. 3–4.

Kommunale Briefe für Ökologie Nr 8/94.

Kuby, Bert (1996) 'Stand der Umsetzung der Lokalen Agenda 21 in Europa. Erste Auswertung einer Umfrage', Rösler, Cornelia (ed.) *Lokale Agenda 21. Dokumentation eines Erfahrungsaustauschs beim Deutschen Städtetag am 29. April 1996 in Köln*, Berlin: Difu, pp. 23–30.

Mäding, Heinrich (1995) 'Kommunale Umweltpolitik unter Veränderten Rahmenbedingungen', *Zeitschrift für angewandte Umweltforschung*, Sonderband Stadtökologie.

Müller, Edda (1986) *Innenwelt der Umweltpolitik*, Opladen: Westdeutscher Verlag.

Petersen, Rudolf und Karl-Otto Schallaböck (1995) *Mobilität für morgen. Chancen einer zukunftsfähigen Verkehrspolitik.*, Basel: Birkhäuser.

Pluckel, Hans (1996) 'Stand der Umsetzung der Lokalen Aganda 21 in den Niederlanden', Rösler, Cornelia (ed.) *Lokale Agenda 21. Dokumentation eines Erfahrungsaustauschs beim Deutschen Städtetag am 29. April 1996 in Köln*, Berlin: Difu, pp. 39-44.

Pohl, Wolfgang (1994) 'Den Gemeinden Geht die Luft aus. Zum Gemeindefinanzbericht 1994', *Alternative Kommunalpolitik* 3/1994, pp. 32-35.

Politische Ökologie, Nr 44/1995, Schwerpunkt Nachhaltige Stadtentwicklung.

Quante, Michael, Schwartz, Michael (1996) *Kommunale Umweltschutzpolitik*, Düsseldorf: Hans Böckler Stiftung.

Rösler, Cornelia (1996) 'Stand der Umsetzung der Lokalen Agenda 21 in Deutschen Städten. Erste Ergebnisse der Difu-Umfrage', Rösler, Cornelia (ed.) *Lokale Agenda 21. Dokumentation eines Erfahrungsaustauschs beim Deutschen Städtetag am 29. April 1996 in Köln*, Berlin: Difu, pp. 45-56.

Schallaböck, Karl-Otto (1993) 'Verkehr, Energie und Klima – Argumente zum Umsteuer'. *Energie-Dialog*, Dezember 1993, pp. 20-23.

Schiller-Dickhut, (1996) 'Machen wir einen Plan! Lokale Agendas 21 in Deutschland', *Alternative Kommunalpolitik* 2/1996, pp. 59- 60.

Schmidt, M., Wortmann, J. and R. Six (1992) *Handlungsorientiertes Kommunales Konzept zur Reduktion von Klimarelevanten Spurengasen für die Stadt Heidelberg*. Heidelberg: Amt für Umweltschutz und Gesundheitsförderung.

Schuster, Franz and Günther W. Dill (eds.) (1992) *Aufgaben der Kommunalpolitik in den 90er Jahren. Band 4: Wohnungsbau, Städtebau, Umwelt*, Köln: Dt Gemeindeverlag.

Sibum, Doris (1995) 'Pläne der AG Stadt- und Regionalentwicklung', Rundbrief, 4/1995, Bonn: Forum Umwelt und Entwicklung.

Simonis, Ernst U. (1991) *Environmental Policy in the Federal Republic of Germany*, Berlin: WZB; FS II 91-403.

Statistisches Bundesamt (ed.) (1992, 1993, 1994, 1995) *Statistische Jahrbücher 1992–1995 für die Bundesrepublik Deutschland*, Wiesbaden: Metzler-Poeschel.

Töpfer, Klaus (1996) 'Städte sind die Zukunft der Menschheit. Ohne nachhaltige Stadtentwicklung wird es keine global nachhaltige Entwicklung geben', BMBau (ed.) *Verstädterungsprozeß und Nachhaltigkeit*, (Bonn: BMBau) pp. 7–10.

Unmüßig, Barbara (1996) 'Mehr als TransFair. Die Rolle der Kommunen für ein Zukunftsfähiges Deutschland', *Alternative Kommunalpolitik* 2/1996, pp. 57–58.

Voisey, Heather, Christiane Beuermann, Liv Astrid Sverdrup and Timothy O'Riordan (1996) 'The Political Significance of Local Agenda 21: The

Early Stages of Some European Experiences', *Local Environment*, Vol. 1, No. 1, pp. 33-50.

Walter, Christoph (1996) 'Zum Stand der Verkehrsentwicklungsplanung für Hamburg'. Vortrag im Rahmen des Workshops 'Klimaschutz durch Veränderte Verkehrsentwicklung' des Forums 'Herausforderung Klimaschutz – Handlungsfelder Energie- und Verkehr' der Umweltbehörde Hamburg zur Erstellung einer kommunalen Agenda 21 am 17. Februar 1996, unpublished.

Wehling, H.-G. (1986) *Kommunalpolitik in der Bundesrepublik Deutschland*, Berlin.

Weidner, Helmut (1995) *25 Years of Modern Environmental Policy in Germany. Treading a Well Worn Path to the Top of the International Field*, Berlin: WZB; FS II 95-301.

Weizsäcker, Ernst U. v., Lovins, Amory B. and Hunter L. Lovins (1995) *Faktor Vier. Doppelter Wohlstand – Halbierter Naturverbrauch*, München: Droemer Knaur.

Wieser, Thomas (1996) Verbal statement of the coordinator of the Local Agenda 21 in Germering at the public inquiry of the Enquete Commission 'Protecting Man and the Environment' on 'Municipalities and Sustainable Development', Bonn 24.9.1996.

Witte, Gertrud (1992) 'Mit dem Grundgesetz die Städte Stärken. Die Vorschläge des Deutschen Städtetages in der Verfassungsdiskussion'. *Der Städtetag*, Nr. 3/1992.

6.

Austria:

A Late Start with a Strong Potential

Otto Schütz

How far have Austrian communities come with the implementation of Local Agenda 21? To what extent have the basic aims of Chapter 28 of Agenda 21 been realised at the local level of governance? How far has the Austrian Government proceeded with dissemination of information about the issue and support for starting the process of LA21 in the communities? On the basis of country reports of Austria from 1994, 1995 and 1996, we can derive the following preliminary conclusions.

Concerning Chapter 28, the report of 1994 describes increasing activities in the field of *partnerships between communities, also across national borders* (especially Hungary). Attention is also given to activities in connection with the Climate Alliance. The initiatives of the federal provinces (*Bundesländer*) in the area of 'village rejuvenation' (*Dorferneuerung*), which was started in the 1970's, are characterised as having particular importance. Besides the preservation of historical objects and the decrease of land-use for buildings and housing, the crucial goals are the maintenance of existing social structures, increasing responsibility, and strengthening social and cultural quality of life in villages.

The report of 1995 tells nothing about activities related to Chapter 28. Furthermore, the reporting on the basis of the guidelines valid at that time was generally found to be not very satisfactory by the National Commission, as certain questions were difficult to answer because of unclear definitions (for example, the meaning of 'poverty' in highly industrialised countries).

In 1996, the report again leaves out any information on implementation processes regarding Chapter 28. Instead it focuses on several

Table I Administrative division of the Austrian federal territory as of 15 September 1996

Federal province	Area km^2	Provincial districts	Communities (Municipalities)
Burgenland	3,966	9	168
Carinthia	9,533	10	131
Lower Austria	19,173	25	571
Upper Austria	11,980	18	445
Salzburg	7,154	6	119
Styria	16,388	17	543
Tyrol	12,648	9	279
Vorarlberg	2,601	4	96
Vienna	415	1	1
Austria	83,857	99	2,353

measures taken at different levels and by different sectors of administration and government relating to topics in the separate chapters (MoE-Austria, 1994, 1995, 1996).

Including the capital city Vienna (which is also a municipality of 23 municipal districts), Austria consists of 9 federal provinces (*Bundesländer*) with a total area of 83, 857 km^2. The country is divided into 99 provincial districts and 2.353 communities (Table 1).

BASELINE CONDITIONS: AGENDA 21 AND AUSTRIA'S NATIONAL ENVIRONMENTAL PLAN

The preamble of Agenda 21 clearly identifies national governments as bearing the primary responsibility for carrying out the action plan: 'Its successful implementation is first and foremost the responsibility of Governments. National strategies, plans, policies and processes are crucial in achieving this' (Agenda 21, Chapter 1, Section 1.3).

At present the National Environmental Plan (NUP) is one of the main guidelines for a national strategy in Austria in this context. The NUP was initiated in 1992 by convening experts and representatives from science, social partnership, communities, administration, environmental organisations and NGOs so as to guarantee representation from a wide range of relevant social groups. The basic aim was to create a vision and to find measures by which to operationalise and implement sustainable development in the related policy sectors in Austria.

This comprehensive task was given to seven working groups: Energy; Industry and Manufacturing; Transport; Agriculture, Forestry and Water Management; Tourism and Recreation; Resource Management and Consumers. In July 1996, the NUP was passed by the Austrian Government. It is going to be revised every four years, and there will be continuous monitoring of goals and achievements, as well as running updates on the current state of development.

The National Environmental Plan is seen as providing long-term guidance and vision, and stipulates specific measures to be implemented. Chapter 1 of the NUP states the long-term nature of practical implementation: 'It is expected that the implementation of the most important measures within a short time period will contribute to finding the right path towards sustainability within the next two decades.'

The key notion of the NUP is the concept of 'sustainable development', and on a wide range of issues the plan covers goals and instruments for a national realisation of the aims of Agenda 21. Table 2 offers an overall view regarding the link between NUP and Agenda 21. It relates the 7 sectoral areas of the NUP to the 40 chapters of Agenda 21 (where connections seem reasonable and relatively clear). This overall comparison provides an idea of the priorities of certain sectors of the NUP from the viewpoint of the separate chapters of Agenda 21.

In brief, it appears that the relevance of the Agenda is strongest in relation to (1) Agriculture, forestry and water, (2) Resource management, and (3) Industry and manufacturing. Tourism, Transport, Energy and Consumers are apparently less well covered by the Agenda, but it must also be noted that particularly Transport and Energy are touched upon in several different chapters of the Agenda. The second section of Table 2 lists the chapters of more general relevance from the four major parts of the Agenda, as well as those chapters which are not directly relevant for Austria.

A major part of the National Environmental Plan (NUP), the Youth Environmental Plan (JUP), was set up as a complimentary initiative to allow Austria's youth to participate in national environmental policy. With this initiative, an attempt has been made to involve the younger generation in a comprehensive environmental policy at the Government level.

While a broad consensus has been attained among experts on many goals and measures, practical implementation is nonetheless viewed within the NUP as inherently difficult, '... since *fundamental structural changes* will be necessary.'

The plan outlines three major responsibilities of Government – the pursuit of environmental policy under the precautionary principle instead of 'end-of-pipe' solutions; the promotion of environmental awareness through education and information; and support for research and development – and describes three general challenges for citizens – greater

Table 2 NUP* chapters and their relation to the chapters of Agenda 21

NUP chapters	Agenda 21 chapters	Ranking
Energy	9, 10	6
Industry and Manufacturing	6, 9, 19, 20, 21, 22, 29, 30	2
Transport	7, 9, 10	5
Agriculture, Forestry and Water	6, 9, 10, 11, 13, 14, 15, 18, 21, 32	1
Tourism and Recreation	6, 13, 14, 32	4
Resource Management	7, 8, 9, 10, 15, 16, 18, 33	2
Consumers	4, 5	6

Agenda 21 sections	Agenda 21 chapters of more general relevance
Section I	1, 2, 3
Section III	23, 24, 25, 26, 27, 28, 31
Section IV	33, 34, 35, 36, 37, 38, 39, 40
Not directly relevant in Austria	12 (deserts), 17 (oceans)

* NUP: National Environmental Plan

self-initiative within the capacities of each individual; a willingness to be open-minded to new information and changing patterns of behaviour; and greater co-operation among affected interests in solving complex problems.

THE ROLE AND REACTION OF CENTRAL GOVERNMENT

The Austrian UNCED-Commission, which was established in 1991, co-ordinated the national preparations for the Rio Summit and continues as the designated forum for the post-UNCED process. The focal point of contact is the Department for International Relations/European Union of the Federal Ministry for Environment, Youth and Family Affairs. The National Commission involves all federal ministries, the federal provinces, the social partnership, and academic as well as nongovernmental sectors. In 1995, Austria became a member of the Commission for Sustainable Development (CSD), and in the years 1994, 1995 and 1996, there were organised a number of meetings to examine the substance of 40 chapters of Agenda 21.

Three national reports basically describe relevant activities of administration and government concerning the contents of the specific chapters of LA21, rather than giving information about progress at community level. The report to the CSD in 1997, prepared by the National

Commission, will also include an additional paper containing a brief summary of an inventory of relevant activities of communities relating to Local Agenda 21 in Austria that have taken place since 1992. The Federal Ministry for Environment, Youth and Family Affairs also intends to use this report as a document for further policy strategies. To date there has been little or no information given to the communities about their possibilities and responsibilities for implementing LA21.

In order to initiate the process of Local Agenda 21 on a broader basis in Austria and to accelerate the few existing initiatives, the Federal Ministry for Environment, Youth and Family Affairs has commissioned a research project to analyse the current status and identify the possible accelerators and barriers to implementing the Agenda 21 process. The study should contribute to initiating and encouraging many Local Agenda 21 activities in the near future.

THE ROLE OF LOCAL AUTHORITIES AND REACTIONS AT THE LEVEL OF THE LOCAL COMMUNITY

With only a few exeptions, the notion of LA21 is little known at the level of local government. In a quick random survey of 16 communities from all over Austria, local authorities were asked the following question: 'Do you have a Local Agenda 21 process in your community/district/town?'

The answer was generally 'no', with none of the interviewed persons – in some cases not even the person responsible for environmental issues – having any idea what a Local Agenda 21 actually is. On the other hand, however, there are numerous communities involved in activities which are similar to those envisioned by a LA21 process. In order to give a brief overview of how many communities have initiated such activities, the present section will summarise various ongoing activities of direct relevance for LA21.

PROnet

The PROnet is a databank of interdisciplinary regional, communal and institutional projects surveyed for all of Austria. The projects may be related to activities concerning community and regional development, and give interesting insights into the variety of activities and major related topics (Loibl, 1996). Initially the PRO*net* databank was created to provide information about environmentally related projects in the area of community and regional development and to foster the dissemination of innovative and creative project ideas.

Table 3 *Ranking of keywords characterising 28 interdisciplinary projects in the field of community and regional development*

Keyword	Number of mentions within the 28 projects
Tourism	I I I I I I I I I I I I I I
Agriculture	I I I I I I I I I I I I I
Energy	I I I I I I I I I I I I
Trade and craft	I I I I I I I I I I I
Traffic	I I I I I I I
Waste	I I I I I I I
Culture	I I I I I I I
Economy	I I I I I
Environment	I I I I
Nature conservation, village rejuvenation, air & climate, water, town development, health, social aspects	I I I (each)
Education, noise, waste water, forestry, industry, infrastructure	I I (each)
Fostering the village community, restaurants and gastronomy, regional economy, youth, finances, community development, development, public relations, public services, telematics, ecology, environmental management, composting, soil, chemical aspects, households	I (each)

The research team contacted 110 communities and 65 institutions which are active in the context of community and regional development. The following criteria were set up for registering projects in the databank: relevance for current community issues; relevance to the environment; and the degree of inderdisciplinarity in the project.

The study points out that the criterion 'interdisciplinarity' is most responsible for the fact that only 28 projects were selected for the first edition of the PRO*net* databank (as of 1996). On the other hand, the projects selected are good examples of what generally corresponds to the practical implementation of Local Agenda 21 issues. As to the time span, it can be said that nine initiatives were started before 1992; nine initiatives since 1992; and ten initiatives where no information was available.

Looking at the keywords characterising these projects, and counting the number of times a certain keyword appears, a simple profile of related sectors and topics can be derived. Although the simplicity of this comparison must be kept in mind, it still gives a picture about the issues of major importance (Table 3).

We can draw the following implications from the exercise: *Tourism* is at the top of the list, followed by *Agriculture*. As long as an area can point to some kind of tourist potential (such as an interesting or pleasant landscape), it seems to qualify for solving current income losses in agriculture with increasing development of tourist facilities run by farmers. This may also be due to the fact that the sector of tourism in Austria, with a decreasing number of guests, particularly in rural regions, generally requires structural changes. The fact that *Energy* ranks third probably has to do with the great number of practical ('value-added') possibilities related to economic benefits for rural communities when dealing with questions of renewable energy using local resources.[1] Different types of biomass (community heating, etc.), wind energy and solar panels are also examples of cross-sectoral initiatives in combination with *Trade and craft*, and which involve increased citizen participation. Solving problems of *Traffic & transportation* and *Waste management* is, of course, of major concern in many communities throughout the country. And finally, it is clear that the *Economy* as a whole is an important issue, and, on the whole, interesting to note that *Environment* takes the ninth place. The latter is, of course, in line with a basic characteristic of LA21, i.e. that it should not only be related to the environment but to 'a more conscious attempt to relate the environmental effects to underlying economic and political pressures.'

Local Agenda 21 and the European Sustainable Cities and Towns Campaign

The cities of Graz, Linz, Weiz, and Vienna have signed the Aalborg Charter and intend to initiate Local Agenda 21 within the framework of the ICLEI/EU program for European Sustainable Cities and Towns. We can use the case of Graz as an example.

The process began with a resolution by the municipal council of Graz and was practically initiated by the Department for Environmental Issues. The framework consists of a comprehensive concept entitled '*Öko-Stadt 2000*' (List, 1996). The goals of the concept were planned and drawn up with participation by local citizens, and are spelled out in nine separate action programmes: private households; public services; businesses and companies; agriculture; water, nature, public green spaces and landscape; waste; traffic and noise pollution, and protection of the atmosphere.

A catalogue of measures was set up and officially adopted by the City of Graz. Based on a number of specific scenarios, parameters of sustainability were established, and targets were set so as to realise reduction goals within the time-frame of the year 2000. Implementation is designed to be more than simple administrative routine, as it calls for widespread contact and involvement among the public in general. For the performance evaluation, a team of experts will audit the process every three years and compile a report.

Initiatives for participation in networks

Participation and the partnerships of Austrian NGOs in international networks (mainly European) is described as an important part of LA21 initiatives by 'Die Umweltberatung' (Eco-Counselling, Austria) which is itself an NGO (Schrefel, 1996). The contents of an LA21 process are here defined by the following points:

* partnerships between communities and other sectors
* an open form of government
* participation of the people
* the integration of social, environmental and economic aspects and aspects of international co-operation.

Several networks of partnerships are listed, e.g.: the Urban Forum for Sustainable Development; the 'Umweltberatung Europa' ('Eco-Counselling, Europe'); the Climate Alliance; ICLEI (International Council for Local Environmental Initiatives); the Green Purchase Club; the Conference of the Mayors of Eastern and South Eastern Cities; the European Cities and Towns Campaign; and the WHO Healthy City Project.
    The degree of success of LA21 in Austria may be measured by counting the number of cummunities affiliated to the Climate Alliance: 95 communities (4 per cent of the total) were affiliated in 1996 (Schrefel, 1996). Once again we see the tendency to automatically equate activities which *resemble* LA21 activities with the LA21 idea, regardless of existing reference to Agenda 21.

Initiatives under the framework of 'The Climate Alliance'

The Climate Alliance stipulates the reduction of CO_2 emissions by 50 percent compared to 1987 by the year 2010 (the Toronto target). The

Austrian Government takes responsibility for this goal in the energy reports of 1990 and 1993. Salzburg was the first Austrian federal province to become a member of the Alliance in October 1990. Since then 8 of the 9 Austrian federal provinces (states) and 142 towns and rural municipalities have entered the Climate Alliance (as of January 1997). The government of the 9th federal province, Vorarlberg, did not join the Alliance itself, but decided to leave the decision as to whether or not to participate to the local community level itself, and several communities in Vorarlberg do, in fact, participate.

The overall activities of the Climate Alliance on an institutional level were, in 1996, as follows:

- *European Climate Alliance Conference:* Held in Linz, Austria for the first time March, 26–27, 1996. Major themes of the conference were national taxes on energy, especially on fossil fuels, and the question of whether to avoid universally the use of tropical timber.
- *Workshops in communities:* Six workhops in communities were held on the topic: 'How to use the guidelines "Protection of Climate in Communities"': Initiating the process', and five workshops on the topic: 'Transport, Traffic and Mobility.'
- *The Climate Alliance and firms:* Conference held on June 20, 1996 to initiate a project among the business firms with the title 'Making Profit with Green Measures.' Successful companies are allowed to enter the Climate Alliance.
- *CO_2 minus 50 Percent:* A competition held for the first time in 1996 to find those communities which set an outstanding example for others. 45 projects were submitted, and the winners were awarded prizes donated by alliance partners in the Amazone. The main winners for 1996 were the communities of: Pfunds (Tyrol), Mäder (Vorarlberg), Schwarz (Tyrol), and Graz (Styria).
- *Conference of mayors of the Climate Alliance communities:* Took place in October 1996 in Schladming for the exchange of information and practical experience. Topics discussed included environmentally compatible tourism, agriculture, transport and traffic, alternative energy sources, saving energy, climate protection and economics and relevant innovative technology.
- *Children's contest:* Children's views and projects related to the Climate Alliance; runs until March 1997.

The implementation of the aims of the Climate Alliance in the relevant sectors covers a wide range of sustainable development issues, and includes an emphasis on citizen participation. By way of illustration, we can look at Grimmenstein, a small village with 1,400 inhabitants in a mountainous region of Lower Austria which joined the Climate Alliance in 1996.

The main task here is the reduction of greenhouse gas emissions caused by agriculture and forestry. Possible reduction strategies focus on the idea that the agriculture and forestry of the village should be able to meet the 50-percent target if woodchips as an energy source can substitute fossil fuels. In addition, the process has initiated citizen dialogues on potential concrete measures in the fields of organic agriculture, renewable energy and energy conservation with the following consequences: Planning and building of a small wind-energy plant; promotion of and financial subsidy for solar panels; initiation of an information campaign on energy conservation; encouraging local products from agriculture and forestry in order to cut down transportation, etc.

This example clearly demonstrates the spin-off effects of initiatives within the Climate Alliance as well as the additional potential which can come into action when such processes take place under the general framework of a Local Agenda 21. During recent years, 15 to 20 new communities per year enter the Climate Alliance.

It remains clear, however, that, if existing processes such as these are going to fulfill the potential of truly promoting sustainable development at the local level of government, information on Agenda 21 must be more widely and effectively promulgated.

SUMMARY, CONCLUSIONS AND FUTURE OUTLOOK

The role of the central government in Austria in preparing and supporting the process of LA21 is relatively modest. Information flows from the central government to public administration at the community level as to their prospective role in implementing LA21 did not take place. There are very few specific relevant initiatives to document. Reports to the Commission in the national reports of 1994, 1995 and 1996 focused mainly on activities of the different levels of administration regarding the separate chapters of LA21.

Austria's National Environmental Plan (NUP) is the major guideline for a national strategy in this context. It was drawn up by experts and representatives from the relevant major groups, and special attention was given to the participation of youth in the planning process, with an extra section entitled the Youth Environmental Plan (JUP). The Austrian UNCED Commission, established in 1991, involves all federal ministries, the federal provinces, the social partner, academic as well as nongovernmental sectors, and has its contact point at the Department for International Relations/The European Union of the Federal Ministry for Environment, Youth and Family Affairs.

Most of the local authorities and governments at the community level have no information about their potential role in a LA21 process.

Numerous initiatives of activities similar to LA21 do exist, however. Some examples are interdisciplinary projects in the field of regional and community development with attempts to 'relate the environmental effects to underlying economic and political pressures.' Regional and community development projects like these are expected to increase within the coming years.

LA21 initiatives in combination with the Aalborg Charter are taking place in the four cities of Graz, Weiz, Linz and Vienna. Austrian NGOs are also participating in various, mainly European, networks. The Climate Alliance is particularly popular and well-known in most parts of the country. 142 communities are participating through different types of reduction strategies, both in resource use and waste deposits, and there are a number of schemes for increased citizen participation with resulting cross-sectoral effects.

In many cases the first step of initiating a process of community development has its source in a local crisis (for example, the closing of a business or firm), or in a resistance movement against a specific project (new power plants or road construction).

Sometimes groups opposing projects (citizens' initiatives) have a wish to go a step further and implement positive ideas. They might even enter into a discussion process with their earlier opponents which ends up in a dialogue about co-operation in future projects.

Regarding interdisciplinary projects in the field of regional and community development, it seems that certain topics such as agriculture, tourism, energy, trade and crafts, traffic and waste, cultural aspects, and the economy are, on the whole, of more concern than others. The connection to the topic 'environment' is given in the sense of addressing 'the underlying economic and political pressures.' It may be that, under the conditions of growing unemployment in Austria, processes of community development on a local level with active self-initiative will increase in the near future.

On the basis of certain positive examples, which took place without the structured guidance of an LA21 process, it can be expected that a well-prepared and well-adjusted program of information from the central government to the local authorities could have a fruitful effect on increasing the number of LA21 initiatives in the not-too-distant future.

The central government could come to view a broad implementation of LA21 as an important multi-sectoral tool for initiating and supporting local activities at the grass-roots level to combat unemployment by mobilising a greater potential for self-initiated projects. Measures to be taken in the near future by the central government in this context will be – information, information and more information: In other words the spreading of 'easy to read and easy to understand' materials on what LA21 is all about.

Finally there remains an important, if hypothetical, question: What if activities labelled 'Local Agenda 21' should have an opposite effect to that intended, i.e. that they increase negative effects rather than promote positive effects? Such a question can only be answered by developing clear baselines and indicators for measuring change vis à vis sustainable development, rather than for change in local environmental conditions.

NOTES

1   A market study of biomass technology in Austria outlines the effects of doubling the use of biomass by the year 2015 to 280 PJ compared to 137 PJ at current state. The increasing market potential would trigger annual investment up to 8 billion ATS (600 million ECU) and create 10,000 to 15,000 permanent jobs. A side-effect would be the increased purchasing power in the region created by the substitution of energy imports (Grübl et al., 1995).

REFERENCES

Grübl, A., R. Hruby, G. Dell and Ch. Egger (1995) *Biomassetechnologien in Österreich* ('Biomass technology in Austria'), Marktstudie, OÖ Energiesparverband, for The European Commission, GD XVII Thermie, BM62, 1995.

List, Daniela (1996) 'Lokale Agenda 21 Graz – Ökostadt 2000', ('Local Agenda 21 Graz: Eco-City 200'), In *Globaler Konsens – lokale Umsetzung; Auf dem Weg zu einemr lokalen Agenda 21*, ('Global Consensus – Local Enactment: On the Road to a Local Agenda 21'), Wien, 20.9.1996.

Loibl, M. C., E. Egger-Rollig, E. Bertsch and G. Tappeiner (1996) 'PRO*net* Datenbank interdisziplinärer Kommunal- und Regionalprojekte' ('The PRO*net* Databank Interdisciplinary Municipal and Regional Projects'), Studie Österreichisches Ökologie-Institut im Auftrag des BM für Wissenschaft, Oktober 1996, Vienna: Austrian Ministery for Science, Transport and the Arts.

NUP (1995), ('National Environmental Plan – Austria') Vienna: Federal Ministry of the Environment.

Schrefel, Christian (1996) 'Partnerschaftsmodelle in der EU' ('Partnership in the EU') In *Globaler Konsens – lokale Umsetzung; Auf dem Weg zu einer lokalen Agenda 21*, ('Global Consensus – Local Enactment: On the Road to a Local Agenda 21') Wien, 20.9.1996.

Other sources (Not cited directly)

Dietrich W., A. Hinteregger, et al. (1996) Endbericht zum Forschungsauftrag Dokumentation: Öko-Partnerschaft der Gemeinde mit den Betrieben in Wolfurt, Wolfurt 1996

MoE-Austria (1994) 'Österreich: Bericht an die 2. Tagung der Kommission für nachhaltige Entwicklung der Vereinten Nationen' ('Austria: Report to the 2nd Session of the UN Commission on Sustainable Development'), Vienna: Minister of the Environment.

MoE-Austria (1995) 'Österreich: Bericht an die 3. Tagung der Kommission für nachhaltige Entwicklung der Vereinten Nationen', ('Austria: Report to the 3rd Session of the CSD'), Vienna: Ministry of the Environment.

MoE-Austria (1996) 'Österreich, Bericht an die 4. Tagung der Kommission für nachhaltige Entwicklung der Vereinten Nationen', ('Austria: Report to the 4th Session of the CSD'), Vienna: Ministry of the Environment.

7.

The Netherlands:

Subsidized Seeds in
Fertile Soil

Frans H. J. M. Coenen

THE POSITION OF DUTCH MUNICIPALITIES

In this chapter we will try to establish whether seeds from Agenda 21 have fallen on fertile soil in The Netherlands. We begin with an overview of the position of Dutch municipalities with regard to administrative structure and environmental policy, and then go on to a description of tendencies in environmental policy-making which are of particular interest for the reception of Local Agenda 21.

The Netherlands is a decentralised unitary state. The administrative structure comprises three layers of government: (1) municipalities and water boards, (2) provinces and (3) national government. Local government is organised in about 600 municipalities. These units have two functions: the implementation of national government policies in certain policy spheres, and the initiation of policy in other spheres where autonomous decision-making is permitted. These functions and the relation with provincial and central government are laid down in Municipal Law. In order to understand the position of Dutch municipalities, it should be recognised that there are constitutional constraints on the activity of local authorities. The mayor is centrally appointed and budgets and other important financial and planning decisions require higher approval. Central government also possesses the power to overrule any act of local government that is considered either against the general interest or illegal.

There are also financial constraints on the activities of municipalities, because over 90 per cent of their income is provided by national government. This can be in the form of an overall grant or in the form of specific payments for the provision of specific services or projects. Dutch municipalities have been involved in environmental policy since the Middle Ages. At first municipalities were mainly considered as mediators in environmental disputes between neighbours. With the growing scale of industry, however, other levels of government became increasingly involved in environmental policy. As a result of the environmental laws introduced in the 1970s, for example, the provinces were entrusted with license-issuing powers in cases involving technically complicated and potentially high-polluting companies. National government concentrates primarily on national legislation and regulations and on the planning of national environmental policy, including targets and norms.

An important milestone in the development of environmental policy was the first National Environmental Policy Plan (NEPP), popularly labelled 'Choose or Lose' (States General, 1989). To realise the ambitious goals of the NEPP, other actors have to become involved. These would, firstly, be the other government layers which have their own responsibilities and tasks in the field of environmental policy. Secondly, there are the other policy sectors with environment-related tasks; and, thirdly, the actors in society who are the actual 'target groups' for the policies in question. NEPP states that:

> *Everyone should be aware of his/her responsibility with respect to the environment and let this influence his/her actions. The large scale on which some environmental problems occur, does not detract from this'. And, further, that: 'Without the dedication of the target groups environmental policy cannot be intensified, and the pursuit of sustainable development becomes a dead letter (p 13).*

As of 1990, municipalities and the provinces were allocated extra funds (under the BUGM and FUN programs) for constructing and expanding the municipal and provincial apparatus.[1] The targets to be achieved at the different governmental levels are based on the notion of 'additional value for funds', and are laid down in the so-called 'Central Plan for Enacting the NEPP' for provinces and municipalities respectively. This implementation plan acts as a kind of contract between the Association of Municipalities (VNG) and the Ministry for Housing, Physical Planning and Environment. To guarantee the minimum level of resources necessary for effective implementation, a population level of 70,000 inhabitants has been set to qualify for funding. This means that smaller municipalities must enter into cooperative alliances with other units to take part in the scheme. The initial targets were set for 1995, with the Environment Inspectorate responsible for annual investigations and monitoring.

The idea was that after 1995 the funding would no longer be earmarked for environmental purposes but would be added to general municipal funding. An evaluation during the funding period (Ringeling Committee, 1993) led to doubts as to whether the environmental tasks were actually being carried out at the municipal level. The Ministry of Environment and the Association of Municipalities then decided to introduce a new funding scheme (VOGM) designed to strengthen the role of municipalities in implementing the second NEPP.[2] The new program provided allocations for the period 1996–1998, and gave municipalities more freedom to choose their own priorities. Among the choices available was an 'action-point' on Local Agenda 21 (which we return to below).

Considering the nature and scope of the environmental responsibilities devolved to the municipalities, supplemented by their own initiatives, Dutch municipalities are clearly among the most advanced in the world. These activities not only include tasks in the field of direct environmental protection, but also activities in related policy fields such as sustainable construction, physical planning, traffic planning and sewage improvement.

Main characteristics of Dutch environmental policy

In the beginning of the 1990's, Dutch environmental policy already contained four aspects which are of particular relevance for Local Agenda 21: the 'comprehensive integral approach', 'cross-sectoral policy integration', the 'target-group approach' and 'open planning'.

A *more comprehensive and integrated approach* to environmental policy is crucial for LA21 (as set out in Chapter 1). From the late 1970's and early 1980's, the Dutch government became increasingly aware of the disadvantages and limitations of compartmentalised environmental policy (air, water, soil). As a result, various efforts were made to integrate policy-making. Environmental policy was no longer prepared along segmental lines, but according to either more general themes (e.g. acidification, the manure problem and desiccation); geographical areas (e.g. vulnerable beach areas); flows of materials (e.g. cadmium); or target-groups (e.g. traffic, industrial sectors and agriculture). The new approach was later called the 'internal integration' of environmental policy. This internal integration was concretised not only in plans, but also in laws and institutions such as the General Environment Act which replaced several more compartmentalised environmental laws.

A LA21 should also be a more conscious attempt to realise *cross-sectoral policy integration*. Next to 'internal integration', this form of 'external integration' is also of key importance for Dutch environmental policy. Many policies on all levels of government have important side effects on the environment which stress the importance of the bases for intra- and inter-governmental decision-making. Since the first National Environmental Policy Plan, much more attention has been devoted to 'external integration of environmental policy'. This entails that matters such as transport policy, physical planning, agriculture policy, economic structure policy, water management, building regulations, energy policy and educational policy, are fine-tuned with the national environmental policy (States General, 1990). This fine-tuning is designed to take place not only at national level, but also at provincial and local levels. Despite excellent initiatives in this respect, however, this form of integration is still making slow progress, due mainly to the 'staying power' of traditional policy objectives. Over the past years, this was particularly clear with respect to important government decisions on infrastructure. In these cases, economic interests invariably take precedence over environmental considerations, either implicitly or explicitly.

A third characteristic of LA21 processes has been identified as *the involvement of stakeholders* in policy-making and implementation. A first aspect of Dutch environmental policy in this respect is the target-group approach. This policy focus means that, after the national environmental objectives have been formulated in the National Environmental Policy Plans, target groups and their representatives are given a strong say in all further stages of the policy process. In creating a consultative structure between the government and the industrial organisations acting on behalf of the polluters (i.e. the target groups), an attempt is being made to internalise environmental responsibility in individual companies. One of the main aims of this consultation is to define the tasks for a specific sector of industry within the framework of the overall national environmental objectives. Usually these arrangements are laid down in covenants and other forms of guidelines, incorporating targets to be realised by the various sectors of industry within a certain time limit.

According to the national planning framework, local authorities should also involve target groups in their planning. At local level there are specific advantages and disadvantages to a target group approach. The main guidelines of environmental policy are largely determined by the state, but policy is mainly executed by the provinces and municipalities. At municipal level there will be less need to arrive at a common policy formulation. Usually there will be a consensus by the time the municipality is confronted with the problem. At municipal level, the tension between what has already been decided between the central government and a particular branch of industry, always plays a key role. For instance, both the municipality and the local garage dealer may be confronted with agreements made between the central government and the Association of Garages (BOVAG).

A target-group policy can also be an active part of municipal environmental policy planning. The new planning system set forth in the General Environmental Conservation Act proposed the concept of *open planning*, with 'open' referring to the involvement of affected interests (stakeholders) in the early planning stages. This is designed to increase the scope and recruiting power of planning, which in turn is related to the goal of 'internalising' environmental responsibility among the plan's target groups. Such internalisation also depends on the way in which the plan is carried through. The combination of 'external integration' and 'internalisation of responsibility' is accomplished by initially publicising the plan so that the affected actors gain an insight into the type of behaviour which is to be expected from the municipalities, so that they can then adjust their own decision-making and allocations. In the beginning of 1993, 82 per cent of the larger municipalities (those with over 30,000 inhabitants) had a strategic municipal environmental policy plan or a mixed strategic and operational plan (Coenen, 1996).

The participation in local environmental policy planning is typical of the way by which participation in municipal environmental policy-making was given shape at the end of the 1980's and beginning of the 1990's. In practice, a local target group policy can be shaped by including representatives from the target group in a guidance or feedback group; organising an informative meeting with the target group; explicitly consulting target groups through interviews with representatives; or requesting a (written) response to planning drafts. Some municipalities set up more permanent 'consultation forums', especially with local environmental NGOs. Participation in local green-planning processes could be either reactive on the basis of a concept plan drawn up by the administration without the involvement of target-groups, or proactive in the preparatory stage of the plan. A telephone survey in June 1992 (Buil, 1992) showed that only one-third of 60 municipalities sampled (all with over 25,000 inhabitants) actually involved the target-groups in the preparatory stage of the planning process. Usually the approach would be to interview the target groups or have face-to-face consultation talks. A written survey held in the beginning of 1993 (Coenen and Lulofs, 1993) showed that roughly 30 per cent were involved only in the initial, preparatory stage; another 35 per cent were involved only in providing reactions to the original draft plan; and only about 21 per cent were involved in both stages. Approximately 14 of the local planning processes covered did not show any form of external involvement.

If we place those municipalities which actually showed involvement on a 'participation ladder', we find that roughly 10 per cent had no more than some form of citizen consultation group as the highest form of participation. 43 per cent had at least hearings and information meetings in addition to consultation, and 33 per cent had some form of additional direct interviews or surveys of target-groups as the highest step on the ladder. These numbers indicate that it was not unusual to involve target-groups when drawing up environmental strategies, but that it happened in a minority of the municipalities and with methods which were relatively limited. The majority of the municipalities relied only on consultation with respect to the draft plans.

Political and administrative modernisation

As with most countries in Northern Europe, there has been a recent tendency in Dutch municipalities toward political and administrative modernisation. The municipal elections of March 1990 showed an all-time low turnout with 61.5 per cent of the voters turning up, a result which was generally viewed as a dramatic decline. What made it even worse was that research (Tops, 1991) also showed that those who had turned up did so mainly because they considered voting to be a duty and not because they were interested or involved in municipal politics. The municipal elections were also shown to be 'nationalised', i.e. voters were led by national issues and voted for the same political party as in the national elections. Dutch citizens were quite satisfied with the services municipalities offered and considered the local authorities as reasonably useful, legitimate and important. But they didn't consider municipal politics as an important political arena were citizens should get involved.

These findings led a number of municipalities to take initiatives for administrative and political modernisation, i.e. to search for new ways of policy-making which (presumably) are better accommodated to the demands of citizens. In general this meant that local administrators and politicians aimed to change modes of interaction with the citizenry. A general diagnosis of the problem was that the 'policy style' of municipalities was too formal and too closed, with public administration directed inwards onto the organisation itself.[3] The policy style was seen as no longer being in line with more general changes in the relationship between municipalities and their citizens. In the first place, political parties had lost much of their post-war role. Fewer and fewer citizens become members of a political party, something which was considered very natural a few decades ago. Furthermore, voters tend to change parties very rapidly, and they don't see that much difference between political parties at the local level. On another dimension, municipalities are increasingly perceived as primarily service providers. Citizens are said to perceive themselves more as consumers than as voters. And, finally, there is a perception that citizens feel themselves increasingly 'left out' because policy making has become a process dominated by experts and an 'inner circle' of sectoral politicians. Citizens develop the idea that there is no need for their general type of competence, and that there are no possibilities for channelling their own needs and problems into local politics.

Survey research shows (Gilsing, 1994) that, by 1994, 96 per cent of Dutch municipalities had taken initiatives which can be considered as experiments with political or administrative modernisation. In general, two approaches can be distinguished – the 'instrumental' and the 'communicative' approaches (Veldboer, 1996) – though a number of the experiments have elements of both categories. The instrumental approach introduces instruments to find out what citizens think, mean and want, such as a referendum or some form of opinion research. With the communicative approach, the mode of policy-making changes. Instead of involving citizens after draft plans have been completed, they are brought in at the outset of the policy-making process. Social scientists refer to these modes as 'interactive policy-making', 'coproduction of policy', or strategic 'bottom-up' policy-making.

Conclusions

These perspectives indicate that, when the RIO-document was published in 1992, Dutch municipalities were already in the process of significantly improving the level of environmental policy performance as prescribed by the national government. This involved mainly being more effective in environmental policy enforcement as prescribed by the 'Central plan for Enacting the NEPP' at the municipal level. In the area of environmental policy implementation, therefore, The Netherlands was, at this stage, one of the more advanced countries in the world. Many of Agenda 21's action points with relevance for local authorities had, in other words, already been introduced into the Dutch policy-making apparatus. There was also considerable experience in communicative and participative procedures in municipalities through innovations with both target-group approaches and open planning. In addition, there were more general tendencies for an administrative and political modernisation of local government towards a more open and flexible interaction between citizens and local politicians and administrators. At first sight, therefore, it would seem that The Netherlands provided fertile soil for the new LA21 'seeds'.

PREPARATIONS FOR UNCED

In this second section, we will briefly discuss the preparations for the RIO conference. In fact these preparations go back to the warm reception of the Brundtland Report in The Netherlands. Almost immediately after the publication of Our Common Future in 1987, the Dutch government designated 'sustainable development' as the major guideline for overall Dutch government policy.[4] The concept was then translated into the first National Environmental Policy Plan (NEPP). Also at the municipal level, there was great interest in the idea. During the local council elections of 1990, environmental issues played a major role. Both NGOs and left-wing political parties (PVDA, 1990) published ideas for a more sustainable municipal policy as input to the election campaigns. In many of the political program's of the newly appointed Boards of Aldermen for the 1990-1994 period, attention was also given to sustainable development.

In the beginning of the 1990's, municipalities showed increasing interest in global problems and in the international dimensions of their policies. Municipalities were influenced by NGOs in this respect. For example, the Inter-Church Peace Platform (IKV) developed a 'Municipal Program for Peace'. NGOs in the field of development aid (NCO, NOVIB, SNV) also prodded municipalities towards trans-urban cooperation with the South. The anti-apartheid movement resulted in a platform for municipalities against apartheid (LOTA). The only part of the 'four-leaf clover' of the international dimension of municipal policy that seemed to be missing was the dimension of environmental policy (Moerkamp, 1992).

NGOs gradually stimulated and heightened interest within municipalities for global environmental problems and sustainable development. In January 1991, the *Vereniging Milieudefensie* (Friends of the Earth, Netherlands) started a campaign against greenhouse-gas emissions aimed at consumers and municipalities. Later the Climate Alliance was incorporated into this campaign, which itself then became part of a broader campaign entitled 'Working for a Cleaner World'. Third-world organisations (NCO, NOVIB) participated in this campaign, along with environmental NGOs, (*Vereniging Milieudefensie, Stichting Milieu-Educatie*), the Ministry of Environment and the Association of Municipalities (VNG). The VNG called upon its members to join this campaign held between Earth day (April 22) and the World Environment Day (June 5) in 1991 (Circular, 8 March 1991).

A similar campaign was held in 1992 dedicated to the UNCED conference and especially to the topic 'climate change' and the possibilities for local greenhouse-gas initiatives. It involved a conference on 'Municipalities in a Sustainable World', the founding of local groups, a model-resolution involving an action program to be signed by municipalities, and actions using postcards supported by international networks (World Life Fund, Friends of the earth) .

Within the campaign 'Working for a Cleaner World', the UNCED connection was largely directed towards the founding of local platforms and programs. These local campaigns received some seed-money (NLG 5,000 per effort), an information package and support from Regional

Centres for Development Cooperation (COS) and Provincial Consultancies for Nature and Environment Education (*Provinciale Consultschappen Natuur- en Milieu-educatie*). The involvement of the municipality was stipulated as a condition for support.[5]

A major step in the preparation for Rio was the formation of the campaign 'Brazil 92', consisting of a large number of organisations including labour unions, employers organisations, church organisations, consumer organisations and environmental NGOs. The goal of the campaign was to contribute to environmental consciousness in The Netherlands, and to participate in the development of Dutch policy for the Rio Summit. In addition to the postcard campaign mentioned above, the campaign organised a conference on 'A Start for UNCED', where the campaign representatives presented their points of view to the Prime Minister and other officials. The conference was also viewed as a preparatory meeting for the World Urban Forum. The campaign also published a booklet (with the same title as the conference) as their contribution to UNCED.

The 'Alliance for Sustainable Development' (a grouping of environmental and peace organisations) also published a Dutch national NGO report for UNCED, entitled 'It Can Be Different'. This report was explicitly presented as an NGO report alongside the formal national report to UNCED from the Dutch National Government. This report was intended to be a list of specific recommendations for society regarding the goal of sustainable development.

Before and after each of the Preparatory Committee meetings for UNCED (PrepCom's), the ministers of Environmental Affairs and Development Cooperation informed Parliament on the positions to be adopted by the Dutch delegation, along with the results from the meetings. Parliament was officially informed on the preparatory process for UNCED in a special white-paper, where the goals and institutional structure of UNCED were explained along with the goals and positions for Dutch policy. In the national governmental papers, little attention was paid to the situation for municipalities, though the Minister for Environmental affairs did state that action on a local level was of crucial importance for sustainable development (PrepCom, New York, 2 March 1992). The Association of Dutch Municipalities (VNG) participated in the preparations conducted within the International Union of Local Authorities (IULA), and the formulation of the 'Oslo Declaration'. The association was also involved in several initiatives and campaigns mentioned earlier as the representative of Dutch municipalities.

Conclusions

The UNCED conference received a great deal of attention from the media in the Netherlands. NGOs played an important role in disseminating the

UNCED theme, and tried to awaken an interest in local groups. The majority of municipalities remained pretty much on the sidelines, with the exception of a relatively small group consisting of those with particularly active local groups; those who became involved in the campaign 'Working for Cleaner World'; and those who became active in the Climate Alliance. The Association of Municipalities was also actively involved in numerous national and international initiatives.

THE FOLLOW-UP TO RIO

The first reactions of NGOs , civil servants and politicians in the media to the results of UNCED were not very positive (e.g.. Van der Kleef, 1992). They ranged from 'very disappointing' (the environmental movement) to 'the best we could get under the circumstances' (Waller-Hunter, 1992). In this section we will sketch the follow-up to Rio in three phases: the initial reactions from the national government and individual municipalities up to 1995; the second phase with the start of a new national campaign; and a third phase where the campaign is expanded and strengthened during 1996.

First reactions from the national government

In a letter on behalf of himself and the Minister for Development Cooperation, the Minister for Environmental Affairs informed Parliament shortly after the Rio Summit about the conference results. The same two ministers followed up this discussion with a white paper on the 'Implementation of the UNCED Results'. A decision was also made to translate the complete version of Agenda 21 into Dutch and to disseminate information on other initiatives of direct relevance for the 'major groups'. These initiatives were of major importance for bringing the Local Agenda 21 idea out to a broader public. It was also decided to transform the preparatory campaign, 'Brazil 92', into a new and more action-oriented 'Campaign ('platform') for Sustainable Development'.

The two ministers also elaborated on the expected relevance of the UNCED outcomes for Dutch policy-making. They promised Parliament an analysis of the changes in policy and law which would be necessary for the Rio follow-up. On the eve of the first meeting of the newly established Commission for Sustainable Development in New York (CSD, June 14–25 1993), the ministers informed Parliament of the progress of Dutch international policy and the Dutch position on post-UNCED implementation. In July of 1993, Parliament was presented with an overview of the changes deemed necessary in Dutch policies and law (States General 1992–1993, 22031, 16). The ministries responsible compared present policies with the contents and prescriptions of Agenda 21 The main conclusion was that the goals and action-points of Agenda 21 were, to a significant degree, already being pursued through present policies in The Netherlands. It was also pointed out, however, that there were numerous recommendations and action-points which still had to be put into effect.

With respect to the municipalities, the white paper emphasised that local government has been given an important role in the implementation of the first NEPP, and went on to state that the municipal role in implementing Agenda 21 would be strengthened in the second NEPP. As soon as the complete translation of Agenda 21 was completed, it was presented to the two ministers responsible, and thereafter widely distributed to the major groups, along with a covering letter and copies of the two documents previously presented to Parliament. On the whole, it is safe to say that relatively little attention was given to the role of the municipalities and provinces in these documents and communications. Municipalities were mentioned as one of the several major groups which had an important role to play in implementation, but they were not given the same amount of attention as a number of other groups (for example youth).[6]

The second NEPP (launched in March 1994) can be seen as the post-UNCED document in which the national government most consequentially discusses the further responsibility of the Netherlands with respect to Agenda 21. (There was, in other words, no separate Dutch implementation plan for the Rio commitments.) In the second NEPP, a more direct reference is made to LA21 and to the role of the municipalities in implementing the Agenda. As a result, key aspects of the idea of 'a Local Agenda 21' were included in the VOGM funding program as a separate point of action, as well as in the second 'Central Plan for Enacting the NEPP' (March 1995).

Reactions from individual municipalities

The idea of LA21 was initially received with little enthusiasm by Dutch municipalities. One reason for this was the feeling that local government was already doing a great deal in the environmental area. International publications documenting 'best cases' of environment-and-development activities seemed to confirm this view, since Dutch municipalities were well represented in areas such as differentiated refuse collection, energy conservation, and sustainable construction practices. There was a general impression that Holland was a front-runner on environmental issues, so that local authorities could not immediately see the 'valued-added' implications of Local Agenda 21.

Secondly, the municipalities felt that their capacity was already overburdened with trying to fulfil the devolved regulatory tasks and responsibilities under the first NEPP. Fulfilling targets so as to retain extra funding proved a difficult and resource-consuming job. Little time, capacity and energy were left to develop new initiatives. A number of municipalities clearly felt that LA21 would simply involve extra responsibilities which they could not face at the time. The Environment Inspectorate had also expressed an expectation that municipalities should give priority to the original targets and the more elemental environmental tasks (Didde, 1994).

Finally, the general atmosphere of environmental enthusiasm which had arisen in most Western countries during the late 1980's, had begun to decline at an earlier date in the Netherlands. Media attention, public interest and political attention were falling off before the final phase of the run-up to UNCED. There remained, however a number of 'pioneers' among the Dutch municipalities. One could easily fill a book with dozens of Dutch examples of sustainable development initiatives which would look good in any country.

With very few exceptions, however, these initiatives did not become associated with or converted in Local Agenda 21 activity. There are only a few cases where the initiative for an LA21 (usually related to the previously mentioned local campaigns for sustainable development) came from the 'bottom-up' (Roosendaal, Etten-Leur). In some cases, the pioneering municipality gave no indication of wanting to become involved in the initiative at all, whereas in others, the first steps were taken by enthusiastic aldermen or civil servants (e.g. The Hague, Schiedam). Of particular interest here is a pilot-project in the province of Noord-Brabant, where a LA21 initiative was started with 20 municipalities in November 1994. Its aim was to promote and gain experience in dialogue processes between local NGOs, business, citizens and local authorities. The project is facilitated by a group of cooperating environment-and-development NGOs and is financed by the province, The National Committee for Development Education and the Ministry of Environment. This pilot-project has resulted in a widely spread scheme for operationalising the LA21 action-point of the VOGM program.[7]

Several international organisations have taken specific initiatives to promote LA21, and a number of the Dutch municipalities opting for LA21 activities have named these efforts as reasons for choosing LA21 among the VOGM alternatives. The first international initiative which really had an impact in the Netherlands is the Climate Alliance that started in 1990. Over one hundred Dutch municipalities signed the Alliance, and this affiliation, along with the signing of the Aalborg Charter, was clearly a contributing factor to several of the municipalities who latter chose the LA21 option under VOGM (see below).

The national campaign

In March 1995, a second stage was initiated in the follow-up to Rio. At the beginning of 1994, the Dutch 'Steering Group LA21' was formed. The Group is directed and coordinated by a national organisation which at the time was called the 'Dutch Program ('Platform') for Sustainable Development'. This initiative functions as a forum for discussions between a wide variety of independent Dutch organisations, with the goal of ensuring and promoting sustainable development. The Program views Agenda 21 as an important source of inspiration in its efforts to bring together representatives for 'major groups' in pursuit of the Rio goals. The Steering Group has members from a wide variety of NGOs, including youth groups, environmental, developmental and health organisations. The Program has published two widely disseminated books on LA21 (PDO, 1993, 1994), and also publishes a newsletter.

The initiative to promote LA21 was given a strong impetus by a conference in March 1995 entitled 'Working with Agenda 21'. The conference received considerable interest from over 400 municipal politicians and administrators, with 150 reserves on a waiting list. This was viewed as exceptional because many people in the field had come to believe that environment-and-development issues were not particularly popular at the time. UNCED seemed to have taken place a long time ago and much had been forgotten. The participants at the conference received a working portfolio with information on LA21 which has since been regularly updated. Before this conference there were other less focused initiatives on a national level. There was a conference organised in June 1994 by an association of professionals working in environmental policy in collaboration with the VNG, mainly on the development of municipal environmental policy within the context of the second NEPP. There were a number of workshops held at the conference on environmental education and information, and LA21 was among the topics covered.

As previously mentioned, the VOGM program was a new form of environmental funding for a three-year period (1995–1998). A draft of the guidelines for the program, including a section on LA21, was circulated to the municipalities in May 1994. Municipalities could receive extra funding for four policy priorities chosen from a list of nine 'action-points', where the LA21 point was the only really new addition. Funding from the program is based on the number of inhabitants (at NLG 4.86 per inhabitant), with a 25 per cent bonus if a municipality cooperates with other municipalities in the region. The municipalities are, in turn, expected to at least double this budget from other means. The program has an annual budget of approximately 94 million Dutch guilders (50 million USD).

According to the leaflet explaining the rules for the program, the goal of the LA21 action-point is to promote sustainable development on a local level. No blueprint has been supplied as how to achieve a Local Agenda 21, but four conditions must be met to receive a subsidy:

* An LA21 should add something extra to the municipality's present activities;
* It should include a debate between the administration and the local population as to how to achieve sustainable development;
* Environmental education should be a key task within the implementation of the action-point; and
* A LA21 should be directed towards concrete projects and activities.

These conditions are set forth and are to be monitored by the Environmental Inspectorate. The municipalities were required to submit a request for funding before March 1995. Eventually, 143 out of over 600 municipalities choose LA21 as one of their four action-points in the first round of allocation. The second 'Central Plan for Enacting the NEPP' (March 1995) also contained a section on environmental education (A-10) which explained the meaning and purpose of the LA21 action-point.

Strengthening the campaign

As a third stage of implementation, we can identify a strengthening of the VOGM campaign for two major reasons: (1) dissatisfaction with the processes already initiated in the VOGM municipalities, and (2) a wish to further spread LA21 among the municipalities which had not chosen the action-point. The Steering Group for LA21 thus declared that their goal now was to achieve a broad-based LA21 process in all Dutch Municipalities within the next five years (Duurzaam, 20 March 1996).

In a progress report in December 1995, the Steering Group had also been critical of developments in those municipalities which had opted for the LA21 action-point. LA21 processes were found to be slow in getting starter. Usually there was a civil servant as project officer from the environmental division of local administration who had to start the process without political backing and support from other divisions. The Steering Group feared that LA21 would become limited to only environmental subjects, leaving out the global perspective and the North-South dimension of sustainable development. In November 1995, the CSTM research institute in Twente surveyed the larger municipalities (over 30,000) by telephone . One of the conclusions of the survey was that some municipalities made a very slow start because they were not sure what the Environment Inspectorate was actually expecting from them.

On a more general level, the Steering Group pointed out that innovation in municipalities is always very difficult. In a new campaign, advisory teams would be assembled to visit municipalities on request, and regional meetings could be organised where front-running municipalities can inform other municipalities on the surplus value of LA21.

On a national level too, new initiatives are being taken to resolve bottle-necks at the municipal level. A committee with representatives from the Ministries of Development Cooperation, Environmental Affairs and Foreign Affairs, has developed some new initiatives. One main effort was a training program for municipal civil servants in the second half of 1996 (IPP, 1996). Parallel to this course, the Association of Dutch municipalities published a new book on LA21 in July 1996 (VNG, 1996). Attention is here given to not only the formal LA21 process, but to working in the general spirit of the LA21 idea. The approach is based on collected experiences in formulating an LA21. Five procedural steps are distinguished: Initiative, Vision, Sustainable Development Audit, Dialogue and Work Plan.

An initial analysis of the Work Plans developed ('*Plannen van aanpak*') gives a general idea of the state of art of LA21 in the Netherlands (VNG, 1996). In summary form:

- A sustainable development audit is carried out or is announced as the first step in the Work Plan;
- The 'vision' aspect tends to be poorly developed;
- Most schemes are municipal but some are regionally prepared. The schemes tend to be either products of the local authorities or a product of one of the partners;
- The duration of the preparatory process varies greatly, with work plans prepared as either general plans for action, stepwise plans, or merely initial statements of purpose;
- The dialogue can be both internally and externally orientated. The number of partners involved varies considerably;
- A LA21 can be part of an environmental policy or a policy of its own, and the LA21 organisation and structure can be based on either existing structures and programs, or be an entirely new initiative.

A Local Agenda 21 can also be viewed as an umbrella for existing initia-tives within the international sphere of municipal policy. Unfortunately, however, coherence is often lacking here between initiatives in the fields of development cooperation, peace and conflict-resolution, human rights and environmental issues (VNG, 1996). Internationally oriented munic-ipal policy is often developed on the basis of contacts related to specific 'partner' projects, twin-city arrangements and other forms of collabora-tive agreements. Dutch municipalities are active in both implementing national initiatives (such as the Climate Alliance), in initiating and funding local initiatives (such as Local 'Platforms' for Development Cooperation), and in different forms of 'green consumerism'.

Conclusions

Assessing the follow-up to UNCED during the first two years, it appears as though municipalities were not really given a central role in implementation. There was a more-or-less 'silent agreement' between the Association of Municipalities and the Ministry of Environment that municipalities were not prepared to take on any extra burdens at that moment. Furthermore, there was a general feeling that Dutch municipalities were, in fact, already doing quite well with respect to environmental policy.[8]

CHARACTERISTICS OF THE MUNICIPALITIES INVOLVED IN LA21

In this section we will try to answer the question as to which municipalities picked up on LA21 first. Are there differences according to size, political profile, and international orientation? Are there any regional differences? What appear to be the major motives for choosing LA21?

The point of view of the Dutch Association of Local Authorities (VNG) is that the impact of Agenda 21 in municipalities is not restricted to the municipalities that are formally engaged in LA21 under the heading of the VOGM funding. In line with earlier viewpoints that, in fact, Dutch municipalities were indirectly complying with Agenda 21 (Dordregter, 1994), the VNG maintains that a number of municipalities are working on LA21 without using the name itself (VNG, 1996). Similarities are particularly clear in the policy-formulation and implementation aspects of some of the other VOGM action points and in other aspects of municipal environmental policy-making. Examples from the VOGM program are sustainable building projects and energy conservation. Other examples include local mobility plans and neighbourhood-oriented policy making.

We will here restrict ourselves to those municipalities which explicitly refer to Agenda 21. We delimit the group to those identified by the ministry as choosing LA21 as one of their four policy priorities from a list of nine possible actions points that could be subsidised by the ministry. We present some facts and figures on these municipalities, although not every municipality engaged in LA21 has chosen for this specific VOGM action point to be funded.

The first relevant characteristic is the *number of inhabitants*. A greater proportion (60 per cent) of municipalities with more than 100,000 inhabitants opted for LA21 as an action point then among municipalities with less than 30,000 inhabitants (where the proportion was 17 per cent). 'Large' municipalities is a relative concept here because the majority of Dutch municipalities can be considered as rather small. Approximately 84

Table 1 *LA21 per province*

Province	LA21				Total
	Yes		No		
Groningen	10	37%	17	63%	27
Friesland	7	21%	26	79%	33
Drente	3	9%	32	91%	35
Overijssel	10	21%	38	79%	48
Gelderland	13	20%	52	80%	65
Utrecht	20	50%	20	50%	40
Noord Holland/Flevoland	21	20%	84	80%	105
Zuid Holland	24	28%	62	72%	86
Zeeland	0	0%	26	100%	26
Noord Brabant	15	12%	108	88%	123
Limburg	15	23%	50	77%	65
Total	138		515		653 (100%)

per cent (547 out of 653 in 1993) are smaller than 30,000 inhabitants, and only 3 per cent (20 units) are larger than 100,000 inhabitants.

A second characteristic could be the *political profile* of the local council and the political affiliation of the Alderman responsible for environmental affairs. The data show, however, that LA21 was not more specifically chosen by left-wing dominated local councils, nor by municipalities with a socialist-leaning Alderman responsible for environmental affairs.[9]

As for *regional differences*, Table 1 shows that there are some interesting variations. There are probably two reasons for this. Firstly, in some provinces such as Noord-Brabant, NGOs have been particularly active in stimulating LA21. Secondly, given the fact that municipal cooperation can be necessary to reach the required level of 70,000 inhabitants (as mentioned above), there are certain regions where (due mainly to a high concentration of small units), more units enter into LA21 activity than otherwise might be the case. If a majority of the municipalities in a certain region want to choose for an LA21, the minority has to follow.

What about leading municipalities on *environmental policy*? Have they also been among the first to opt for an LA21? The Ministry of Environment published a list (10 September 1993) which divided all the municipalities into three categories: Those which the Environment Inspectorate expected to reach the BUGM targets for adequate environmental policy performance ('achievers'); those who were *not* expected to meet this deadline ('stragglers'); and those who were not meeting the targets at this time – but who might comply ('strugglers').

Table 2 *Environmental policy performance and the choice for LA21:*
(Municipalities with more than 30,000 inhabitants)

	Type of municipality by criteria for environmental policy achievement		
Opted for LA21?	*Achievers*	*Strugglers*	*Stragglers*
Yes	17 (38%)	24 (44%)	3 (30%)
No	28 (62%)	31 (56%)	7 (70%)
Total	45 (100%)	55 (100%)	10 (100%)

One would here expect that those municipalities showing good records on regulation and environmental control would be among the first to be interested in LA21. Surprisingly enough, however, Table 2 shows that of the 110 municipalities with more than 30, 000 inhabitants, relatively more 'strugglers' than 'achievers' actually opted for LA21.

We mentioned above the involvement of Dutch municipalities in international initiatives To see if this variable has had an effect, we compared the group who choose LA21 with 68 municipalities who did not choose LA21. Only 54 per cent of the municipalities which were involved in international initiatives like the Climate Alliance and the Aalborg Charter chose for LA21, compared with 72 per cent of those municipalities which were not involved.

Further information is available from a telephone survey (CSTM, 1996) where the responsible civil servants in all of the 43 municipalities with over 30,000 inhabitants were asked about their motives to choose LA21 as a VOGM action point. Their responses are here broken down into nine categories.

1. *Policy continuity:* LA21 was chosen because it was seen as a logical consequence of an already established policy in the Environmental Policy Plan or the political program of the Alderman. This motive is largely connected with the nature- and environmental-education component of the LA21 VOGM tasks.
2. *New possibilities:* LA21 is here seen as an opportunity to apply innovative environmental policy. Innovation is especially mentioned in the context of dialogue and participation.
3. *VOGM-stimulation:* The availability of VOGM funding is mentioned as a motive.
4. *Local stimulation:* Pressure from local groups (political parties, environment-and-development groups.

Figure I *Reasons given by local environmental officials for choosing LA21 within the VOGM program*

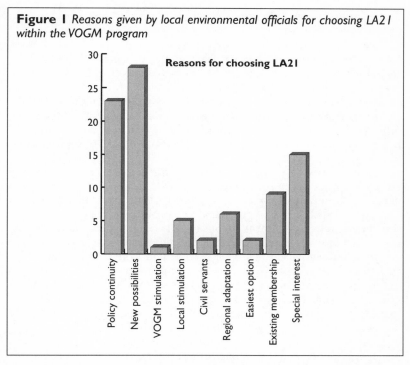

5. *Civil servants:* Civil servants are seen as pushing the subject onto the political agenda.
6. *Regional adaptation:* Other municipalities in the region took the first initiative, thereby obliging the municipality (more or less) to make the same choice.
7. *Easiest option:* LA21 is viewed as the easiest of the VOGM tasks to carry out.
8. *Existing membership:* Membership in, for example, the Climate Alliance made LA21 a logical option.
9. *Special interest:* The motive for LA21 is a special interest in one of the aspects of the VOGM LA21 option, for example environmental education or environmental communication.

Note that the purely monetary aspect of the VOGM program was seldom mentioned. 'Policy continuity' and 'new possibilities' were the main reasons stated for starting a LA21.

THE IMPACT OF LA21

In this section we will try to assess whether changes are visible in the Dutch situation in the direction of the essential characteristics of LA21 as set out in Chapter 1. We will also deal with factors which have an inhibiting influence on these characteristics.

We have above described the baseline conditions for some of these characteristics. A major enhancing factor in the Netherlands is the possibility of funding for LA21. But this funding can also be an inhibiting factor because of the very specific definition of LA21 in the VOGM program.

It is to early to judge if LA21 has changed the relation between *economic and political pressures and environmental effects*. Research on municipal environmental planning (Coenen, 1996) shows that the overall economic growth target of municipalities is of major importance for the way they handle environment and sustainable development. Municipalities with a high growth targets, where several thousands new jobs have to be created and thousands of houses have to be built with the necessary infrastructure, show a more reserved environmental policy. There are even examples of municipalities trying to set the national environmental policy aside in the name of economic growth. On the other hand, there are municipalities with a low-growth rate and fewer employment problems, which advertise themselves as 'green cities'. They are able to make choices in attracting new businesses and refuse environmentally unfriendly businesses. These are often municipalities which prove to be very popular for locating new offices and business. It remains a question, therefore, as to whether LA21 changes this pressure from day-to-day political practice in order to give the environment greater preference with respect to economic growth.

Immediately prior to UNCED there already existed a growing interest in *the global aspects of municipal policy*. In 1994, research was conducted (Bie, 1994) on the factors influencing 'failure' and 'success' in global environmental policy in municipalities. Global activities were found to take place within different frameworks such as the already mentioned campaign 'Working for a Cleaner World', the Climate Alliance and the UNCED campaign. Other initiatives are the rain-forest protection (tropical wood) campaign and North-South city-relations. More recently, local sustainability 'charters' and schemes for joint implementation have been added.

The fact that global municipal environmental policy is generally viewed with scepticism in the Netherlands is a major inhibiting factor. As one Alderman puts it: 'It is not a task of our municipality to do something about the melting polar ice caps'. In the research carried out in 1994, it was expected that an LA21 might be an important framework for the municipal global environmental policy. Research in the province of Limburg showed that joining the Climate Alliance did not mean that the municipalities involved took more substantive actions in policy areas such as energy, traffic, usage of tropical wood and refuse treatment.

The third characteristic is a more conscious attempt to achieve *cross-sectoral integration*. We have previously mentioned some of the problems in this area. If we consider the excellent examples in sustainable building, sustainable physical planning, traffic planning, sewage building, purchasing of office goods, etc., however, policy integration is quite successful on a local level.

A major inhibiting factor is the relation with national policy. Cross-sectoral integration should be more effective at the local level because this is where policy areas really intersect. But in a number of areas integration is given shape on a national level and then implemented on a local level. This applies, for example, to physical and traffic planning where sustainability principles are formulated at the national level and then implemented on a local level.

A second inhibiting factor is the resistance from other policy sectors to the infringement of environmental policy on these sectors. LA21 is thus often rejected and turned back on the environmental sector. Although it is intended as a much broader concept, it is handled as if it were simply another initiative from the environmental department. The problem arises because an LA21 initiative often means that a civil servant from the environmental department gets time off as a project officer, because LA21 is financed by the Ministry of the Environment. The effect is, therefore, seen as an 'environmental initiative'.

A third inhibiting factor comes from the specific definition of the VOGM action point were LA21 is primarily associated with environmental education and dissemination. Municipalities tend to view LA21 as a question of environmental information and not as an initiative for administrative and community change.

Has LA21 led to increased involvement on the part of average citizens and major stakeholder groups, particularly business and labour unions, in the planning and implementation process? This is clearly a major goal of Chapter 28 of Agenda 21, and we have previously discussed the issues and problems involved. In the present context, we would point out the particular problems with getting business involved. The evidence indicates that whereas a broad spectrum of other groups would show up for hearings and open meetings, there were seldom representatives from business present.

A major inhibiting factor here is that municipalities, as well as the environmental policy target-groups, have problems getting used to the new role municipalities have to play in LA21 processes. Instead of a local government which lays down the rules as to what is right and wrong, the municipality is here intended to play a role as facilitator of a process and as a partner in an open dialogue.

Another restraining factor is, from a converse perspective, that a bottom-up LA21 process depends very much upon the quality and power of the actors involved. NGOs and other actors need to be well organised to play a role in LA21. Municipalities sometimes find it difficult to find well-matched partners for the dialogue.[10]

The fifth characteristic of LA21 is the attempt to define and work with local problems within *a broader framework and an expanded time frame*. We have already seen that in a number of municipalities LA21 is restricted to environmental subjects, leaving out the global perspective and the North-South dimension of sustainable development. The evaluation of the 1996 training course (IPP, 1996) showed, for example, that the North-South dimension was still under-developed.

A LA21 should be *future-oriented, towards a sustainable municipal community for future generations*. The development of a sustainable vision or future projection is in this sense crucial. In practice, there are two pressures working against the development of such a sustainable vision. In the first place, the VOGM regulation states that an LA21 should be directed towards concrete projects and activities. This is then interpreted by some municipalities and consultants as meaning that a sustainable vision should be secondary to direct and short-term results so as to keep the process going. Secondly, there's a general tension between short-term gain on specific action points and a long-term sustainable vision, because politics requires immediate successes (at least within the next four years) and consultants want to deliver quick and concrete results.

CONCLUDING REMARKS

On the eve of UNCED, the baseline conditions for Dutch municipalities for a rapid and broad diffusion of LA21 looked very promising in the Netherlands. Dutch municipalities were in general well ahead on environmental policy. Sustainable development had become a political issue; experience with participation in environmental policy had been gained; and there was a tendency towards political and administrative modernisation.

Not much happened the first two years after Rio, except in a few pioneering municipalities. The main reasons for this lukewarm reception of the concept of LA21 were the external pressure to concentrate on basic environmental tasks (regulation and certification), as well as a misconception that LA21 required little more than what Dutch municipalities already were doing.

As it turns out, the baseline conditions were not as good as they at first appeared to be. Target-group policies were not a positive stimulus for LA21 in practice. There is a fundamental difference between the Dutch target group policy and Agenda 21: 'Local authorities' (as one of the 'major groups' identified by Agenda 21) are not target-groups in the Dutch sense, but intermediaries or partners (Second NEPP, p 44, 102). They do not formulate a local target-group policy, although some municipalities try to do so, but are mainly the executors of *national* target-group policies.

A further problem with political and administrative modernisation is that it is much easier to profess one's *faith* in political modernisation than to actually practice it. Both politicians and civil servants have difficulty with the new roles these modernisation processes demand. But their partners in the process also have difficulty with the new role. The manner by which LA21 has taken form may also have complicated things. We have already discussed some of the advantages and disadvantages of the VOGM program as a financial incentive. It is clearly an advantage that it can solve capacity problems in manpower and money, but just as clearly a disadvantage in that, like every form of funding, it creates certain expectations on the part of the subsidy-provider and specific obligations on the part of the subsidy-receiver. It is the municipality which receives the funding and has to account for its use, but implementation is difficult because it is not clear to the municipalities what, in the end, is expected of them

And what is the perspective for, say, the next five years? In general we should probably not expect that the Netherlands will move to a situation with a 100-per cent coverage with a formal LA21 within a period of five years. The Steering Group on LA21 has as its goal that the next five years will see a broadly based LA21-plan for all Dutch municipalities, and that, in the majority of municipalities, implementation will have been initiated. Coverage is expected to increase considerably because, for a number of municipalities, it will only be a small step from the existing practice in other VOGM tasks to an LA21. For the VNG and the Ministry of Environment, the main issue will be LA21's international dimension. A crucial juncture will come with the disappearance of the special environmental funding on January 1 1998. The funding will not disappear completely, but it will no longer be ear-marked. This means that environmental goals will have to compete with sports, welfare or whatever else for the same general funds. What the municipalities will do in this situation, and whether the goals of sustainable development will be sufficiently institutionalised to maintain both funding and progress towards change, remains to be seen.

NOTES

1   BUGM in Dutch refers to a government-sponsered program 'Funding implementation municipal environmental policy'; and FUN to 'Funding Implementation National Environmental Policy Plan'

2   VOGM in Dutch refers to a Government-sponsored program for 'Continuation of support of municipal environmental policy'.

3   There were several symposia, conferences, committees and research efforts which led to publications with differences in both analyses and possible solutions for the crisis in municipal politics.

4   The points of departure and goals of the Brundtland Report (World Commission on Environment and Development, WCED) were endorsed by the Dutch government in a provisional report on the Brundtland Commission (TK, 1987-1988, 20298).

5   This led to 25 new 'platforms' (action programs) besides 13 already existing platforms. An important output was the learning process in cooperation between municipalities and NGOs, and the publicity this provided (COS and *Provinciale Consultschappen Natuur- en Milieu-educatie* , 1992).

6   In 1993 there was established a National Youth Council for Environment and Development (a campaign directed toward joint actions among youth groups) and a 'sustainable development treaty' was signed.

7   The leaflet was disseminated through the 'Working Files LA21' of the Joint Platform for Sustainable Development. The pilot-project substantially influenced the schemes for LA21 and later publications.

8   In the first two years, there was still considerable confusion on the concept of LA21. Interviews with civil servants in 15 municipalities in the region of Twente showed that 10 out of 15 said that they had a limited knowledge of the content of the UNCED-documents. Only two could answer the question as to who were the 'major groups' referred to in Agenda 21, and their answers were only partially correct.

9   Dominance was indicated on the basis of the two largest parties in the local council. Left-wing dominated are the PVDA, D66 dominated councils. Right-wing dominated are led by the VVD and/or small Christian local parties.

10 It is interesting in this respect that in one case of preparing a municipal environmental policy plan, the local association of trade and business hired their own consultant to help them comment on the environmental policy plan which was prepared by the municipality with the help of another consultancy firm!

REFERENCES

Arnstein, S. (1969) 'A ladder of citizen participation', *Journal of the American Institute of Planners*, 216–224.

Buil, V. (1992) *Een open planning van het gemeentelijk milieubeleid?* ('An open planning of the municipal environmental policy?') Een onderzoek naar de participatie van doelgroepen aan de totstandkoming van gemeentelijke milieubeleidsplannen, ('Research into the participation of target groups in the realisation of municipal environmental policy plans') Msc-thesis, University of Twente, Enschede.

Bie, M. van der (1994) *Mondiaal denken, Lokaal handelen!* ('Think globally, act locally') *Een onderzoek naar succes- en faalfactoren van mondiaal milieubeleid in gemeente,* ('Research into the succes- and fail factors of global environmental policy in municipalities') Utrecht: Stichting Milieu Educatie (Foundation for Environmental education).

Coenen, F.H.J.M. (1992) 'The role of municipal environmental policy plans in environmental management', paper XXIInd IAAS-Conference, 13–17 July 1992, Vienna.

Coenen, F.H.J.M. en Lulofs, K.R.D. (1993) Resultaten enquête naar gemeentelijke milieubeleidsplanning en gemeentelijk milieuzorg-beleid ('Results of a survey on municipal environmental planning and municipal environmental management policy') CSTM-Studies and reports 93-11, Enschede.

Coenen, F.H.J.M. (1996) 'The effectiveness of municipal environmental policy planning', CSTM-Studies en reports 96-53, Enschede.

COS Brabant (1995) 'Aan de slag met een lokale Agenda 21, verslag van een werkconferentie 19/5/95', 'Starting with a local agenda 21, report of a working conference', COS Brabant (Centre for Development Cooperation Province Brabant).

Didde, R. (1994) 'Agenda 21 van Schiedam' ('Agenda 21 of Schiedam') Heidemijtijdschrift, 2.

Dordregter, P. (1994) 'Draagvlak voor gemeentelijk milieubeleid en milieudraagvlak door gemeentelijk beleid' ('Basis for municipal environmental policy and environmental basis for municipal policy') Inleiding congres vaksectie milieu ('Presentation conference civil servants in environmental professions') June 1994.

Gilsing, R. (1994) 'Bestuurlijke vernieuwing in Nederland' ('Political modernisation in the Netherlands') *Acta Politica*, 1.

Institute for public and politics (IPP) (1996) 'Evaluation trainingscourse LA21 for civil servants', unpublished

Kakebeeke, W.J. (1994) 'Nederland en het internationale milieubeleid, Agenda 21 als leidraad' ('The Netherlands and international environmental policy, Agenda 21 as a guide') *Internationale spectator*, 1.

Kleef, M. van, UNCED (1992) 'Teleurstellende uitkomst met lichtpuntjes' ('Disappointing results with bright spots') and 'Nieuwe wereldorde nog meer anti-milieu en anti-mens' ('New world order even more anti-environment and anti-human') *Milieumagazine*, 5.

Klima-Bündis (1992) 'Der Europanische stadte mit indigenen Volkern der Regenwalder zum erhalt der Erdatmosphare', Klimaatverbond.

Platform voor Duurzame Ontwikkeling (PDO) (1993) 'Duurzame ontwikkeling op de Lokale Agenda 21. Ideeën voor gemeentelijk milieu en ontwikkelingbeleid'.

PDO (1994) 'Een lokale Agenda 21, zo werkt dat. Op weg naar een duurzame gemeente', ('A Local agenda 21, this is the way it works') Platform voor

178

THE NETHERLANDS

Duurzame Ontwikkeling ('Platform for sustainable development').

PvdA (Socialist party) (1990) 'Duurzame ontwikkeling: de mogelijkheden voor lokaal beleid, Adviescommissie Milieu en energie' ('Sustainable development, the opportunities for a local policy, Advisory Committee on Environment and Energy').

Ringeling Committee (Adviescommissie Evaluatie Ontwikkeling Gemeentelijk Milieubeleid) (1993) Stappen verder ... (Advisory Committee on the Evaluation of the development of Municipal Environmental Policy, Steps forwards ...)

VNG (1994) 'De ontwikkeling van het gemeentelijke milieubeleid in het perspectief van het NMP2' ('The development of municipal environmental policy in the contect of the second NEPP') Vaksectie milieu (Environment Section civil servants) VNG-publisher, The Hague.

VNG (1996) 'Praktijkboek Lokale Agenda 21' ('Handbook on Local Agenda 21') VNG-publisher, The Hague.

Waller-Hunter, J.H. (1992) *De VN conferentie over milieu en ontwikkeling,* ('The UN conference on environment and development') Milieu en recht, 11.

Veldboer, L (1996) *De inspraak voorbij,* ('Beyond participation') Institute for public and politics (IPP).

Tops e.a. (1991) *Lokale democratie en bestuurlijke vernieuwing* ('Local democracy and administrative renewal') in Amsterdam, 's-Gravenhage, Utrecht, Eindhoven, Tilburg, Nijmegen and Zwolle, Delft.

8. The United Kingdom:

A Mirage Beyond the Participation Hurdle?

Stephen Young

THE PRE-RIO BASELINE

Between the publication of the Brundtland Report in 1987 and the Rio Earth summit in 1992, there was a sudden and considerable growth of interest in environmental issues and how sustainable development could be applied, amongst some local authorities in Britain (Ward, 1993). This was the period of Friends of the Earth's Environment Charter; the launch of the Environment Cities programme; and the appointment of the first Environmental Co-ordinators. So by Rio, a small but significant number of pioneering authorities had done a lot of work on how to apply the themes inherent in sustainable development within their areas. However, this was mainly at an enthusiastic, exploring stage. Little real evaluation was attempted.

This activity was supported by some significant changes in policy taking place within the Department of the Environment (DoE). This reflected the need to respond to the 15 percent Green Party vote in the 1989 European elections; to EU directives, as over Environmental Impact Assessment; and to the growing interest in sustainable development in local government. A new planning framework began to emerge in 1991/2 in the wake of the 1991 Planning and Compensation Act (Stoker & Young, 1993, Chapter 4). In February 1992 Planning Policy Guidance 1 (PPG1, DoE, 1992a) was published; and PPG12 (DoE, 1992b) followed a little later. The latter instructed councils to take account of the environment in a wider sense than before. Para 6.3 said that plans need to go further than they had before to ensure that newer environmental concerns, such as global warming and the consumption of non-renewable resources, are also reflected in the analysis of policies that forms part of the plan preparation.

Para 6.8 explicitly states that, 'Attention must be given to the interests of future generations', and goes on to mention topics that had not been central to the preparation of plans before – coastal flooding, health, protecting groundwater, and the implications of policies on transport and energy for global warming. The framework within which councils had to operate had begun to change in significant ways before the Rio Earth Summit. The baseline with regard to attempts to promote sustainable development and to prepare what came to be called LA21s, had started to move forward in important ways before UNCED.

However, the baseline with regard to environmental conditions in Britain in the late 1980s was quite different. Britain was labelled 'The Dirty Man of Europe'. Many of the details, with some evaluation, were set out in *This Common Inheritance* (DoE, 1990). Britain was starting from a baseline that was far behind most other European countries. The limited scale of ambition was apparent before Rio too. Rydin points out (1995, p 134) how the 1990 revisions to the building regulations on energy conservation and other issues brought Britain up to where Sweden had been in the 1930s!

INVOLVEMENT WITH THE LA21 IDEA IN PREPARATION FOR UNCED

The interest in sustainable development in a few individual authorities in the pre-Rio era led to pressures on the local authority associations to take the concept more seriously. This had three results. First, the associations' research and training organisation, the Local Government Management Board (LGMB) was given the remit to promote the concept. It is important to stress that LGMB was an existing body, taking on a new task – not a newly created organisation. There was thus in-house experience of the whole process of promoting research and spreading knowledge about new approaches out to policy-makers in local government. The initial work led to a report which was submitted to the Earth Summit – *A Statement to UNCED on Behalf of UK Local Government* (LGMB, 1992a).

Second, local government organisations lobbied the DoE, arguing the need to take the local government dimensions of sustainable development more seriously. Ministers were looking for positive ideas to take to Rio, and this led to close co-operation. A Central and Local Government Environment Forum was set up in 1991 to promote co-operation and co-ordination by bringing together ministers and local government leaders. As a result – and somewhat unusually – local government representatives were included in the UK Government delegation to Rio.

Finally, the local authority associations got involved in international local government networks. Whitehall was pressured by British local government interest in the series of international local government associations' conferences and PrepComs during the run-up to Rio to discuss their ideas (LGMB, 1992b). The most important part of this activity was an invitation from the Secretariat of UNCED to the International Council for Local Environmental Initiatives (ICLEI). ICLEI was asked for a draft chapter on the role of local government in promoting sustainable development to go into the Earth Charter to be discussed at Rio. The close links that ICLEI had begun to develop with the pioneering authorities created the opportunity for influential figures from the LGMB, from the associations, and from councils like Lancashire to play a role. British local government thus played a part in setting up the situation in which local government across the world went to Rio with its own agenda. This became the basis of Chapter 28 in the Agenda 21 document.

As mentioned above, NGOs like WWF and Friends of the Earth had been active in the late 1980s and early 1990s in promoting the idea of local government taking the concept of sustainable development more seriously, and in working out how it could be applied at the local level. Their media campaigns, their lobbying efforts in Whitehall, and their involvement at the pre-Rio PrepComs and at Rio itself all complemented the involvement of central and local government in promoting the LA21 initiative within the UNCED process.

CENTRAL GOVERNMENT'S RESPONSE TO LA21

After Rio, central government was positive in encouraging British local government to pick up the challenge posed by LA21 and the need to work out how to apply the concept of sustainable development at the local level. This was largely due to the civil servants in the unit in the DoE who had been involved in the pre-Rio push on sustainable development in the early 1990s; had prepared the UK delegation's papers; and had guided the UK input into the discussions at Rio. Much of their energy was sustained over the next eighteen months. In January 1994, *Sustainable Development: The UK Strategy* was published (DoE, 1994a: the UK Agenda 21 Report), together with three separate reports on climate change, biodiversity, and forestry. This included a positive statement about the role of local government.

Both central and local government acknowledge the importance of working in partnership to help identify priorities for action and the ways in which this can best be delivered. Local government's ability to innovate, to anticipate problems, to provide local leadership and processes for involving other groups, represents an important contribution towards

the development of strategies for sustainability which reflect local needs
and priorities (DoE, 1994a, para 30.4).

In the light of the conflicts between central and local government, not
just after 1979 but after the cuts imposed by Labour in 1976, this was
surprisingly positive. It amounted to a list of strengths, a list of things that
ministers had spent years accusing councils of not being able to do.

The next section shows how Whitehall did play a positive, if
secondary, role in promoting local-authority involvement in the preparation of LA21s. But this encouraging stance has to be set against the
government's approach on a range of policy issues where councils have
repeatedly accused it of failing to develop coherent, supportive policy
frameworks.

A general pattern has emerged whereby the central government
departments and agencies take time in discussing policy options as they
affect local councils, and then take some tentative steps in developing
programmes and allocating supportive funding.

On energy, for example, lack of resources handicapped the ability of
the much trumpeted Energy Savings Trust to promote energy efficiency.
The government hoped that private funding would be forthcoming, but it
had to take extra-legal powers to give the Trust financial help for 1995/6. In
1996/7 it received £25 million. It also took until 1995 to pass the Home
Energy Conservation Act. This requires councils to submit energy conservation reports to government, identifying cost-effective ways of tackling
the problem in residential accommodation (DoE, 1996a, paras 83-4, & 87).

A similar kind of saga developed in the sphere of waste. In 1993,
councils were instructed to prepare waste disposal plans. Targets were set
up – for example, to recycle or compost 25 percent of all household waste
by 2000. But only £66.4 million of local council borrowing was approved
during 1991-6 for investment in recycling and composting. (DoE, 1996a,
pp 35 & 81, Ref 233). The new land-fill tax did not become operational
until September 1996. A similar story emerged here with lack of money
and capacity-building programmes to support the growth of community-
based partnerships in the social economy (as discussed below).

Transport is a worse example. This is also discussed in more detail
below, but the essential point is that, since before Rio, there have been
fairly open disagreements between the Secretaries of State for
Environment and Transport over the problems that unrestrained car
growth has brought, and there has been a great deal of discussion in
Government, Parliament, the media, and amongst the NGOs about all the
inter-related issues (Young, 1994). In particular, debate centred around
the huge and comprehensive Royal Commission on Environmental
Pollution report published in 1994 (RCEP, 1994). But the government
failed to move beyond welcoming the report, calling for a National Debate

on Transport, and a commitment to 'examine its recommendations carefully' (DoE, 1995a, para 13.9 & Ref 290). Nothing will happen until after the 1997 election when another RCEP report will be published (Economist, 18/1/97). Meantime, urban congestion and lack of investment in public transport repeatedly crop up as issues in LA21 participation programmes. Without a coherent strategy from the centre, councils can do very little to tackle the problems.

The slow, rather tentative pace, at which central government has been developing its programmes has made local-authority lobbying of Whitehall departments to amend policies even more important than usual. Much of this is political posturing by politicians from opposing parties. But ultimately, Whitehall needs to know when its policies are not working so that they can be amended and made more effective. Lobbying is at its most effective when a dialogue is established and maintained. In the environmental sphere, the creation of the Central and Local Government environment Forum in 1992 marked a recognition of the value of dialogue, and of its institutionalisation (Stoker & Young, 1993, Chapter 7). Waste provides an example. The government was persuaded to set up a review of the recycling Supplementary Credit Approval Programme. When this revealed a range of problems, the review was broadened in 1996 to examine a number of related dimensions (DoE, 1996a p 83, Ref 245). The government's reaction is as yet unclear, but such reviews usually lead to improvements.

PROMOTING THE INVOLVEMENT OF LOCAL AUTHORITIES IN LA21

The LGMB has been the leading organisation on Local Agenda 21, building on the pre-Rio interest and involvement of central government, and on the work of the pioneering councils in the early 1990s. After Rio, it highlighted the growing realisation that much of the implementation of Agenda 21 would depend on action at the sub-national level. It claimed that two-thirds of the statements adopted by national governments 'cannot be delivered without the commitment and co-operation of local government' (LGMB, 1993a, p 1). After Rio the local-authority associations established the LA21 Steering Group, which included representatives from other sectors, to oversee and develop what was now called the 'LA21 Initiative', complete with its own logo. The aims of the Initiative were to interpret Agenda 21 for local councils; define what sustainable development means at the local level; help councils prepare sustainable-development strategies; develop local environmental initiatives; promote information exchange on 'best practice'; assist with education and training initiatives; and help to create local partnerships with the business and voluntary sectors (DoE, 1994a, paras 30.6, and 30.10).

Although limited resources were available within LGMB, those involved set about establishing an energetic programme – organising conferences and round tables; drawing up a Declaration on Sustainability; developing contacts with academics and promoting research; and spreading best-practice ideas. As individual councils got involved with LA21, LGMB developed a system of sending out monthly mailings to all local authority environmental co-ordinators.

During 1993-6, its publications list included a series of fairly short papers pooling knowledge and experience on such issues as greening local economies and promoting participation in the LA21 context. It provided guidelines and training packs explaining the basics of sustainable development to chief executives and councillors, as well as more substantial reports on the practicalities of promoting sustainable development. *Sustainable Settlements: A Guide for Planners, Designers and Developers* (Barton et al, 1995), for example, put into one publication a great deal of technical information, drawing in particular from the Dutch and Danish experience. It explains in detail such things as the criteria needed to help decide the optimum location in a conurbation in environmental terms for different kinds of businesses, and how to design shelter-belts to shield housing from major roads and major industrial neighbours. As a result of reading journals, attending conferences and going on study tours, the professionals who had been interested in these issues knew about them and were aware that their counterparts in Europe were routinely doing things that were not even considered in Britain. Gathering and presenting the detail in a readily accessible form in English, however, was an important step. The knowledge has now at least been made available, even though it will clearly take time to affect daily working practices.

The Central and Local Government Environment Forum also contributed – via its newsletters – to the spread of knowledge and information in the post-Rio period. It initiated work on energy efficiency, environmental publicity, environmental management and the role of local charters (DoE, 1994, para 30.13).

Other factors were also at work to draw local authorities more closely into the LA21 sphere. The growing interest amongst professions such as planning and environmental health was reflected in the articles in their journals. The vagueness of sustainable development helped here. There was no single model to follow, no package of knowledge to simply acquire. It was all an intellectual puzzle. It was new and stimulating. Individual officers developed their own personal networks with NGOs, people working for other councils, and through such organisations as the Ålborg signatories. A high point on the conference circuit was the Global

94 gathering in Manchester (Whittaker, 1995). Increasingly this all fed into academic activity, which in turn fed back into the journals and the conferences.

There was also an underlying political reason why council interest in the environment and LA21 grew. Both elected councillors and some officers moved into the environmental policy arena as it grew before and after Rio simply because it gave them a role. From 1976 onwards, local government in Britain had faced round after round of spending cuts; the imposition of further controls; loss of powers to non-elected bodies; and changes in the law forcing them to privatise services (Stoker, 1991). The environment emerged as an arena where they could take the initiative. What's more, this was at a time when public interest in the environment was growing.

The role and influence of the national NGOs was not as significant at the level of local government after Rio as it had been before. Some, like the WWF, got involved with participation experiments in, for example, Reading and Bradford. Friends of the Earth retained its interest to some extent, but its campaigns on issues like air pollution in cities had a national rather than a local focus, although it highlighted specific cases like Greenwich. Broadly speaking, the national NGOs focused on broad policy issues, such as transport, energy and the Brent Spar affair, as these affected national policies.

As a result of all this activity, and especially because of LGMB's role, the numbers of councils preparing their LA21s grew sharply. Lancashire County Council was one of the first in the world to complete – in 1994. Although the aim agreed at Rio was for all LA21s to be completed by the end of 1996, LGMB fell back on trying to get all councils *started* by the end of 1996. LGMB carried out a survey in February and March 1996, sending questionnaires to all 542 councils. The situation was complicated, however, by the fact that local government reorganisation was being carried out at the same time, so that by April 1st 1996, there were 478 authorities. A total of 275 questionnaires were returned. 111 councils said they were aiming to complete their LA21s by the end of 1996; 39 said they would be producing an LA21 at a later date; 62 said they intended to produce a strategy document but had not decided on the details; and 17 said they were not producing an LA21, but would feed the work into other plans (Tuxworth and Thomas, 1996, Q 3).

Although the situation is complicated by local government reorgani-sation, it seems, in summary, that the question on the council's approach to LA21 was answered by 271 out of 478 councils – or about 57 percent. Adding 111 and 39 together means that 150 out of 478 UK councils intend to produce an LA21 – about 32 percent. This figure might go up slightly. A government report published in March 1996 claimed that 'the UK is recognised as a world leader with more than 300 of its local authorities having embarked on the process' of producing an LA21 (DoE, 1996a, para 166). This would mean about 63 percent of all councils post April 1996, but the basis for this higher figure is unclear.

THE IMPACT OF LA21 AND RELATED ACTIVITIES

Local authority responses to Brundtland and to Agenda 21 have led to a number of different areas of activity. The key point here is that LA21s have only been one part of councils' attempts to respond to Rio and promote sustainable development.

Green housekeeping

Many authorities have analysed their own impact, as organisations, on the environment. Environmental audits have been carried out to examine the variety of ways in which a council's routine operations affect environmental conditions through, for example, the use of energy and the generation of traffic. Some actions have impacts far from the town hall. Life-cycle analysis and other techniques have been used to analyse where the goods and services the council purchases have come from; and how the suppliers of those goods and services have, in their turn, affected environmental conditions when, for example, producing cars or paper. Nottinghamshire County Council is but one example of an authority that has introduced energy-saving programmes; changes to purchasing policies; schemes to get its employees to use public transport, bikes and car-sharing arrangements when travelling to work; and a range of other green house-keeping arrangements.

State-of-the-environment audits

A parallel activity has been the development of environmental audits. The aim here has been to survey the range of local environmental conditions with a view to identifying the worst problems and those most amenable to action. This creates a baseline against which progress can be measured. It also helps with both the development of programmes, and the prioritising of resources. Tackling car congestion for example is far more difficult and expensive than replacing lost tree cover. The latter can be tackled incrementally over time for a relatively small cost. Another function of state-of-the-environment audits has been to identify how far, and in what ways, the routine application of council policies has had detrimental effects on the local environment. Wildlife has benefitted for example from reducing the routine mowing of grass verges, and the frequent use of herbicides.

Developing more broadly based policies to link sectors

During the 1970s and 1980s policies on issues like parks, recreation, tourism, transport, housing, industry, shopping and so on were developed in a rather narrow way which did not reflect an understanding of the links between these different policy spheres. The Brundtland Report and the Rio accords have had an important impact in highlighting the links. For example policy-makers now have a greater understanding of the need to appreciate the links between, for example, environmental conditions and health (Crombie, 1995). The links between air pollution and traffic congestion and asthma have received lots of attention. In a similar way, policy towards waste collection and disposal have become more broadly based. Reducing the volume of waste going to landfill has become more important, as has the need to prevent leakage from land-fill sites to protect ecological conditions around a new site. This has all led to new approaches to waste minimisation, and to reviews of the balance at the local level between recycling, incineration and land-fill. Combined Heat and Power (CHP) plants have also become more common. What these examples have in common is the need to think more broadly about the whole range of environmental impacts when developing policy, an approach which, in contrast with much of western Europe, is relatively new in Britain.

Environmental education

Many councils have realised the fundamental importance of environmental education in raising awareness of environmental issues, and of the need to devote resources to this. This is usually understood to mean focusing on leaflets and other means of persuading people to save energy, garden for wildlife, leave the car at home more often, and so on. The aims are to change people's life styles and to educate them so they can contribute more effectively to participation programmes. People in Britain find it also difficult to judge whether their actions will make any difference; and find it difficult to trust government on these issues (Harrison et al, 1996).

Many councils have interpreted environmental education more broadly. A prominent theme has been changing routine planning guidance and planning briefs to encourage architects and builders to pay more attention to energy efficiency, the use of indigenous species when designing landscaping schemes, and so on. Another approach has been to try to persuade hospitals, water companies and other large landowners to manage land in environmentally more sensitive ways. Resources have also gone into demonstration projects – 'ecohouses' (Bolton); centres of excellence (Lancashire); environment shops (Leicester); and centres providing training, education, and environmental information for businesses, and accommodation for local environmental groups (Bristol).

Developing new tools and appraisal techniques

The promotion of sustainable development has taken the more advanced councils into new fields. One of the problems has been developing new tools to move on from Cost Benefit Analysis and conventional environmental economics approaches. Lancashire, for example, has carried out a 'Green Audit'. Two of the most discussed approaches have been sustainability indicators (LGMB, 1995) and environmental assessment at the level of a plan (DoE, 1993). The extent to which these have been used, however, is still very limited, especially when compared to Environmental Impact Assessment. However, exploring the potential and practice of such techniques has been an important part of how policy-makers are trying to puzzle out what sustainable development means in practice.

The planning process

It seems clear from the early LA21s, and from the drafts, that they vary considerably in their scope (Church, 1995; Whittaker, 1995a & 1995b). They have incorporated some of the State of the Environment Audit work; and they identify problems and priorities. Some are quite specific whereas others are fairly vague. They vary in their ambition and the extent to which they relate in realistic terms to prevailing national policies; local authority powers; and available resources. In some policy spheres, they will undoubtedly influence the development of council programmes because they will be pushing at open doors. Examples where councils are reassessing their approaches and priorities are biodiversity, housing renewal, and waste.

However, it is as yet too soon to assess the impact of LA21s on issues where they are in conflict with council and/or Whitehall priorities. In the context of the British political and planning system, LA21s are a new breed of plan. The system of structure and local plans, and, in metropolitan areas, Unitary Development Plans (UDPs), provide the legal basis of the planning system. They set out policies on land release, minerals, housing investment, transport infrastructure, tourism and a whole range of other issues. They reflect major central government policies, as over airports, power stations and motorways; as well as setting out the council's conclusions from its own survey work and public consultation programmes. Once they have been formally approved, these are the statutory plans against which planning applications are judged. When appeals against the refusal to grant planning permission are considered, their status is of almost overwhelming importance. It seems clear that where the LA21 is at variance with the existing statutory plan, it will be the latter which will almost always have more influence.

During the late 1990s, many current statutory plans will come up for review. The process of integrating LA21s with the statutory plans, and rearranging priorities in the light of the LA21's lead, will determine their significance. But during that review process, the LA21 document is likely to be in conflict with minerals plans, the road building programme, and the priorities of other organisations.

Similarly, LA21s envisage change in the public expenditure programmes of councils, Whitehall departments, government agencies, and the privatised utilities. It is not just the council's own budget that will have to be rearranged in accordance with the priorities within the LA21 document. It is the budgets of a range of other organisations which individual councils will have to try to influence. Meanwhile, the outlook at the national level, irrespective of which party wins the 1997 election, is for further cuts in revenue and capital budgets.

In the context of LA21 participation programmes, transport has attracted a great deal of attention. It provides a good example of the complexities of trying to assess the significance of an LA21 document. Such a plan will carry some weight, but the implementation process is very fragmented and difficult to influence, let alone control. Councils can draw up proposals to tackle local problems – park and ride schemes, road improvements, traffic calming measures, bike paths, and so on. But decisions as to the amount of available funding are largely taken in Whitehall. Any action on introducing road pricing will also depend on a central government lead. The Department of Transport determines the road-building programme, and buses and trains are now largely privatised. The impact of LA21 proposals on transport will thus depend to a considerable extent in many cases, on councils persuading others to act differently.

Preparing LA21s, and producing the final document is a significant step. But it is likely to be several years before that significance can be tested by analysing the influence of LA21s on the statutory plan review process; and on the budgets of a range of organisations. In the British context, LA21s provide a new agenda on which decisions will be made during the late 1990s. The realisation of the LA21 idea will depend in large part on this process.

ENVIRONMENTAL EFFECTS AS AN EXPRESSION OF ECONOMIC AND POLITICAL PRESSURES

The attempts to unravel the different dimensions of sustainable development during the period since the Brundtland Report has led to more conscious attempts to relate environmental effects to the underlying economic and political pressures. Several examples have been mentioned above. Non-decisions in Whitehall have, for example, led to the lack of a clear political lead on transport policy. Similarly, cities like Manchester and Cambridge have tried to avoid imposing car restrictions. The Government has also talked a great deal – from the 1990 white paper *This Common Inheritance* (DoE, 1990, Appendix A) onwards – about the need to use economic instruments to tackle pollution costs passed on as externalities by private firms (Young, 1994b). But this strategy has still had little impact. The 1996 land-fill tax is an exception. This gives firms an incentive to reduce the waste they send to landfill sites. The 1995 Environment Act continues the long-established command-and-control approach with regard to air pollution (DoE, 1996a, paras 15-28). Privatisation of bus and rail has exacerbated market pressures and made integrated transport planning more difficult. In summary, this dimension has been understood, but not often acted upon in ways that remove the problems.

Linking local issues to global effects

There is a much greater understanding than before Brundtland as to how the local affects the global (with respect, for example, to the effects of local greenhouse gas emissions on global warming and ozone depletion), but the extent to which there is a conscious attempt to tackle this at the local level is limited to isolated cases. Oxford's attempt to reduce traffic congestion through park and ride schemes and electric buses is one example. There is a certain complacency in Britain on this issue as CO_2 emissions have been reduced to 1990 levels long before the target date of 2000, an effect achieved through the earlier decision to run down the coal industry, and the replacement of coal-fired power stations with gas-fired ones (DoE, 1996a, paras 7-14).

With regard to global solidarity and justice, some authorities have developed 'twinning' arrangements to share experiences with local councils in Eastern Europe, Africa and elsewhere. This has been done under the auspices of the Healthy Cities Programme, WWF, ICLEI, the International Union of Local Authorities, and the Foreign and Commonwealth Office. Britain's restricted and much criticised overseas aid programme has been linked more explicitly to equity and environmental issues during the last decade (DoE, 1994a, para 30.16-8; & DoE 1996a, pp 106-8). In the North/South context, Britain's LA21 programme makes a very limited contribution to global equity issues.

Decision-making and policy integration

The promotion of sustainable development, and the preparing and implementing of LA21s, depends to a considerable extent on establishing integrated inter-departmental decision-making processes. It is then possible to construct multi-disciplinary, holistic approaches so that the principles underlying sustainable development can infuse every aspect of what a council does. It is clear that only a small proportion of councils fully appreciate this. The problem is made worse by the fact that the need for integrated inter-departmental decision-making flies in the face of much of the experience of British local government since the Bains Report, arguing this case, was published in 1972. With some exceptions, the attempts to create processes that genuinely integrate all aspects of a council's work have been erratic and limited (Stoker, 1991). Compartmentalism has been a continuing problem.

However, the problem is certainly understood by a sizeable minority of the UK's 478 authorities. A 1996 survey (LGMB, 1996) reported that of the 275 councils that responded, 70 had signed the Local Government Declaration on Sustainability (Q 4); 54 had signed the Ålborg Charter for Sustainable Cities and Towns (Q 20); and 106 were committed to changing their operations (Q 1). Understanding the problem is, however, clearly not the same as solving it.

Attempts to adapt decision-making processes are most evident in councils like Mendip and pre-reorganisation Cardiff, where the environment unit was put into the Chief Executive's Department; or in Lancashire, where a strong and influential Planning/Environment Department was established. Committed political leadership – as in Kirklees, the council based around Huddersfield – also drives change. The LGMB survey found that 111 councils have established new officer-liaison groups to promote LA21, while 113 are using existing officer working groups (Q 6). In Scotland, Marston found that 14 of the 32 post-reorganisation councils had established inter-departmental working groups (1996).

In a small proportion of councils it seems that potentially significant changes are being established. But perhaps Manchester's experience is more typical. The legacy of compartmentalised approaches has haunted the LA21 initiative, with attempts to establish holistic approaches breaking down in a tangle of departmental and committee rivalries.

The broadening of ecological and temporal horizons

The regional offices of government departments in England were reorganised during the early 1990s into Integrated Regional Offices. One of their jobs is to provide strategic guidance within which local councils can prepare their land-use plans. A range of documents have been produced; and sustainable development has been referred to. However, the concept has been applied to a very limited extent. Again this lack of clear guidance has been criticised at the local council level. Government projections suggest that an additional 4.4 million households will be looking for homes during the period between 1991 and 2016 (TCPA, 1996). How this will be resolved through a balancing of urban infill on reclaimed land; expanding small towns and villages; and perhaps building new settlements has not been resolved. The problem needs a strategic approach at the regional level. However, this issue and that of 'ecological footprints' have remained the concern of academics. The use of the precautionary principle is, however, attracting more attention from policy-makers though.

In the case of policies on biodiversity, there has been a more conscious attempt to relate local problems to a broad ecological context, and to a longer time horizon. The late 1980s and the early 1990s was a controversial period for British wildlife policy (Young, 1995), with numerous problems at the national level leading to some gains and some setbacks. However, biodiversity issues have become a more important factor in policy-making processes in many town halls. Ecology units have done surveys, often in partnership with local NGOs, and produced many reports. Plans for nature reserves often look ahead for up to 400 years as this is the time it takes an oak tree to mature. Programmes are being developed to increase woodland cover through community forests and similar schemes. Trends are emerging to protect green spaces within urban areas, and to avoid building on sites that are of local value for wildlife even if they are not outstanding in national terms.

LOCAL AGENDA 21 AS A PARTICIPATORY REFORM

It is the participatory aspect of the UK approach to LA21 which has received most international attention. Chapter 28 of Agenda 21 identifies nine so-called 'minorities' which are to be drawn in as stake-holders to the process of creating consensus-based local strategies for sustainable development. This area has seen a ferment of activity (Young, 1996). Many councils have tried to move away from 'top-down' consultation strategies towards 'bottom-up' approaches that aim to empower local communities (Figure 1). An imaginative range of approaches have been used. These include visioning techniques, village appraisals, parish maps, 'Planning-for-Real' exercises, community profiling, small-group discussions, focus groups, Environment Forums, Round Tables and 'citizen juries'.

Perhaps about 40–50 councils out of the post April 1996 UK total of 478 have made a conscious effort to promote these more ambitious strategies. In many cases the participation programme has actually become more important than the LA21 document itself. This reflects the growing concern in Britain about the need to regenerate local democracy. Together with some of the estate regeneration and urban renewal programmes, LA21 has been in the forefront of a frenzy of experimentation. However, as very few LA21s have as yet been completed, it is too early to assess the participation programmes against the documents that are produced.

Economic interests account for three of the nine minorities – business, farmers, and trades unions. Many of the concerns of a fourth minority – the scientific and technical community – also relate to economic issues. However the attempts to integrate economic interests into consensus-building processes have had a weak and erratic impact. Chambers of commerce and similar representative bodies cannot commit their members; and the firms that get involved tend to be enthusiasts for the environment anyway. The trouble is that companies that belong to greening business clubs and so on can only speak for a sympathetic and converted minority (Roberts, 1995).

In general, the features of the programmes which stand out most are *variety* and *imagination*. Traditional approaches based around leaflets, exhibitions and public meetings have been submerged in a riot of experimentation. They involve new ways of sharing information; local residents designing questionnaires and doing the house-to-house interviews; arts-based approaches; and other attention-grabbing events. The central aim is to draw in the views of all local stakeholders.

Visioning techniques are used to get people to discuss how they would like a neighbourhood to be, prior to discussing the action needed to change it. Community profiling and village appraisals involve local people doing surveys to identify local needs, and available resources; and priorities for

Figure 1 *Dimensions of local authority participation strategies for LA21*

Participation strategy	(1) Extent of dialogue	(2) Aim and attitude of the Local Authority	(3) Agenda setting and control	(4) Direction of policy and choice of priorities	(5) Balance of power during the process	(6) Scope for changing Local Authority's approach after the participation process	(7) Stage at which participation process becomes introduced into policy-making process
Top-down strategy	One-way process	Pass information out to the public and interested parties	Local Authority sets and controls the agenda	Determined by the Local Authority	Local Authority dominates	None	Grafted onto policy-making processes
Limited-dialogue strategy	Two-way process, but within limited parameters	Local Authority aims to get some feedback on details of proposals	Local Authority sets the agenda	Determined by the Local Authority	Local Authority holds balance of power and controls process	Changes mostly marginal, but some may be important	Grafted onto policy-making processes
A 'yes … but' strategy	Two-way dialogue	Local Authority aims to open things up and give participants a real role in shaping decisions – but subsequently reasserts control	Local Authority relinquishes control of agenda and welcomes additions	Open to discussion, but Local Authority is committed to some positions	Some power-sharing, but Local Authority remains in control	Significant change is possible, but Local Authority has some positions it will not budge from. These may surface only after the participation process	Sometimes grafted on – sometimes inserted at outset
Bottom-up strategy	Two-way dialogue based on a sharing of information	Local Authority aims to empower people, giving them an effective role in shaping decisions; adopts a listening and learning stance	The agenda is left open to be set by participants	Open to discussion	Power is shared; participants 'own' the process	Left very broad so participants have a real role in taking decisions	Comes at start with no pre-set agenda. Local Authority avoids fixed positions

change. Small group discussions and working groups are used to get people together for a meeting or to divide up a large meeting. Visioning and profiling techniques are then used to identify key issues. Focus groups draw in individuals from specific backgrounds to discuss pre-set agendas. Planning-for Real exercises bring local people together for short intensive periods to promote consensus about the nature of neighbourhood change. Environment Forums, Round Tables and a range of advisory committees are used to get stakeholders together to generate discussion, commitment and consensus.

Probably about 50 or 60 councils have aimed at something like a bottom-up strategy. These include Kirklees, Reading, Gloucestershire, Derbyshire, Vale Royal, Nottinghamshire, Mendip, Croydon, Merton, and Leicester. Others have tried similar approaches in the context of the Single Regeneration Budget (SRB) and estate regeneration programmes. In practice however, councils have fallen back on a 'Yes ... But ...' strategy. This occurs where the council adopts the rhetoric of the bottom-up strategy, but finds it difficult to let go of the agenda. What happens gets summed up by a senior figure as follows – 'Yes let's aim at a Bottom-Up Strategy, but the issue of the ring road/opencast mine/landfill site is too important to compromise on'. The council thus changes the nature of its approach as the participation programme develops. It evolves into a more limited and controlled exercise.

This widespread interest in participation has certainly had an impact on participation processes. Councils adopting the more innovative approaches have had positive responses from a wider range of people getting involved than the usual self-presenting groups. However, by the end of 1996 very few LA21s had actually been completed. It was thus too soon to assess fully the impact of the participation programmes. Although great claims were being made, we were probably at that point still not yet at the peak of what might be termed the 'enthusiasm stage'.

It is always necessary when assessing participation to identify the perspective a programme is being judged from. Thus a council adopting a top-down strategy would judge 'success' in terms of its out-of-town industrial estate proposal not being irreversibly damaged. On the other hand, a council pushing a bottom-up strategy would focus on the extent to which it was empowering local communities and putting their views at the heart of policy-making processes. In the latter case though, it is only possible to judge success in the longer term. It is too soon, as yet, to assess the impact of the LA21 participation programme on the LA21 document itself; and that document's influence on the revision of a council's statutory plan and the restructuring of its budget in ways that reflect sustainable development principles.

Promoting community-based partnerships

At Rio, partnerships between local communities and other agencies were picked out as having a significant contribution to make to the implementation of LA21s. This idea needs to be linked to the growing numbers of such organisations emerging in Britain during the last twenty years (Young, 1996). LA21 participation and environmental education programmes, and other council programmes have encouraged this increase.

The range of these organisations is set out in Figure 2, in the way they are seen in Southern Europe. The focus is on the concept of a 'social economy' operating between the public and private sectors, with three distinctive sets of families of organisations in the social economy. This is a useful analytical approach as it is the one being promoted by DG23 of the EU Commission to analyse the contribution of social-economy organisations and in the development of programmes to support their growth.

These organisations take many forms, but they have three main features in common. First, they operate on a not-for-profit basis. Second, they focus on the level of the local community. Usually this is meant in the geographical sense of the village, the estate, or the urban neighbourhood. But it also refers to communities of need, interest and experience across a wider area – as with disabled groups across a city for example. Finally, these organisations emphasise local democracy and the involvement of local people in defining their needs, shaping programmes, and controlling the development of the organisation. The significance of these organisations is that they function where locality, sustainable development and participatory democracy interact.

Difficulties underway

A number of difficulties have emerged with LA21 participation programmes. People have been asked about the promotion of sustainable development and priorities in a situation where the extent of future resources is not clear. For example, shifts to energy supplies from more environmentally friendly sources and to better and more extensive public transport require substantial capital investment. With regard to urban traffic congestion, participation programmes have produced extensive calls for change. But it is very difficult for councils to respond positively because of the Government's lack of response to the urban traffic agenda as set out in the report from the Royal Commission on Environmental Pollution (1994). In addition, privatisation has led to the fragmentation of public transport undertakings and made it much more difficult to promote integrated investment programmes.

Figure 2 The scope of the 'social economy' at the local level

	Private sector	Social economy			Public sector
		Co-ops	Mutuals	Associations and Foundations	
Legal structures:	Specific legal structures for companies				
Types of organisation:	Firms of all kinds and sizes from trans-nationals down to small firms; Profit-oriented public/private partnership companies, as in urban renewal	Worker co-ops; Food co-ops; Community businesses	Credit union; LETS;* Permaculture schemes; Danish community windfarms; Training & managed workspace projects; Neighbourhood development trusts; European Community forest projects; Community co-ops	Neighbourhood-based mutual aid organisations with restricted membership; Housing co-ops; User groups; Alternative health projects; Recycling schemes; Environmental improvement projects	Self-help organisations with open membership; Heritage trusts; Wildlife bodies; Community arts projects; Traditional voluntary sector organisations; Small housing associations	Departments, corporations, and government agencies at the national level; Municipalities, regional and city councils, and other sub-national and local governments

*Local Exchange Trading Systems (LETS)

Some councils have found it difficult to maintain momentum. Some of the early enthusiasm for the Environment Forums, for example, has ebbed away amidst criticisms that they have become fossilised talking shops. In some places it has proved difficult to draw lower income groups and young people into the participation programmes. The problems of raised expectations haunts some councils as well. The businesses that have got involved tend to be committed to different forms of sustainability anyway. The disinterested firms that have ignored the calls to give their views are the ones it is important to influence. But organisations like chambers of commerce – and in farming areas the National Farmers' Union – can only speak for their members. They cannot commit them to using less fertiliser or transporting more goods by rail.

The other main problem is that it has proved difficult to integrate the participatory experiments with the need for strategic planning. Many of the pioneering councils' participation programmes have focused on the micro-level – the level of the village and the urban neighbourhood. However, work on LA21s has also clarified the need for a strategic level of analysis. On waste, for example, a council needs to decide the balance between landfill, recycling, and incineration (including the CHP option) within its programme for the next decade. Promoting recycling, reuse and waste minimisation can help, but this does not remove the need for new landfill sites. Transport also has to be planned at the strategic level. Similarly a city-wide or county-wide approach has to be taken to identifying land that needs to be released for housing or industry or a new site for a major football club. The use of vacant urban sites can help reduce, but not remove, the demand for land release. In practice, many LA21 participation programmes have been taking place in something of a vacuum without the implications of strategic issues like these being fully integrated.

The strategic approaches and the micro-level approaches have been running in parallel. This sometimes makes it difficult to reach consensus as the two have to be reconciled and the strategic approach may well limit options at the neighbourhood level. What is needed is more of a linear approach to participation over years, not months. If people are presented with proposals for a new reservoir or landfill site on their doorstep they are understandably horrified. But if they are involved via citizens juries and similar arrangements, then they can understand the technical details that lie behind the proposals being made and see if different conclusions can be drawn. Such an approach is used with regard to water planning in the US; and work is being done on it in the context of waste management in Britain (Walesh, 1995).

Why does LA21 work as a participatory reform?

A number of factors contributed to this growth of interest in the participation aspects of LA21. First of all, Chapter 28 of Agenda 21 stresses the need to involve all groups in society when preparing LA21s. Particular mention was made of drawing in women and young people; involving all groups in society and not just the more articulate ones; and of trying to generate consensus. Participation was thus promoted to being an integral part of the LA21 policy-making process. In the LA21 context it was no longer – as so often in contemporary politics – an optional extra. Rio thus elevated community involvement to a new status.

Interest in participation was further promoted by two other factors. To begin with, the LGMB has stressed the importance of promoting community involvement in its publications about LA21 and in its monthly mailings to environmental co-ordinators. This has encouraged individual councils to give it more attention and be more innovative.

In addition, those involved within individual councils in promoting the participation aspects of LA21 have brought new approaches to the task. They have come in with experience of community development, running adult education programmes and directly involving people in countryside and recreational projects (as via the Groundwork Trusts). There has also been an influx of people from the NGO world with detailed ideas about how to promote participation. Collectively the attitudes of all these people towards involvement reflects much more of a bottom-up, people-centred perspective than that of planners who have previously been running top-down structure-plan consultation programmes. The views and values of these people have decisively influenced the nature of the participation programmes being pursued by the more innovative councils.

Finally, there has been a broader change of attitude towards community involvement amongst some policy-makers. The resulting exploration of new ideas has not just been directed at LA21. It has also found expression in the contexts of housing renewal and estate regeneration; City Challenge; and the SRB programmes. The attempts to promote bottom-up style strategies reflect a growing recognition of the need to move on from the top-down, bureaucratic paternalist approaches that predominated during the 1960s and 1970s. The process of imposing projects with minimal consultation programmes created schemes that did not work, such as the high-rise flats and the Hulme crescents. A range of subsequent inner-city regeneration programmes did promote economic renewal and make a physical impact in terms of new buildings and landscaping projects. But they did not produce social renewal and tackle local unemployment, housing deprivation, crime and other dimensions of urban poverty.

dis

As a result, a small but growing number of policy-makers began to argue the need for a new approach. Their starting point was that top-down solutions do not relate effectively to peoples' perceptions of what is wrong. They argued that the lesson from previous decades was that it was important to start with a blank agenda, and ask local people to define the problems as they perceived them. It then becomes possible to produce relevant and creative solutions. These have more chance of working because they draw from local peoples' knowledge and experience. The solutions that emerge are promoted and supported by the people themselves. These arguments are reflected in the discourse of City Challenge and the SRB in the early 1990s about the importance of drawing in all the stakeholders, and empowering local communities.

The new emphasis on bottom-up approaches has also found support from another constituency. The early 1990s produced a debate in the media and amongst academics about social exclusion, alienation, a loss of trust in local government, and a loss of faith in the capacity of local political institutions and processes (Wheeler, 1996; Macnaghten et al., 1995); Commission for Local Democracy, 1995). Despite the attempts to communicate more effectively with local people and the experiments with decentralisation and neighbourhood offices, many were increasingly concerned about the growing disillusionment with local democracy. Discussion amongst media commentators, academics, politicians and leading local government figures focused around the need to regenerate local democracy. These people were not specifically interested in the environment or LA21. They were drawn to the bottom-up approaches to participation from a different perspective. They were interested in the experiments because of the opportunity to experiment with ways of communicating with the public and promoting community involvement. These new approaches thus offered a way of breathing new life and vitality into the institutions and processes of local government itself.

CONCLUSIONS

The clear conclusion seems to be that, although there are some exceptions, only a small proportion of council activity to promote sustainable development has focused on preparing LA21s. The discussion shows that few have as yet been completed, and that it is too soon to assess the quality of the documents and their impact. It is not yet clear, for example, whether the LA21s in place are genuine action plans, with specific time frames and targets – or much vaguer visioning documents. Some see LA21s as a distraction. Stockport for example argues that it can achieve more by greening programmes and promoting sustainable development across the range of its activities. Others are passing off what they have been doing outside of LA21 and prior to Rio as LA21 activity. Southampton's promotion of community-based partnerships and usage of Community Action Forums is an example here.

More generally the significant point seems to be that policy-makers in a small but growing number of councils are thinking more broadly and ambitiously about adapting programmes to incorporate priorities suggested by sustainable development. Much of this activity is novel in the context of British local government. It is important to stress how much has been achieved – especially by the pioneering councils – despite the cuts, the loss of powers, and the increasing trend towards centralisation, in what is one of the most centralised unitary states amongst the OECD countries.

In terms of constraints on local councils, the development of less tentative, more ambitious policy frameworks in Whitehall would help, together with clearer guidance from the centre. Lack of local council powers are also a handicap. This means that councils often have to fall back on working through partnerships with a variety of other organisations. These are time-consuming to set up, and often fail for lack of public-sector financial input. More financial resources are also needed in such spheres as transport infrastructure and environmental education. Here a longer term approach is needed of the kind developed in the context of managing US water resources (Walesh, 1995). One other suggestion has been to give councils a general power that can be used to promote LA21 activity. This would be an incremental step forward. It would encourage the pioneers, and make it easier for others to follow in their footsteps. Such an approach certainly has had an impact in the sphere of economic development, where local authorities have developed a more positive, wide-ranging role.

REFERENCES

Barton, H, Davis, G. & R. Guise (1995) *Sustainable Settlements: A Guide for Planners, Designers and Developers*, Luton: LGMB.

Breheny M & P Hall (eds) (1996) *The People – Where Will They Go?*, London: Town and Country Planning Association.

Church, C (1995) *Towards Local Sustainability: A Review of Current Activity on Local Agenda 21 in the UK*, London: United Nations Association.

Commission for Local Democracy (1995) *Taking Charge: The Rebirth of Local Democracy*, London.

Crombie, H (1995) *Sustainable Development and Health*, Birmingham: Public Health Trust.

Department of the Environment (DoE) (1990) *This Common Inheritance*, Cm 1200, London: HMSO.

DoE (1992a) 'Planning Policy Guidance 1', London: HMSO.

DoE (1992b) 'Planning Policy Guidance 12: Development Plans and Regional Planning Guidance', London: HMSO.

DoE (1993) 'Environmental Appraisal of Development Plans: A Good Practice Guide', London: HMSO.

DoE (1994a) 'Sustainable Development: The UK Strategy', Cm 2426, London: HMSO.

DoE (1995a) 'This Common Inheritance: UK Annual Report 1995', Cm 2822, London: HMSO.

DoE (1996a) 'This Common Inheritance: UK Annual Report 1996', Cm 3188, London: HMSO.

Harrison, CM, Burgess, J. & P. Filius (1996) 'Rationalising environmental responsibilities: A comparison of the lay publics in the UK and the Netherlands', Global Environmental Change, Vol 6, No 3, pp 215-34.

Local Government Management Board (LGMB) (1992a) *A Statement to UNCED on Behalf of UK Local Government*, London: LGMB.

LGMB (1992b) *Earth Summit: Rio '92 – Information Pack for Local Authorities*, London: LGMB.

LGMB (1993a) *Agenda 21: A Guide for Local Authorities in the UK*, Luton: LGMB.

LGMB (1995) *Sustainability Indicators Research Project: Consultants Report of the Pilot Phase*, Luton: LGMB.

Macnaghten, P., R. Grove-White, M. Jacobs and B. Wynne (1995) Public *Perceptions and Sustainability in Lancashire: Indicators, Institutions, and Participation*, Preston: Lancashire County Council for the Centre for the Study of Environmental Change.

Marston, A. (1996) 'Local Agenda Progress: A survey of the New Councils', *Scotland's 21 Today*, Autumn, Issue 10, pp 6-7.

Roberts, P. (1995) *Environmentally Sustainable Business: A Local and Regional Perspective*, London: Paul Chapman.

Royal Commission on Environmental Pollution (1994) *Transport and the Environment*, London: HMSO.

Royal Commission on Environmental Pollution (1994) 18th Report: *Transport and the Environment*, Cm 2674, London: HMSO.

Rydin, Y. (1995) chapter in M. Bhatti et al (eds) *Housing and the Environment: A New Agenda*, Coventry: Chartered Institute of Housing.

Stoker, G. (1991) *The Politics of Local Government*, second edition, Basingstoke: Macmillan.

Stoker, G. & S.C. Young (1993) *Cities in the 1990s: Local Choice for a Balanced Strategy*, Harlow: Longman.

Tuxworth, B. & E. Thomas (1996) *Local Agenda 21 Survey, 1996*, Luton: LGMB.

Walesh, S.G. (1995) 'Interaction with the public and government officials in urban water planning' in van Engen, H et al (eds) *Hydropolis: The Role of Water in Urban Planning*, Leiden: Backhuys Publishers.

Ward, S. (1993) 'Thinking Global, Acting Local? British Local Authorities and their Environmental Plans', *Environmental Politics*, Vol 2, No 3, pp 453-78.

Wheeler, R. (ed) (1996) *Local Government Policy-Making: Special Issue on Empowerment and Citizenship*, March 1996.

Whittaker, Stella (ed) (1995a) *Local Government Policy Making: Special Issue on LA21*, Vol 22, No 2, October 1995.

Whittaker, Stella (ed) (1995b) *First Steps – Local Agenda 21 in Practice: Municipal Strategies for Sustainability as Presented at Global Forum 94 in Manchester*, London: HMSO.

Young, S.C. (1994) 'The Environment', in P Allan, J Benyon & B McCormick (eds) *Focus On Britain 1994: A Review of 1993*, Oxon, Deddington: P Allan Publishers, pp 217-223.

Young S.C. (1994b) 'An Agenda 21 Strategy for the UK?', *Environmental Politics*, Vol 3, No 2.

Young S.C. (1995) 'Running up the down escalator: Developments in British wildlife policies after Mrs Thatcher's 1988 speeches', in T Gray (ed) *UK Environmental Policy in the 1990s*, Basingstoke: Macmillan.

Young, S.C. (1996) 'Promoting Participation And Community-Based Partnerships In The Context of Local Agenda 21: A Report For Practitioners', EPRU Paper, Govt Dept, Manchester University.

9. Ireland:
Does the Road from Rio Lead Back to Brussels?

*Ger Mullally**

INTRODUCTION

The United Nations Conference on Environment and Development (UNCED) held in Rio de Janeiro in June 1992 was by many accounts 'a historic event', 'an epoch making universal attempt at global sustainability'. The Irish delegation was one among 176 signatories to 'Agenda 21', committing the Irish Government to the development and implementation of a national plan of action for sustainable development. Agenda 21, according to the current Irish Minister for the Environment, is best described as 'a blueprint for global sustainable development in the 21st century':

> *With Agenda 21, governments agreed to translate global sustainable development principles into new and practical policies and programmes. Agenda 21 is a document of far reaching ambition, but it is recognised that a global partnership for sustainable development must be built on the broadest public participation. This involves the best efforts of government at local, regional and national levels, as well as the support of international agreements'.[1]*

The juxtaposition of global and local approaches in the Minister's statement mirrors the emphasis on localising the 'global partnership for sustainable development' which pervades many of the 470 pages of 'Agenda 21'. The role and contribution of local authorities is explicitly addressed in Chapter 28 of this voluminous document. By comparison with many of the other chapters of the action plan, the objectives of 'Local Agenda 21'(LA21), are procedural though not excessively prescriptive, and are tied to a specific time frame (see Lafferty and Eckerberg, this volume). Despite, or rather because of this, an environmental campaigner was prompted in June 1995 at a national conference on 'Local Agenda 21', to note that three years after Rio 'most of us in Ireland are still asking: What on Earth is Local Agenda 21?'[2] The upcoming special session of the United Nations General Assembly in New York of this year ('Earth Summit +5') is devoted to a review of progress of Agenda 21 in its entirety. Perhaps this affords us the opportunity to reconsider the question and ask: Five years after Rio, where in Ireland is Local Agenda 21? The short answer is that five years down the road, with the benchmarks now gone past, the journey towards Local Agenda 21 is just beginning in earnest

In this review of the Irish experience of Local Agenda 21, the focus is necessarily couched in the language of 'latent potential' rather than 'visible progress'.[3] It proceeds by means of a reconstructive account of baseline conditions for the integration of environmental concerns at the local level of government prior to, and in the aftermath of Agenda 21. A number of key questions are also posed to determine the future potential of Local Agenda 21, and to provide the basis for future investigation. This includes the following questions: What reforms or social experiments were in place at the time of Rio, and how could they affect the successful implementation of Local Agenda 21? What was the antecedent role of central government within UNCED, and how did government react to and interpret the Local Agenda 21 initiative? What has been the role of leading non-governmental organisations (NGOs)? Where and how have Local Agenda 21 initiatives made the greatest impacts? Finally, what are the short-term prospects for the further development and realisation of the Local Agenda 21 idea?

In addressing these questions, I want to suggest that Local Agenda 21, despite the unimpressive attempts at progress to date, still represents a potent mechanism for change in Ireland. The direction of this change is not simply 'moving towards sustainability' in a global sense, but has the potential to enhance existing attempts to re-invigorate an enfeebled structure and culture of local democracy in the Republic of Ireland. If the agenda set in Rio is to have a meaningful impact on 'the social and technological arrangements upon which sustainability depends' the challenge is to find a positive means of relating local initiative to the global debate (Irwin, 1995: 116). This can only be achieved if the local implementation of sustainable development is understood 'as a discursively created rather than authoritatively given product (Barry, 1996: 116).

CONTEXTUALISING RESPONSES TO LA21

The 1970's comprised two distinctive approaches to environmental discourse. On the one hand, there was the 'radical environmental discourse' which demanded radical social change, and, on the other, 'a pragmatic legal-administrative response' which brought Ministries of the Environment into existence all over the Western world (Hajer, 1996; Weale, 1992). In Hajer's account, 'ecological modernisation' is a discourse that breaks with both previous tendencies. It recognises the structural character of the environmental problematic, but breaks with the analysis of deep ecology by placing technical and procedural innovation above the prescription of a total break from modern industrialism (1996:249). Hajer situates the growing dominance of this discourse in the period from 1984 onwards. In his view, the concept of sustainable development has become the 'leitmotif' of this discourse.[4]

Drawing on Christoff (1996), we can classify the normative reference point of Ireland's current response to ecological discourse as 'weak ecological modernisation'.[5] The evolution in Ireland of environmental discourse and corresponding institutional forms, though similar in character to other European countries, occurred in a much more condensed time frame. Ireland underwent a period of a rapid institutional innovation in the late 1980's and early 1990's in the run-up to UNCED. The *Environmental Action Programme* initiated in 1990, was the *first* comprehensive environmental programme ever adopted by an Irish Government. The Irish Presidency of the European Communities was the immediate focus and occasion for many initiatives of the *Action Programme*.[6] The Programme now acts as the co-ordinating mechanism for environmental policy in Ireland.[7] The document commits the Irish Government to the following:

- the principle of sustainable development
- the 'precautionary principle'
- the integration of environmental considerations into all policy areas

The formulation of this policy document and subsequent innovations occur in the context of a number of discrete but intersecting forces. Increased environmental concern in the political and administrative system can be related to systemic responses to pressures transmitted from: (1) below (extra-systemic political challenges; increased public salience of environmental issues/cultural learning); (2) within (implementation crises, legislative innovation, political competition); and (3) above (increased exposure to discourses of global responsibility, international conventions and supranational regulation and directives) (Mullally, 1995).

Analyzing these pressures along their different dimensions will perhaps show the extent to which much of the innovation in environmental protection in the run-up to UNCED, rather than representing social experimentation, was, in the Irish case, primarily reactive or defensive in the Irish case. Approached in this way, we can also identify both the reception context for Local Agenda 21, and the social actors crucial to its implementation, and then make some tentative remarks concerning its prospects for success. The notion of participation which is central to the official rhetoric of sustainability in general (WCED, 1987; UNCED, 1992), and Chapter 28 of Agenda 21 in particular, will provide the central focus for this account.

INNOVATION AND CHANGE IN THE INSTITUTIONAL LANDSCAPE PRIOR TO AGENDA 21

The forces driving the Irish Government to a rhetorical embrace of the principles of sustainable development can be summarised as localised pressure, *implementation crises*, and *international influence*. Commentators frequently remark that 'exceptionalism' distinguishes the Irish relationship to broader environmental discourses and events (Yearly, 1995; Baker, 1987). Therefore, despite the very specific focus here on Chapter 28 of Agenda 21, it may be appropriate for comparative purposes to describe the key elements that gave rise to a period of intense innovation relative to the situation which prevailed prior to the formulation of a policy for the environment in 1990.

Localised pressure

Extra-systemic pressure for institutional innovation for environmental protection reflects the essentially local nature of protest mobilisation by the Irish environmental movement in the 1980's and 1990's . In effect, despite the penetration of the Irish social-movement sector by international organisations in the late 1980's, much of the pressure for change has come from a series of localised conflicts. A variety of commentators have attributed this to the patterns of 'dependent industrialisation' pursuant to the state's development trajectory from the 1960's onwards (Baker, 1987, 1990; Allen and Jones, 1990). The transformation of the Irish Republic from a predominantly rural agricultural base to an urban-industrial society was precipitated by a period of 'rapid industrialisation'. This in turn was accompanied by an expansion of the print and broadcast media, bringing

the cultural production of meaning into more immediate contact with international developments after a prolonged period of isolation.

The trans-national pharmaceutical industry was one among several
sectors (chemicals, mining, electronics) to arrive in Ireland subsequent to
the Government's development strategy of 'foreign direct investment'
(FDI). This sector's predilection for greenfield sites (and in many cases
it's international environmental record) brought it into direct conflict with
the values, norms, cultural practices and economic interests of rural
Ireland.[8] On the other hand, we have a gradual emergence in Ireland of a
more principled relation to nature which was extended by (1) public
communication strategies of recently arrived international environmental
organisations and, (2) increased public awareness of high profile environmental events locally, nationally and internationally which were widely
disseminated in the media. The implication of this sector in a debate which
intertwined a 'cultural politics of national identity', and a 'cultural politics
of nature' laid bare the institutional vacuity of administrative arrangements for environmental protection. While the trajectory of Irish
environmentalism is not the focus of this chapter, it is important to understand that conflicts about planning and pollution very quickly translate
into questions about democratic decision making, the locus of political
representation, patterns of interest mediation, and, perhaps most crucially,
democratic participation.[9]

The structural arrangements for public participation prior to the period
of intense policy innovation were exclusively re-active. Participation
resided primary by way of objection and appeal through the planning
system or by recourse to the legal system. A series of high-profile planning
and legal controversies which put the environmental effects of industrial
policy under the microscope also exposed the incapacity of the administrative system to adequately deal with those effects.[10]

Implementation crises

Among the achievements of the Irish environmental movement was to draw
attention to the fact that, despite the existence of a large body of environmental legislation: (1) the Government had no coherent environmental
policy, and (2) a crisis of implementation existed in the area of environmental protection. The main arena in which this implementation crisis
unfolded was in the structure of local government as revealed in its dual
mandate for both economic development and environmental protection, and
in its dependent relationship with the Department of the Environment.

The accession of Ireland to the EEC in 1973 marked the beginning of
almost two decades of development of environmental legislation which

has impacted on Irish law. In the period since Ireland joined the EEC/EU, community-action programmes on the environment have resulted in nearly 200 pieces of legislation related to the environment. There were also a number of significant developments in relation to indigenous legislation in the 1970's and 1980's. The most significant development in terms of institutional structures for environmental protection in the late 1970's was the transformation of the Department of Local Government to the Department of the Environment (DoE) in 1977 .

Chubb (1992) argues that the metamorphosis of the Department symbolises the essentially environmental character of local government, while Coyle (1996) points out that, when contrasted with other European countries, the range of functions performed by Irish local authorities is very limited, being primarily concerned with the physical environment in terms of (1) planning and development and (2)] environmental management and control. Local authorities have no constitutional basis in Ireland. They derive their power and function from central government. The Department of the Environment (DoE), exercises control over the financial, administrative and technical affairs of local authorities, and also regulates relationships with central government (Coyle, 1994:69).[11]

Implementation of centrally ordained policy is the responsibility of Local Authorities:

> *The principal agencies for the local implementation of environmental policy and regulation remain the 34 major local authorities (29 county councils, 5 county borough councils) operating under the co-ordination and supervision of the Department of the Environment. Some 54 borough and urban councils also operate as authorities in relation to physical planning, litter control and the licensing of discharges into sewers in some cases (DoE, 1995b).[12]*

A number of factors have historically impeded the ability of local authorities to implement environmental policy effectively. These broadly speaking can be defined as *institutional arrangements, resources* and *conflict of interests.*

Institutional arrangements

Coyle (1996), identifies the structural relationship between the Department of the Environment and Local Authorities as significant to the weakened capacity to implement policy. If we summarise the elements of the problem that Coyle presents, four main points are evident:

(1) Local Authorities have little function on the input side of environmental policy or negotiations on EU directives. There is, therefore, a linear process of policy directive from the top down which takes no account of the local-authority perspective.
(2) Following the first point, there is a considerable vacuum between the policy-making culture of the DoE, and the pragmatic considerations and constraints of implementation.
(3) The institutional connection with the DoE precludes direct co-ordination between local authorities and other Departments directly implicated in negotiations with the EU on environmental policy.
(4) Disaggregated policy styles within the DoE (due to the fragmentation of functional responsibilities for EU dossiers) results in the lack of a co-ordinated understanding of EU policies in local authorities.

These problems of horizontal and vertical co-ordination of environmental policy in Ireland have been accentuated in the implementation process on the local level by a diminution of local-government resources.

Resources

The transformation of the Department of Local Government into the Department of the Environment took place in the context of a reduced capacity for local authorities to generate income. The abolition of the domestic rating system in 1978 largely removed the fiscal autonomy of local authorities. The result has been a weakened capacity for local authorities to monitor and police environmental regulations. Coyle (1994) makes the point, in regard to staffing, that an embargo on public sector recruitment in the 1980's coincided with increased environmental responsibility being placed on local authorities.

The managerial resources available to local authorities regarding environmental problems is severely constrained by their narrow functional remit. Coyle (1994) argues that their policy scope, and consequently their autonomy for environmental management, is thus limited. The organisational capacity of local authorities for environmental management is severely constrained by the problem of limited resources which Coyle argues is demonstrated by the range of functions for which they rely on outside expertise.

Conflicts of interest

A significant factor in undermining public confidence in the capacity of local authorities to regulate the environment has been the perception that there is a conflict of interests between the various functions which are imposed upon them. The dual function of local authorities with regard to economic development on the one hand, and environmental regulation on the other, has been central to the legitimacy crisis endured over the past period. This has been compounded by the fact that local authorities rely heavily on business for their discretionary income. Scott (1992) concludes that this situation has given rise to conditions under which local authorities have a clear incentive to 'to be very pro-business'. Another problem pointed out by Coyle, is that local authorities act as both 'gamekeepers' and 'poachers' in respect of water quality and waste disposal since, under existing arrangements, they are responsible for the environmental impact and control of their own operations. In other words, the legitimacy of local authorities as environmental regulators has been undermined by the perception that they are major polluters in their own right.

From implementation crisis to legitimation crisis: The need for reform

Recently, many of the above criticisms have been acknowledged as weaknesses in the structure of local government which require a substantial programme of reform. The implementation crisis alluded to is exacerbated by an insufficiently embedded cultural attachment to local government in Ireland. The recently published reform programme *Better Local Government*, links this legitimation crisis to the historical origins of Irish local government introduced under a colonial regime (DoE, 1996a: Para 2.3). Local government is here seen as lacking the 'deep community roots' that legitimise its continental European counterparts.

The implication is that the ideal of citizen participation which LA21 seeks to extend is currently disengaged from the experience of representative democracy in Ireland. It is not adequate to simply ascribe the poor articulation between local communities and local government to exterior causation alone.[13] The atrophy of local government in Ireland is the result of a persistent lack of attention and of being victim of a succession of counter-productive election promises by parties of all political hues in the past. However, the reform programme signals central government's intention to engage in a process of fundamental renewal that would give local government a more meaningful role in the overall system of governance. The principal motivating factor for this renewal is to facilitate the recognition of local government as 'the legitimate voice of communities' (DoE, 1996). If realised in practice the reform programme would could create a more sympathetic reception context for LA21. Moreover *'Better Local Government'* explicitly calls for more accelerated action towards the development of LA21:

> *Local authorities will be requested to intensify action to*
> *accelerate the adoption of Local Agenda 21 programmes*
> *and to seek more systematically to develop joint action and*

partnerships with other interests, including the business and
farming communities and the voluntary sector in promoting
sustainable development. (DoE, 1996a: Para 8.23.12).

The emphasis on accelerating LA21, and particularly on developing a
strong partnership approach, must be seen in the context of the increasingly influential role of international events in the internal government of
Ireland. The most pertinent of these being, of course, Ireland's membership of the European Union. It is primarily within this relationship that
the Local Agenda 21 process in Ireland is being shaped.

International influence

The elevation of the environmental debate to the global level has resulted
in ratification of a host of international protocols and agreements including the Earth Summit Agreements and Agenda 21. The Irish Government
enjoys and actively propagates the reputation of being proactive in the
international arena and, in particular, of being a good European 'citizen'.
The language of the UNCED process and Agenda 21 has undoubtedly
made an impact on the policy programmes of the Irish Government, at
least on a semantic level. A more fundamental catalyst, however, has been
the need to conform to the various EU action programmes on the environment; to draw down structural funding; and to respond to specific EU
directives. Without rehearsing these developments here, it is sufficient to
remark that directives such as 85/337/EEC (Environmental Impact
Assessment), and 90/313/EEC (Freedom of Access to Information on the
Environment), represent significant developments conditioning the
context for receiving and enacting LA21 in Ireland.[14,15]

Membership of the EU has contributed to a number of institutional
innovations with regard to both environmental protection and economic
development. These innovations merit discussion here since they represent some of the key institutional conditions pre-figuring the diffusion of
LA21.

Institutional innovation and the environment: Before and after Rio[16]

The legitimation and implementation crises of local government's capacity to protect the environment coincided with the need to co-ordinate with
the development of the European Environmental Agency, and the increasing electoral salience of the 'green' vote after 1989. This culminated in an
increase in environmental policy-making in 1990; the creation of the
Environmental Protection Agency (EPA) in 1992; the initiation of mechanisms to disseminate information and increase public awareness; the

creation of specific policy supports; and, a series of manoeuvres to shift the emphasis from 're-active' participation to a more 'pro-active' (and neo-corporate) representation.

Coyle concludes that Ireland stands out in a European context in that it has not implemented any major reform of local government since the second world war. Despite the huge volume of legislation that has come with EU membership, the tendency has been towards the formation of single-function executive agencies rather than local government reform (1996:283).

Social innovation and the economy: Before and after Rio

In tandem with the influence of EU membership on institutional innovation towards environmental protection, has been the importance of Ireland's status as an 'Objective 1' region for the purpose of EU Structural Funding.[17] Matthews argues that the reform established: 'clear priority objectives and introduced the principles of geographical concentration on regions whose development is lagging behind, programming, partnership and additionality to which the disbursement of funds must conform.' (1994:16). It is the particular emphasis on 'partnership' that the Funds demand of the beneficiaries which is of specific interest to the prospects for Local Agenda 21.

The Irish government, aided by EU Structural Funds, has been involved since 1991 in an experiment to reduce the incidence and mitigate the effects of long-term unemployment by promoting 'local partnership and social innovation'. The eponymous OECD evaluation of this experiment argues that these partnerships are 'at the core of a new localism in Ireland' (Sabel, 1996:10). This, by definition, makes them important contextual variables for the evolution of LA21 in Ireland. The core of the experiment was the creation of 38 (originally 12), urban and rural area-based partnerships to 'address social exclusion in a more flexible, decentralised and participative way'. Theoretically, these models of 'partnership' could contribute to the 'fertile ground' (see Coenen, this volume) in which to grow a Local Agenda 21 process.

The conclusion of the report notes more somberly, however, the disparity between 'innovative potential and institutional reality' that could impede more widespread societal diffusion. These partnerships are independent corporations under Irish company law. Their boards comprise a wide variety of community interests from representatives of the unemployed to representatives of labour and business. The boards also include local and regional representatives of the national social welfare, training and economic development administration. The OECD report notes that such partnerships act both as 'independent local entities', and as 'the local mandatories of sub-national units of the central administration'. In normal circumstances, the report concludes, these partnerships would act as the complements and competitors of local government (Sabel, 1996:85). The problem is that these entities lack the fundamental legitimacy and accountability at the local level that could allow for wider relevance among the community and for further diffusion throughout Irish society. These partnerships, according to the OECD report:

> *simultaneously pursue area-based economic development and the local, integrated implementation of national programmes connected to it; and they do so in a way that blurs familiar distinctions between public and private, national and local, and representative and participative democracy (Sabel, 1996: 9).*

In the view of the report, these arrangements are beset by problems of horizontal and vertical forms of co-ordination which reflect 'a fragile democratic legitimacy and administrative status'. This is particularly the case where a diversity of partnerships exist between an emergent variety of layers of governance and a constellation of single-function agencies in a situation of increasingly complex social and administrative relations.[18] This disjunction between local development and local democracy has meant that these partnerships are often seen as a threat rather than a complement to democracy at the local level of governance.

The report argues that the answer does not lie in the integration or subordination of local initiatives to central or local government control. Rather, the suggestion is for the creation of a project of 'democratic experimentalism' which could be formalised by providing 'organised comparisons' of benchmarks for individual projects and benchmarks for the design of partnerships as a whole. The ideas of fostering local initiative, benchmarking progress and partnership recommended by Sabel in the OECD report, are all important elements in building an LA21 process.

In the next sections, when we move more directly to the unfolding logic of Local Agenda 21 in Ireland, it should become evident that problems of horizontal and vertical integration in both environment and development innovations are also visible in the tentative efforts to proceduralise 'sustainable development'. This will involve a discussion on the role and reaction of actors central to co-ordinating LA21 processes to date on the local and national level. Finally, in considering the short term potential of LA21 in Ireland, we will focus on *Better Local Government* (BLG), the programme for the reform of local government. This document sets out a programme to modernise the structure of local government and outlines the procedural vision of local sustainable development being promoted by central government. As we will argue, however, there are certain features of the programme which require closer scrutiny with respect to the participatory aspect of the LA21 idea.

INPUT AND REACTIONS FROM CENTRAL GOVERNMENT

Ireland appears to have had very little input in terms of the development of the Local Agenda 21 initiative. Ireland's definitive input in terms of preparation for Rio was two-fold. Ireland took over the EU presidency in 1990, just as sustainable development was gaining policy prominence with the EU. The government in Dublin actively supported this change, and, in January 1992, acted as host for the International Conference on Water and the Environment. The 'Dublin Statement' adopted by the conference significantly influenced Chapter 18 of the Agenda on freshwater resources, but official publications lay no claim to significant input to any other aspect of the action plan. The preparation for Rio involved 'extensive consultation with interested government Departments and State bodies, as well as with the non-governmental sector'. Local authorities are not given explicit mention as having made any significant input in official publications.

As part of the preparatory process for UNCED, countries were requested to prepare national reports which presented national perspectives as well as information on policies, activities and issues. In addition to the initial National Report to UNCED in 1992, the Irish Government has prepared a number of subsequent reports to the UN Commission for Sustainable Development (CSD). Ireland officially joined the CSD on January 1 1997. Prior to this date, Ireland reported to the CSD and only attended meetings as an observer. According to the review of progress in the governmental White Paper on 'Moving Towards Sustainability' (1995b), much of the follow-up to Rio and implementation strategies for Agenda 21 has taken place in the context of EU membership.

Until relatively recently, Local Agenda 21 has not appeared high on the list of priorities of central government. Central government's own evaluation of progress in all aspects of Agenda 21 is contained within the 1996 report to the CSD. This evaluation is perhaps the most illustrative indication of the current level of information available for the implementation of Chapter 28 of the Agenda. (Table 1)

The Department of the Environment circulated copies of 'The Earth Summit's Agenda for Change: A Plain Language Version', as well as other Rio agreements, to local authorities in October 1993. A more focused approach to LA21 came with the publication of a booklet of guidelines in May 1995 (DoE, 1995c). The booklet provides local authorities with a variety of philosophical justifications, participative possibilities, and

Table I *Evaluation of progress in Agenda 21 by central government*

Very good	Good	Some good data (but many gaps)	Poor
Chapter 6	Chapter 2	Chapter 10	Chapter 4
Chapter 7	Chapter 3	Chapter 12	
Chapter 9	Chapter 5	Chapter 13	
Chapter 18	Chapter 11	Chapter 22	
Chapter 19	Chapters 14–17	Chapter 25	
Chapter 20	Chapter 24	Chapters 27–34	
Chapter 21	Chapter 26	(including Ch 28)	
	Chapters 35–39	Chapter 40	

Source: The Report of Ireland to the 1996 Session of the UN Commission on Sustainable Development (DoE, 1996b)

practical suggestions for action. The guidelines were described as 'suggestions' to give 'a common focus to the different initiatives of the individual local authorities, because it is open to the local authorities to decide exactly how they will go about Local Agenda 21.'[19] In order to place the response to LA21 in a comparative context, it should be noted that the guidelines are closely modelled on the those brought out by the LGMB in Britain. However, unlike the experience in Britain, the guidelines are the product of a government initiative emanating from the centre rather than representing a co-ordinated attempt by local authorities to collectively participate in the steering process.[20]

Despite the clear financial dependence of local government in Ireland, there is no indication of any special financial provision or allocation from central government for the implementation of LA21 included in the document. Local authorities appear, therefore, to be accorded a degree of decisional and procedural autonomy which in reality is not matched by fiscal autonomy or access to financial resources independent of central government.The 'Better Local Government' programme does, however, indicate the there will be alternative means of financing the activities of local government in the future.[21] To some extent, the 'suggestions' in the LA21 Guidelines are superseded by the more prescriptive proposals contained within *Better Local Government*, and the *Strategic Management Initiative* (SMI).[22] However, it is valuable to consider these suggestions in the context of the currently existing situation.

Aspiring to multi-level co-ordination

The aspirational and exemplary tenor of the Guidelines for LA21 suggests a number of possible ways in which co-ordination might take place. These can be summarised as follows:

• The involvement of recently formed regional authorities designed to 'facilitate coherence and co-ordination between the initiatives of their constituent local authorities';
• Integration of sustainability objectives into existing partnerships such as County Enterprise Boards, Area-Based Partnerships, LEADER groups, EU Regional Operational Committees;
• The creation of new partnerships in the form of LA21 fora; and,
• Maximising opportunities for the diffusion of 'best practice' through national representative bodies for local authorities, the EU Committee of the Regions, and the Council of Europe Congress of Local and Regional Authorities.

Theoretically, these regional and supra-regional (EU level) bodies represent potential resources for the implementation of LA21. However, in practice there are a number of obstacles to the actual realisation of their potential.

Both the regional authorities and the structures co-ordinating local partnerships represent layers above and beside local government. These bodies act as elements among other layers of functional mechanisms to draw down European Structural Funds. Ultimately, the deployment of these funds is formally controlled by central agencies. Sabel (1996) notes, however, that the profusion of initiatives has given rise to a situation of increasingly confused jurisdiction. Eight regional authorities were established in 1994, with a specific mandate to promote co-ordination of public services at the regional level, and to monitor and advise on the implementation of EU funding in the regions. The membership consists of county/city councillors from the region who are appointed by the constituent. These authorities have no direct representative democratic mandate and contribute thereby to compound the public perception of a lack of democratic legitimacy in the context of the present structure of local government. The regional tier of government in Ireland is primarily administrative.

Conditioning the Spread of Local Agenda 21

At present, there is a distinctive absence of systematic and accurate research regarding the extent of Local Agenda 21 in Ireland. Anecdotal evidence, as much as inconclusive responses to investigation, suggest that the actual incidence of specific LA21 partnerships in Ireland is minimal.[23] However, many local authorities are beginning on the road to creating LA21 processes. There are currently only two local authorities signed up to the Ålborg Charter as participant members of the European Sustainable Cities and Towns Campaign. A third local authority, although not in the campaign, has a standing LA21 forum in Cork. In the latter case, this forum arose in the context of regionally concentrated environmental conflict. In this case, action was precipitated as a means to mediate a series of high-profile conflicts that were negatively impacting on economic development objectives. Regardless of its origins, however, the LA21 process in Cork is being built up incrementally as part of the implementation of other aspects of national and international obligation. For example, under the Waste Management Act, 1996, local authorities are required to adopt systematic 'Waste Management Plans'. As part of a communication strategy, Cork Corporation and Cork County Council established the '20/20 News', a newsletter aimed at increasing awareness and involvement in the waste management process. Other initiatives, such as the Healthy Cities Project, which embody a local partnership model are also beginning to take root.[24]

More disparate elements of a Local Agenda 21 can also be seen in other parts of the country. These appear to lack a strong concept of a 'process' such as the creation of an LA21 forum, or at least this is not stressed, but local authorities are starting to make explicit conceptual connections between the global 'agenda' and the local level. For example, South Dublin County Council, publicising its Environment Strategy, stated that its key objective was the promotion of sustainable development which; 'improves the quality of life for people today and into the future, while cherishing, conserving and promoting the built and natural environment'. Despite its embellishment for the urban context this is clearly a derivative of the WCED and UNCED definition of sustainable development.

Macro-regional co-ordination within the EU

There has, until recently, been a marked absence of the type of mobilisation by sub-national government which seems to characterise the relationship to Brussels in many other EU countries (Marks et al, 1996). This is due to the fact that for structural-fund purposes the Republic of Ireland *is* a region and that direct contact by local authorities with Brussels has only lately shifted from a situation of explicit prohibition to a situation best described as an implicit lack of encouragement (Coyle 1996).

Irish local authorities may, therefore, not yet have sufficiently adapted to the strategic exploitation of diffusion mechanisms supporting LA21 and related initiatives operating more broadly within the European Union.[25] Lately there has been somewhat of a shift in this regard, however. The Institute of Public Administration (IPA) has recently developed a training programme for the creation of a European Liaison Officer in local authorities which provides the authorities with a more direct route for drawing down information from Brussels.

Although Irish local authorities have been slow to participate in the European networks and diffusion mechanisms for LA21, they have been very active with regard to the up-take of Community Initiatives since 1991.[26] Coyle (1994b) estimated that around 70 percent of local authorities were involved in some Community Initiative project. Individual local authorities are also making use of funding through European Programmes to 'get their own house in order'. One example is Cork County Council's involvement in the 'Eurosynet Network' under the European Union's RECITE programme. The network has prepared an Environmental Audit Model which Cork County Council is drawing upon for the purposes of preparing for its Local Agenda 21 process. The type of activities being adapted for local use include the implementation of 'green housekeeping measures', and the improvement of communication among departments within the local authority. While these are all crucial steps forward, they have to be placed in the context of the limited range of local authority functions. The administrative capacity of local authorities to implement LA21 beyond their specified function is, despite the explicit desire of central government for multi-level co-ordination, bound up in residual structural arrangements for environmental policy and the co-ordination of cross-sectoral integration of sustainable development into all areas of policy making.

Cross-sectoral integration and structural co-ordination

Cross-sectoral policy integration remains very much the preserve of central government. A 'green network of government departments' was established in October 1994. This network was created to facilitate horizontal co-ordination between the environment units established within each of the economic ministries and to facilitate the exchange of information. The vertical integration of local authorities into such cross-sectoral initiatives continues to be strategically regulated by the Department of the Environment despite the fact that local authorities are charged with the implementation of centrally ordained policy.

Recent research by Skillington (1996), has indicated a lag between the rhetorical embrace of sustainable development and the language of participation and the creation of participative structures and procedures. With respect to cross-sectoral policy actors, this can be related to a conceptual misapprehension of participation that emphasises 'reaction' , or at best 'consultation' at the expense of more pro-active and deliberative understandings. It is, furthermore, rooted in a defensive policy-making culture which is suspicious of public involvement and protective of the 'expert /citizen' dichotomy. This is borne out by the 1996 report of the DoE to the Commission on Sustainable Development, where participation is characterised as access to the planning and legal system (including EIA), public consultation through submissions on policy issues, and neo-corporatist enrolment of some environmental actors by the state and state agencies. There is as yet no evidence of a broadly based discursive, pro-active understanding of participation at the national level which LA21 processes are supposed to re-produce at the local level.

On the national level, there are mechanisms in place which facilitate the on-going exchange of experience between Government and major economic groups. These have recently expanded to include representatives of environmental and other NGOs. These include: the National Economic and Social Forum (NESF) established in 1993 to develop economic and social policy initiatives to combat unemployment; the Advisory Committee to the Environment Protection Agency; and the National Forum on Development Aid (NFDA) which considers the Overseas Development Aid (ODA) programme and broader aid issues. The inclusion of NGOs in these types of fora indicates a recognition that a wider definition of 'social partnership' is required for sustainable development.

The national partnership model has a potentially supportive role to play as an institutionalised structure for debate on the direction of national policy. However, because of the limited scope for inclusion, the national steering of LA21 has taken place informally through conferences, seminars and workshops. These types of fora are a step beyond a neo-corporate Agenda, but are in equal measure removed from a lasting dialogue with policy makers.

There are no similar mechanisms at present on the local level outside of the limited examples of LA21 fora that exist. Nor is there any repre-sentation of local representatives on the National Economic and Social Council (NESC). Individual local authorities which are pioneering LA21 remain just that, individual local authorities. As we saw in the case of 'local partnership and social innovation', the national diffusion of innova-tion or 'good practice' has, with the exception of interventions by environmental NGO's, remained 'hostage to chance'. In the past, the lack of concerted efforts towards national co-ordination of Local Agenda 21 has been lamented as a lost opportunity on the part of Irish local authorities. There are now indications that this situation is about to change. The IPA has sought to remedy both of these deficiencies by co-operating with local authorities to disseminate information and begin the process of national co-ordination. This began with the staging of a seminar series devoted to Local Agenda 21 which was well attended by local authorities. This has, in turn, contributed to a situation whereby a meeting of a sub-committee of the City and County Managers Association (CCMA) on Local Agenda 21 was convened in early 1997 to discuss the possibility of a national steering mechanism similar to that in operation in the UK. The IPA is also involved in a network of 'National Co-ordinators for Local Agenda 21'. This network was established by the Council of European Municipalities and Regions (CEMR), one of the networks participating in the European Sustainable Cities and Towns Campaign. The purpose of the network is to allow for an exchange between national co-ordinators responsible for encouraging and assisting Local Agenda 21 processes in their respective countries. Through these types of activities, the IPA is playing a crucial facilitating role in encouraging the diffusion of LA21 processes. Perhaps more importantly, it is contributing to the creation of stabilising mechanisms for the horizontal co-ordination of LA21.

The role and reaction of environmental groups

The reaction of environmental groups has been varied and can be related very much to their historical patterns of mobilisation, their organisational strategy and the degree of integration into policy networks and neo-corporate arrangements. Recent government attention to LA21 (on both central and local level), comes at a time when the environmental social-movement sector in Ireland is undergoing a widespread transformation (Mullally, forthcoming). Trans-national environmental organisations such as Greenpeace and Friends of the Earth (FoE) have been central to placing environmental issues on the global agenda. However, the Irish branches of these organisations are currently undergoing changes which are partially due to their success in raising the profile of environmental issues internationally. The international board of Greenpeace has decided to concentrate its efforts on the issues of global warming and deforestation. Since the Irish branch is both financially dependent and structured around individual campaigns, the international organisation has taken the strategic decision to discontinue their support for the Irish office. Earthwatch, which is affiliated to FoE International, has begun to concentrate its scarce resources on campaigns to bind the Irish government to supranational and international obligations on sustainable development. These organisations have played an important role in both raising environmental awareness and in reshaping the boundary conditions of environmental decision making in Ireland.

The types of interaction that are currently on the rise with direct consequences for LA21 are those that include organisations or individuals who: (1) mediate between the initiatives of local authorities on the one hand, and locally based sectoral initiatives on the other; (2) have a history of co-operation/partnership; and (3) involve new environmental groups with a specific LA21 focus who perform as *de facto* consultants to local authorities and promote sustainable lifestyles for local citizens and communities.

The first type of relationship is often represented by former movement activists who have embraced sustainable development and recast themselves strategically as 'experts' with the aim of co-ordinating the efforts of local authorities and the local market in the pursuit of environmental goals.

The second represents a type of environmental discourse which embraces sustainable development precisely because it resonates with its own organisational culture. *An Taisce* (the gaelic name for The National Trust for Ireland) has always attuned its strategy to the particularity of both localised and national patterns of intermediation in Ireland. A neo-corporatist interpretation of LA21 fits in very well with this historical pattern of mobilisation. Consensus and co-operation, discussion and dialogue, argument and 'informed' persuasion, represent the key strategic emphases of the organisation. *An Taisce* has attempted to promote the 'partnership' dimensions of sustainable development and LA21 through interaction with a variety of social actors in conference settings. In 1994, in conjunction with the European Commission and the WWF, *An Taisce*, held a series of regional workshops on sustainable development in Ireland. This type of exchange has acted as an informal mechanism for steering the activities of actors and institutions. In 1995, in conjunction with Dublin Corporation, the Department of the Environment and the European Foundation for the Improvement of Working and Living Conditions, *An Taisce* organised the first national conference on LA21 ('Our Environment – The Future').

The Global Action Programme (GAP) represents a newly emergent type of organisation among environmental NGO's which attempts to change individual and community behaviour towards more sustainable practices. GAP is an international organisation that deals with sustainable development and Agenda 21 by addressing global environmental issues at the level of household and community. GAP works closely with local authorities and local communities through practical steps to address global issues such as waste production and disposal, CO_2 emissions, water quality and natural resource use. In Ireland to date, GAP appears to have had the greatest impact among local authorities that have already embarked on a Local Agenda 21 process.[27]

A hybrid organisational structure transcending many of the other types identified is a network of organisations formed as response to the growth of global ecology. The Network of Irish Environment and Development Organisations (NIEDO) was formed in the run-up to the Earth Summit to co-ordinate the response of major environment-and-development organisations to the Earth Summit. The approach of the UN special session on Agenda 21 (June, 1997) has seen a re-activation of this network as well as a parallel effort to mobilise local citizens groups in a national network to give a focus to the 'partnership' dimension of LA21.

The developments represented by the efforts of *An Taisce*, GAP and NIEDO, have positive implications for promoting and developing LA21 towards a partnership approach. Whereas NIEDO attempts to globalise the local by targeting international events, GAP localises the global by implementing practical local actions to respond to global priorities. This has been an important way of connecting local action to the global level in the absence of a concerted effort from local authorities and will be just as important if and when this type of co-ordination arises. These organisations will need to continue their efforts even with the emergence of horizontal forms of co-ordination. Apart from the periodic activation of the broadly based NIEDO in response to global events, the current trend among the larger environmental organisations represents a shift towards the privatisation of protest or the de-publicisation of conflict. The 'sustainability' of the countervailing force of demands for ecological responsibility made in the public sphere, although crucial as a democratic safety mechanism, appears to be increasingly fragile. It is difficult to see where this public pressure will come from as the larger organisations face increasing financial difficulty. This trepidation has recently been echoed by a journalist who asks: 'As Ireland's two major environmental groups continue to flounder, people are beginning to ask just who is keeping an eye on the issues?'[28] If environmental groups are to play a definitive role in LA21, they need to enter a sustained dialogue with the community development/voluntary sector to overcome difficulties in this regard.

The role of the community-development sector

The community development sector, while largely concerned with redressing social exclusion is also well aware of the negative environmental impact of 'development' particularly in urban areas. Much of the negative experience of 'urban renewal' and 'necessary infrastructural development' has tended to impact directly on the more vulnerable sectors of society. One leading community activist, speaking at the National Conference on LA21, noted there are examples of local sustainable development initiatives which could be built on to form the basis of full NGO participation of a Local Agenda 21 process. He went on to note that although all of these initiatives are concerned with the smallest community organisations, they are all administered at National Government or at EU level. The connections made between the global strategy of Agenda 21, the effects of the EU in everyday life, the negative environmental consequences of social exclusion, and the positive potential for social change based on ICLEI guidelines in this contribution to the debate, demonstrate the intimate connection between sustainable development as a global ethic and LA21 as a local process.

These connections are made in the context of the experience of the community/ voluntary sector in local and national partnerships. In addition to the involvement of individual groups in the type of social partnership discussed earlier, the sector is also nationally organised through the Community Workers Co-operative (CWC). The CWC is a national network made up of over 400 individual and organisational members, North and South, involved in a broad range of community based projects. This network has been involved in providing representation to many of the monitoring committees of local initiatives and, in developing community representation in the National Economic and Social Forum (NESF).

It is important to stress, of course, that the observations of one community activist are not representative of the sector as a whole, despite the potential affinity of this sector with the LA21 idea. There is a lot of work to be done to bridge the gap between the predominant environmental framing of LA21 and the broader connection that sustainability could have with the concerns of community-development organisations. This not only requires a dialogue between the environmental and community sectors, but also needs a more targeted communication effort on the part of those agencies promoting LA21. The potential combination of this sector with environmental groups in 'partnership' with local government could be an important source of democratic legitimacy for authorities attempting to pioneer Local Agenda 21.

'BETTER LOCAL GOVERNMENT': REALISING LA21, OR EXTENDING NEO-CORPORATISM?[29]

The basis of the account up to now has been heavily dependent on a variety of terms like co-ordination, steering mechanisms and participation, and on the pre-condition for fundamental reform of local government. In particular I have raised the notion that much of the potential for LA21 is contingent on the implementation of aspects of the programme of reform contained in the document *Better Local Government* (BLG). The conjunction of a variety of elements within the reform programme represent an important first step toward reconciling the participative thrust of LA21 with the representative and administrative function of local government. *Better Local Government* also goes some way towards providing the conditions under which the horizontal and vertical co-ordination of the process are possible. This represents a significant contribution to creating a more favourable institutional environment for LA21, but there are some difficulties that could negate the broadly positive implications of the reform programme. In general terms, this problem can be expressed as the apparent conflation of *structure* and *process* for LA21.[30] More specifically, it relates to the potential narrowing of the participative ideal from the broader more inclusive idea of an LA21 Forum to a reformed committee structure. These two institutional forms are qualitatively different but they need not be mutually exclusive.

The creation of the Strategic Policy Committee (SPC) mechanism is undoubtedly a useful innovation that could conceivably give procedural form to the concept of 'shared responsibility'. The intention to localise the national 'partnership' model within this mechanism has the potential to embrace the idea of participation which is so central to Agenda 21. The SPC mechanism has the function of enhancing the role of democratically elected councillors in the management of local authorities, and in drawing the national level 'partnership approach' into local governance. Each county and city authority and the larger urban authorities will be required to establish SPC's. The SPC proposal will involve an overhaul of the current committee system through the creation of strategic committees to mirror the major functions of local authorities (BLG, para. 2.20). Each committee would include representation from a variety of social partners. In this system, the SPC on the environment, made up of councillors and representatives of business, farming interests, voluntary groups and environmentalists, would have the opportunity to consider programmes to implement LA21. The chairperson of each of the SPC's will combine with the chairperson of the council to form a Corporate Policy Group (CPG). This group would link the work of different SPC's, and 'act as a sort of cabinet, and provide a forum where policy positions affecting the whole council could be agreed for submission to the full council' (BLG, para. 2.21). Under the reform programme the disjuncture between local development and local government is being addressed by the creation of a Community and Enterprise Group (CEG). The chairperson of the CEG will form part of the Corporate Policy Group of the local authority in order to create a more co-ordinated approach.

The question that the partnership model raises for local democracy, however, is the same question that it raises on the national level: What are the criteria for inclusion and how will this be decided? The non-prescriptive language and content of Chapter 28 of Agenda 21 implicitly recognises that the implementation of sustainable development will vary over time and space and in accordance with local circumstance and needs. It follows that participation in Local Agenda 21 cannot be legislated in a rigid fashion. However, the question of minimum criteria for inclusion is a dimension of the new structural arrangements for Irish local government which requires careful reflection. This is important because the creation of a 'partnership' approach is taking place at a remove from the partnership idea and establishing an institutional context which will have long-term implications for LA21.

Proposals to convene a 'special group' at national level to revise the current committee structures; to create a network of SPC chairpersons; and to strengthen the centre/local dialogue between government departments and the representative associations of elected councillors, are crucial building blocks in creating the basis of horizontal and vertical forms of co-ordination for LA21 (BLG, paras. 2.24-2.30). These developments are being complemented by the Institute of Public Administration's training seminar series on LA21, and that body's efforts to bridge the gap between local authorities and the diffusion mechanisms supporting LA21 on the EU level. When we consider these developments in the context of moves by local authority managers to create a co-ordinating mechanism like the LGMB model in the UK; their new operational role in regional authorities; and the new responsibilities that regional authorities will have in promoting sustainable development – the potential for stimulating LA21 improves immeasurably (BLG, paras. 7.4, 7.6). This is, however, as seen from an administrative viewpoint with respect to the creation of structures and procedures within, across and above local authorities. But how will the participative dimension of LA21 function in this framework-steering process? If it is just a role in a committee at a level below the Corporate Policy Group, then –   even if it does represent a progression from the current model of local government – it still will not have grasped the meaning of 'partnership', let alone participation.

In short, 'a funny thing seems to have happened on the way to the forum'. The new SPC mechanism, while allowing the 'partners' access to policy discussions at a level below the Corporate Policy Group (CPG), seems to involve a qualification of the broader participatory aspirations of an LA21 forum. The word 'forum' is only used in the BLG in relation to the Corporate Policy Group, which does not include representation from outside the council. If this is the case, and a corporate arrangement is to be passed off as an LA21 forum, then the structure may well *inhibit* the development of LA21 rather than supporting it.

This raises the entire issue (mentioned earlier) of whether Local Agenda 21 is to be 'discursively created' or 'authoritatively given'. The issue is particularly relevant in Ireland, where there is an obvious danger that LA21 will become a localised 'pale green' version of neo-corporatism. What is currently lacking emphasis in the institution-building phase of LA21, is a 'deliberative' conception of politics that could mediate between the administrative, representative and participative dimensions of implementing Agenda 21 at the local level of governance.

Of direct relevance here is Barry's observation (1996) that, as a normative principle, sustainability does not come with its own rules of implementation. Realisation of the concept in practice requires deliberation in public discourse and debate. If sustainability is to become a co-ordinating social value and institutionalised mode of action, it cannot be 'left up to specialists alone since it is not simply a matter of 'expertise' but, fundamentally, one of ethical consideration' (1996:118). Lafferty identifies the same ethical and political implications in the development of the concept from the Brundtland Report to Agenda 21. The transition from concept and values to operationalisation and implementaton requires an 'analogue of public discourse and debate' since: 'the politics of sustainable development are not only the politics of UNCED, UNEP, CSD and the EU (but) ... the *potential* politics of national and local change under the onus of supranational commitments' (Lafferty, 1996:193-194).

Local Agenda 21, and the potential institutional correlate contained in the reforms proposed for local government, have not yet reached this crucial stage of public discourse in Ireland. The absence of a more widespread public debate amounts to a deficiency of communication; a crucial co-ordinating mechanism foregone. A reconsideration of this steering deficit in light of a deliberative conception of politics could provide the opportunity to question not only how *Better Local Government* contributes to the LA21 process, but how the process itself contributes to the democratic viability, sustainability and impact of Irish local government into the future.[31]

One of the major possibilities that LA21 provides in this respect is the preparation of a comprehensive 'action plan' which considers the long-term impacts of problems and the long-term sustainability of solutions, and which sets specific targets for achievement. Moreover, LA21 aims at proceduralising a monitoring and reporting framework, including indicators to measure progress, which can be used by all stakeholders to evaluate progress towards targets.[32] The proposed SPC mechanism, with suitable modification, could meet this practical requirement half way. However, a lasting response to a moral commitment made in Rio, requires the counter-weight of sustained moral pressure on the local level in order for an LA21 process to in earnest. This moral pressure in the deliberative conception of politics (Dryzek, 1990, Habermas, 1996, Benhabibi, 1996), would have to emanate from the public sphere. The idea of an LA21 forum provides an institutional form where practical implementation could meet moral pressure in constructive although not necessarily consensual dialogue on the local level.[33]

CONCLUSION

This review of the Irish LA21 experience, although intended to be primarily descriptive, has of necessity dealt more in the currency of 'latent potential' than 'visible progress'. Lacking the benefit of an insight into the proposals of the National Sustainable Development Strategy and the overview of the general state of progress which the ICLEI survey on Local Agenda 21 may provide, predictions of LA21 prospects for the next five years becomes all the more precarious. The review of Agenda 21 by the UN General Assembly may give new impetus to the LA21 process, but there are also more tangible, and perhaps more immediate, stimuli that will surely influence the process.

Firstly, beginning from the 'bottom-up', is the fact that despite the current change in the structure of the environmental social-movement sector, environment-development conflicts are just as widespread as before. Contention over environmental issues is beginning to transcend a multitude of social and economic endeavours and it is becoming increasingly obvious that the command and control model of environmental regulation alone is insufficient to cope.

Secondly, there is the impact of the reform of local government outlined in detail here. The Strategic Management Initiative which paves the way for the introduction of the new structure of local government is due for completion in March 1997, and much of the legislative reform required for its statutory basis is due in 1998.

Thirdly, there are the factors involving macro co-ordination – factors which indicate that the road to Rio currently points back towards Brussels. Despite the recent moves by Government to become more explicitly identified with the UNCED by joining the CSD, the spatial horizon of its gaze is firmly fixed at the level of the EU. Without the enticement of the Structural Funds it is arguable whether the social innovation described in the OECD report or the gradual emergence of a regional level in Irish administration would have taken place. The attempts to link the systems of local government and local development represent a move towards consolidation at a time when Ireland's automatic qualification for this aid is no longer guaranteed.

The partnership/participation dimension of the reforms are every bit as much a result of external stimuli as the national partnership model was in the last decade. On a European level, the emphasis on partnership and shared responsibility is no less crucial as a symbol of legitimacy as the European Commission has to contend with its own 'democratic deficit'. The irony here is that the potential conflicts between time and environmental amelioration (as recently outlined by Barbara Adam (1996) for example), may, in the Irish case, act *for* rather than against LA21. Two temporal cycles are drawing to a conclusion as LA21 gains momentum in Ireland. The electoral cycle ends in 1997 with an election drawing closer; and the current round of structural funds ends in 1999. Normally, an election would threaten any initiative at such a tentative stage as this one is. However, there is very little divergence among any of the political parties on the importance of the European Union to Ireland, nor on the continuing importance of structural funds to development, sustainable or otherwise. Meeting the eligibility criteria for structural-fund purposes will not be guaranteed solely by having a 'partnership' or participative approach to economic development in place. However, as an expressed principal of much of EU policy, and particularly of the goals outlined in the program 'Towards Sustainability', not being able to point towards new forms of participation may act as a disqualifying factor. It is reasonable to assume, therefore, that the emphasis on participatory reform, in one form or another, will remain an important signifier in Irish economic and political discourse.

The answer to the crucial question for LA21 as to what type of participation we are talking about is less obvious without the benefit of hindsight. This will be contingent on a number of variables, such as an increased communication output by the state agencies and analogues promoting Local Agenda 21; heightened communication within and between public spheres; a more enlightened and elaborated means of funding local government; and an augmented programme to co-ordinate the activities of individual local authorities and the diffusion of LA21 initiatives more broadly on a European and global level. All of these elements of an LA21 programme will, however, arguably remain diffuse and fragmented without the benefit of a deliberative conception of politics. By making the connection to the EU explicit, my argument is not that the prospects for LA21 in Ireland should be seen as contingent on a continuation of EU economic largesse. Rather it is that, at some point, Ireland's membership of the EU should be less about the building of roads, and more about the facilitation of decisions as to what type of 'roads' we, and sustainable development, need.

NOTES

*   This chapter originates in part from a larger comparative project on the institutionalisation of environmental issues in five western European Countries, directed by Klaus Eder at the European University Institute, and sponsored by the European Commission-DGXII (Grant PL210943). The overview of LA21 has benefited from involvement in a pan-European research project on sustainable urban mobility, directed by Patrick O' Mahony at the Centre for European Social Research, also funded by the European Commission-DGXII (PRVI-CT-005-IRL). The author would like to acknowledge the research assistance of Stephanie Schmidt and the help of Tara Dennehy in completing the current account of LA21 in Ireland. He would also like to thank William Lafferty and the members of the LA21 research network for the invitation to take part in this endeavour.

1   Mr. Brendan Howlin , T.D. (M.P), Minister for the Environment, in the opening address to the National Conference on Local Agenda 21, June 1995.

2   See Leslie O Dowd, 'Local Culture, Local Knowledge, Local Power: Locating an Irish Local Agenda 21' in the proceedings of 'Our Environment the Future: A National Conference on Local Agenda 21'.

3   This is particularly the case where progress in Local Agenda 21 is explicitly linked to target dates and objectives which have now long since passed by (see Lafferty and Eckerberg this volume).

4   In the context of this chapter, the term 'sustainable development' denotes the programme embodied by the World Commission on Environment and Development (WCED), the UNCED process and the documents agreed at the Rio Summit, particularly *Agenda 21*. We are concerned here, in the first instance, with progress in the implementation of Chapter 28 of the Agenda, and as such refer to the concept of 'sustainable development'. There is a long-standing debate regarding the merits and demerits of conceptualisations of 'sustainability' versus 'sustainable development', where the former places a stronger emphasis than the latter on normative and ethical issues and on the 'non-technical, extra-economic dimensions of the debate, particularly those which relate to democracy' (Barry, 1996: 129). Lafferty (1996:190) has argued that the follow-up to the Earth Summit has been less focused and impressive than anticipated in Rio. Much of this, he argues, comes from the lack of analytic attention to the concept's [sustainable development] ethical and political possibilities. Therefore, while the descriptive tenor of this chapter is focused on the local level implementation of sustainable development the normative content of the argument is very much rooted in the environmental discourse of 'strong' or 'reflexive' ecological modernisation (Christoff 1996, Hajer 1995, 1996).

5   In Christoff's typology (1996:490), 'weak ecological modernisation' has the following characteristics: economistic, technological, instrumental, technocratic/neo-corporatist/closed, national, and unitary (hegemonic). In counter distinction to this 'strong ecological modernisation', is ecological, institutional/ systemic (broad), deliberative, democratic/open, international,

diversifying. Despite the somewhat static nature of these classifications, the former adequately describes the Irish situation as it currently stands.

6　An Environment Action Programme, 1st Progress Report, Department of the Environment, June (1991:2).

7　The Government's Action Programme may well be superseded by the long awaited 'National Strategy for Sustainable Development'. This document was due for completion by mid-1996. However, up to the time of writing the strategy had not been made publicly available.

8　For a full account of the dimensions of these conflicts, see the work of Peace (1993), Tovey (1992), and Baker (1987, 1990).

9　See Adrian Peace (1993).

10　See Susan Baker (1990).

11　This is important when considering the prospects for Local Agenda 21. Coyle (1996:280-1) notes that beyond the narrow functional remit identified, local authorities effectively have no involvement in the major policy areas of education, agriculture, social welfare, police, public transport and public utilities. Local authorities are seen as being within the sole remit of the Minister and Department of the Environment. However, institutional arrangements regarding the environment tend to be fragmented and dispersed throughout various governmental departments.

12　Until recently, there were only 27 county councils. However, in 1994, Dublin County Council was reorganised into three new administrative counties to respond to the difficulties of rising population trends in the Dublin region.

13　Garvin, in his account of local government in Ireland from 1919 to 1922, notes that the centralising tendencies of the state were to become a permanent distinguishing feature in the structure of Irish governance: 'The impulse behind the centralising and streamlining of local government was powerful and was not to expend itself in 1923. On the contrary, the Irish state, consistent with its beginnings in the Dail government, was to impose central controls and standard practices on local government' (1994:30). He goes on to note that the lack of community attachment to the institutions of local government was perpetuated by a political culture in which: '[n]either side truly believed in secular participant local democracy. Local government was a British invention, expensive, anti-national and incompetent' (ibid.: 31)

14　Directive 85/337/EEC was adopted by the European Council in 1985, brought into operation with effect from July 3rd 1988, and passed into Irish law in February 1990. The 1976 Local Government (Environment and Development) Act had previously provided a framework for the operation of Environmental Impact Assessment (EIA). Projects in excess of five million pounds were subject to EIA, with the exception of certain projects including those carried out by local authorities. The adoption of the European directive added a limited right to participation to the 'repertoire of contention' of Irish citizens in the case of controversial large-scale developments, albeit in a negative rather than pro-active sense. EIA is primarily an information-providing tool rather than a decision making tool.

15　Council Directive 90/313/EEC was adopted during Ireland's EC Presidency in 1990. It required public authorities to make available to any person, on

request, subject to certain exceptions, information which they hold relating
to the environment. The Directive took effect from 31, December, 1992 and
implemented in Ireland by the Access to Information on the Environment
Regulations, 1993. A review of the first year of operation of the Regulations
was carried out in 1994 by means of a call for public submissions and a
questionnaire was administered to over 120 public authorities. By far the
most interesting result was that only 57 percent of public authorities
responded, despite their obligations under the regulations.

16   For a comprehensive account of the relationship between Irish and EU
environmental policy, see Coyle (1994a), Peace (1994) and McCarthy and
Yearly (1995). An official account of these developments is contained in
'Moving Towards Sustainability', (DoE, 1995b).

17   The 1988 reform of Structural Funds assigned five 'objectives' to the Funds.
Ireland is among the countries that are classified under 'Objective 1' which
is concerned with promoting the development of regions (Matthews: 16-17).

18   The focus of these partnerships varies from situation to situation. Some are
primarily economically driven and reproduce the interests of established
business actors in an area. Other projects focus on problems of social
exclusion and deprivation. The potential for exchange of experience is
limited to informal exchange which the report argues 'makes the diffusion
of innovation hostage to chance' (Sabel, 1996: 90).

19   The relevant text from the Guidelines is as follows: 'consultation and
consensus building are essential elements (of sustainable development), but
local authorities may choose different means to develop the process, and
different ways of reporting its outcome and defining an appropriate Local
Agenda 21 for their areas' (1995c: 3).

20   See the Chapter by Young (this volume) for the evolution of the steering
mechanisms for LA21 in the UK.

21   The programme proposes that, in future, local authorities will supplement
their revenue from the proceeds of motor vehicle tax which previously was
directed towards the national exchequer.

22   The Strategic Management Initiative (SMI) is a multi-faceted programme
for reform and renewal of the public service as a whole. As part of this
process, local authorities were asked by the DoE in March 1996 to develop
strategy statements (corporate plans) in the context of general governmental
policy generally and the DOE's Operational Strategy. These plans form the
basis of the preparation of local government for the reforms proposed in
'Better Local Government'. The precise implications for Local Agenda 21
are explored in the section on the proposals for the reform of local government.

23   The International Council for Local Environmental Initiatives (ICLEI) has
undertaken an international Local Agenda 21 survey designed to assess
progress in the implementation of Agenda 21 at a local level. The results of
the survey are anticipated in June of 1997 and may provide a more definitive picture. (Editor's note: The ICLEI survey was made available just prior
to the publishing deadline and is commented upon in the concluding
chapter.)

24   The World Health Organisation's (WHO Europe) Healthy Cities Project is

aimed at establishing a Multi-City Action Plan on Health and Sustainable Development within the framework of the WHO Healthy Cities Project and the European Sustainable Cities and Towns Campaign. At present, Sligo Corporation is the most far advanced in this regard and other cities are beginning to follow.

25 In a survey regarding the degree of influence of agencies and other bodies on the EU activities of the local authorities, Coyle (1994b) found that national administration was deemed overwhelmingly the most influential and active. The only other bodies attributed with real influence were the County and City Managers Association (CCMA) and the Institute of Public Administration (IPA). In May 1993, the IPA set up a consultant service for the dissemination of EU information to local authorities.

26 For a descriptive overview of the networks operating within the framework of the European Sustainable Cities and Towns Campaign, see the handbook issued by the Campaign in March 1996.

27 Cork County Council is an active member of the GAP programme and has a local GAP co-ordinator. '20/20 News'. Volume 1, Issue 2, March 1997.

28 Denise Hall, 'Eco-nomics signal the end of green rainbow', *The Examiner*, Tuesday, March 4, 1997.

29 Unless otherwise stated all paragraph numbers refer to *Better Local Government* (BLG) (DoE, 1996a).

30 The phrase 'apparent conflation' is used here deliberately to indicate recognition that, while there may be an inherent contradiction in the conceptualisation of LA21 in 'Better Local Government', this is not necessarily the case. The objectives and provisions of the reform document are much wider than the reference it makes to LA21, but insofar as it makes an explicit connection between the new SPC structures and the LA21 process, it is crucial to comment on what I see as the possible corruption and narrowing of the idea of a forum.

31 An extended discussion of the deliberative conception of politics and a theory of deliberative democracy is well beyond the scope of this chapter. Its importance to the ideas of LA21 lies, broadly speaking, in its formulation by Jürgen Habermas: that is, as a normative concept which emphasises communication and the crucial importance of the 'public sphere' to democratic politics. Habermas's most recent elaboration of the concept, in English, is his book 'Between Facts and Norms' (1996). Its relevance for the discussion of LA21 is justified by, first, reference to the emphasis that deliberative democracy places on the importance of institutional procedures and practices for attaining decisions, and, second, the recognition of the existence of conflicts of values and conflicts of interest in social life for which these procedures are required (Benhabib, 1996: 73). As referred to here, deliberative democracy (following Barry, 1996: 122), implies a 'demand for a participatory democratic practice, where representative democratic institutions can be supplemented with more discursive institutional forms and greater citizen involvement in political and non-political spheres'.

32 These possibilities are contained in a communication from the United Nations Department for Policy Co-ordination and Sustainable Development

(UNDPCSD) dated April 9, 1996. The communication to the Department of the Environment concerns a request for participation in the joint UNDPCSD/ICLEI international Local Agenda 21 Survey, and was distributed to Irish local authorities in a circular dated April 25, 1996 (Circular EPS 2/96).

33   The 'Briefing Document for Potential Participants' to the proposed 'Cork Environmental Forum' issued by Cork County Council which preceded the announcement of the SPC mechanism, could act as a guide for other local authorities embarking on an LA21 process. Whatever its operation in practice – and this will be the object of more critical attention at some future date – its philosophy is entirely consistent with both the narrower SPC model and the wider idea of a forum. The progression moved sequentially from the establishment of a broad-based steering committee, to the agreement of substantive objectives and to the proceduralisation of the process. The proceduralisation involved the appointment of a forum chairperson, the establishment of working groups on a geographical basis and the establishment of a plenary session. The working groups have the function of both reporting to the plenary session and of hearing detailed submissions from interested parties. It is too early at this stage to judge how effective this will be over time, especially in light of the novelty of local government reform, but as an operational model it is worthy of attention.

REFERENCES

Adam, Barbara (1996) 'Beyond the Present: Nature Technology and the Democratic Ideal', *Time & Society*, 5(3) 319–338.

Allen, Robert and Tara Jones, (1990) *Guests of the Nation: People of Ireland versus the multinationals*, London: Earthscan.

Baker, Susan (1987) 'Dependent Industrialisation and Political Protest: Raybestos Manhattan in Ireland', *Government and Opposition*, 22(3) 352–358.

Baker, Susan (1990) 'The Evolution of the Irish Ecology Movement' in Wolfgang Rudig (ed.) *Green Politics One*, Edinburgh: Edinburgh University Press, 47–81.

Barry, John (1996) 'Sustainability, Political Judgement and Citizenship: Connecting Green Politics and Democracy' in Brian Doherty and Marius de Geus (eds.) *Democracy and Green Politcal Thought: Sustainability, Rights and Citizenship*, London: Routledge, 115–131.

Beck, Ulrick (1992) *Risk Society: Towards a New Modernity*, London: Sage.

Benhabib, Seyla (1996) 'Towards a Deliberative Model of Democratic Legitimacy' in Seyla Behahib (ed.) *Democracy and Difference: Contesting the Boundaries of the Political*, Princeton, Princeton University Press, 67–94.

Community Workers Cooperative (CWC) (1996) *Partnership in Action: The Role of Community Development and Partnership in Ireland*, Galway: CWC.

Coyle, Carmel (1996) 'Local and Regional Administrative Structures and Rural Poverty' in C. Curtain, T. Haase, and H. Tovey (eds.) *Poverty in Rural Ireland*, Dublin: Combat Poverty/Oak Tree Press, 276–305.

Coyle, Carmel (1994a) 'Administrative Capacity and the Implementation of EU Environmental Policy in Ireland' in S. Baker et al. (eds.) *Protecting the Periphery: Environmental Policy at the European Periphery*, London: Frank Cass Co., 62–79.

Coyle, Carmel (1994b) 'Local Government in Ireland: A Crisis but not quite a Catastrophe' in Maurice R. O' Connell (ed.) *Decentralisation of Government, Proceedings of the Fourth Annual Daniel O' Connell Workshop*, Dublin: Institute of Public Administration/DOCAL, 32–42.

Christoff, Peter (1996) 'Ecological Modernisation, Ecological Modernities', *Environmental Politics*, 5(3) 476–500.

Chubb, Basil (1992) *The Government and Politics of Ireland* (Third Ed.) Essex: Longman.

Dalal-Clayton, Barry (1996) *Getting to grips with Green Plans: National Level Experience in Industrial Countries*, London: Earthscan.

DoE (Department of the Environment) (1990) 'An Environment Action Programme', Dublin: DoE .

DoE (Department of the Environment) (1991) 'An Environment Action Programme: 1st Progress Report', Dublin: DoE, June.

DoE (Department of the Environment) (1992) 'National Report to the United Nations Conference on Environment and Development, Rio de Janeiro: June'.

DoE (Department of the Environment) (1994) 'Ireland Report to the Commission on Sustainable Development 1994', Dublin: DoE.

DoE (Department of the Environment) (1995a) 'Access to Information on the Environment: A Review', Dublin: DoE. April.

DoE (Department of the Environment) (1995b) 'Moving Towards Sustainability: A Review of Recent Environmental Policy and Developments', Dublin, May.

DoE (Department of the Environment) (1995c) 'Local Authorities and Sustainable Development: Guidelines on Local Agenda 21', Dublin June.

DoE (Department of the Environment) (1995d) 'Ireland Report to the Commission on Sustainable Development 1995', Dublin: DoE.

DoE (Department of the Environment) (1996a) 'Better Local Government: A Programme for Change', Dublin: Government Stationary Office, December

DoE (Department of the Environment) (1996b) 'The Report of Ireland to 1996 Session of the UN Commission on Sustainable Development', Dublin: DoE.

Dryzek, John. S (1996) 'Political and Ecological Communication' in Freya Mathews (ed.) *Ecology and Democracy*, London: Frank Cass and Co.,13–30.

Garvin, Tom (1994) 'The Dail Government and Irish Local Democracy, 1919–22', in Maurice R. O' Connell (ed.) *Decentralisation of Government, Proceedings of the Fourth Annual Daniel O' Connell Workshop*, Dublin: Institute of Public Administration/DOCAL, 20–31.

Habermas, Jürgen (1996) *Between Facts and Norms*, Cambridge: Polity Press.

Hajer, Maarten (1995) *The Politics of Environmental Discourse: Ecological Modernisation and the Policy Process*, Oxford: Clarendon Press.

Hajer, Maarten (1996) 'Ecological Modernisation as Cultural Politics in Bronislaw Szerszynski et al. (eds.) *Risk Environment and Modernity: Towards a New Ecology*, London: Sage, 247–268.

Hewett, Jonathan (ed.) (1995) *European Environmental Almanac*, Earthscan, London.

Irwin, Alan (1995) *Citizen Science: A Study of People, Expertise and Sustainable Development*, London: Routledge.

Lafferty, William A. (1996) 'The Politics of Sustainable Development: Global Norms for National Implementation', *Environmental Politics* 5(2) 185–208.

Marks, Gary et al. (1996) 'Competencies, Cracks and Conflicts: Regional Mobilization in the European Union' in Marks et al (eds.) *Governance in the European Union*, London: Sage, 40–63.

Matthews, Alan (1994) *Managing the EU Structural Funds in Ireland*, Cork: Cork University Press.

McCarthy, Elaine, Yearly, Stephen (1995) 'The Irish EPA: the early years', *Environmental Politics*, 4(4) 258–264.

Mullally, Ger (1995) 'Entering the Stage, Strategies of Environmental Communication in Ireland', in Klaus Eder (ed.) 'Framing and Communicating Environmental Issues', Research Report, Commission of the European Communities, DGXII, Florence/Cork: European University Institute/Centre for European Social Research.

Mullally, Ger (forthcoming) 'Re-locating Protest: Environmental Organisations in Late Twentieth Century Ireland', in Mario Diani and Klaus Eder (eds.) *Movement Organisations in the Information Society: A comparative Analysis of Environmental Groups in Five West European Countries*.

Sabel, Charles(1996) Ireland: Local Partnerships and Social Innovation, Prepared by Professor Charles Sabel and the LEED Programme, Paris: OECD.

Peace, Adrian (1993) 'Environmental Protest and Bureaucratic Closure: The politics of discourse in rural Ireland', in Kay Milton (ed.) *Environmentalism: The view from Anthropology*, London: Routledge, 189–204.

Peace, Adrian (1994) 'Chemicals, Conflicts and the Irish Environmental Protection Agency', *CEA News*, No. 9, Spring, 17–22.

Rein, Martin and D.A. Schon (1994) *Frame Reflection: Towards the Resolution of Intractable Policy Controversies*, New York: Basic Books.

Scott, Sue (1992) 'Jobs versus the Environment: A local authority perspective', *Administration*, 40, (4).

Skillington, Tracy (1996) 'Sustainability and Institutional Innovation in Ireland', in Patrick o' Mahony (ed.) 'Sustainable Development and Institutional Innovation', Research Report, Commission of the European Communities, DGXII, Cork: Centre for European Social Research.

(An) Taisce (1995) Proceedings from Our Environment the Future: A National Conference on Local Agenda 21, Co-sponsored by An Taisce: The National Trust for Ireland, Dublin Corporation, European Foundation for the Improvement of Living and Working Conditions, and, the Department of the Environment, Dublin Castle Conference Centre, Dublin, 9th and 10th of June.

Tovey, Hilary (1993) 'Environmentalism in Ireland: Modernisation and Identity', in Patrick Clancy et al. (eds.) *Ireland and Poland, Comparative Perspectives*, Dublin: 275–287.

Yearly, Steven (1995) 'The Social Shaping of the Environmental Movement in Ireland', in Patrick Clancy et al (eds.) *Irish Society: Sociological Perspectives*, Dublin: Institute of Public Administration, 656–674.

10. Conclusions:
Comparative Perspectives on Evaluation and Explanation

Katarina Eckerberg and William M. Lafferty

DESCRIPTION AND EVALUATION: THE PROBLEM OF CRITERIA

The major purpose of the studies here presented has been to grasp, in a systematic way, the steps taken in eight European countries to implement Chapter 28 of Agenda 21. The goal has been to report on the most salient aspects of the implementation process within a set of common descriptive and evaluative categories. As the reader will now fully understand, it has not been easy to maintain a distinction between these two dimensions. To describe, one must define and delimit — and therein lie the first steps towards evaluation. As a research network, we have developed an initial set of distinctions and categories (as set forth in the Introduction), the aim of which has been to guide our common reporting effort. We have maintained that an implementation of the UNCED-Rio program for change is best understood as a potential transition across four stages of environment-and-development policy. These stages can now be made more explicit as follows:

1. *Pre-environmental policy:* 'Business as usual', with no active attempts to ameliorate the negative environment-development consequences of industrialism and open-ended materialism;
2. *Environmental policy:* With an emphasis on the conservation of nature and technological, 'end-of-pipe' solutions to environmental damage;
3. *Sustainable-development policy:* With direct or implied reference to the Brundtland Report and a greater emphasis on both the underly-

ing socio-economic causes of environmental damage and the inter-
dependence between environment and development in a North-South
perspective;

4. *UNCED policy:* With direct reference to the values and goals of the
Rio documents – in this particular case Chapter 28 of Agenda 21.

We have also tried to identify (in very general terms) the step-wise implementation procedure implied by Agenda 21 for this area (its 'adequate
causal theory'); as well as the distinguishing characteristics of 'a Local
Agenda 21 process'.

Given the relatively brief period that the research network has been in
operation, we have not had the opportunity to further standardise and operationalise these criteria. The network can be seen as a developmental research
process, where we are moving from description through evaluation towards
explanation. The challenges for policy-implementation research of the
sustainable-development idea in general, and of the UNCED program in
particular, are only now being confronted (Lafferty and Meadowcroft,
1996). Work on monitoring frameworks and indicators is actively underway on a number of different fronts, but the progress to date with respect to
Local Agenda 21 is still both general and open-ended. The problem can be
illustrated by briefly looking at the status of indicator development and
application within the general UNCED frame of reference.

Indicators for sustainable development and LA21

Although work on environmental indicators has been going on for a
number of decades, efforts to develop more specific indicators of sustainable development are of a much more recent date. Projects are underway
within the OECD and EUROSTAT, as well as within 'leading-edge'
national departments of the environment in, for example, Canada, the
Netherlands, Sweden, Norway, the United States, Japan and Costa Rica –
to mention but the most active. There are also numerous research institutes, international organisations and agencies, and other non-profit and
for-profit organisations involved in comprehensive programs for indicator
development.[1]

Within the CSD system itself, the task of indicator development has
been given high political and scientific priority. There was early on established a separate Advisory Group on Indicators for clarifying the status
which indicators are to have within the CSD monitoring process (an issue
which has proved to be of touchy political relevance), and the Scientific
Committee on Problems of the Environment (SCOPE) was given the task
of co-ordinating and further developing indicators within the scientific

and academic communities.[2] In 1995, the CSD initiated a separate work programme on indicators, and in 1996 the DPCSD published a manual of 'methodology sheets' with detailed references to the chapters of Agenda 21.[3] It is expected that further efforts at conceptual clarification and operationalisation will be given high priority in the second five-year phase of the Earth Summit follow-up. With respect to Local Agenda 21, it is interesting to note here that the DPCSD manual contains no specific references to Chapter 28 or Local Agenda 21.

One indicator effort which is of particular interest for the present perspective is a sub-project of the indicator programme being conducted at the International Institute for Sustainable Development (IISD) in Canada (see note 1). In an attempt to both promote and systematise indicator development at the local level, IISD took the initiative to bring together representatives of leading indicator and evaluation projects in Bellagio, Italy in 1996. The conference resulted in the so-called 'Bellagio Principles' ('Guidelines for Practical Assessment of Progress Toward Sustainable Development'). Printed here as Appendix 3, the principles provide general criteria for distinguishing the difference between assessments of local *environmental policy* and *sustainable-development policy*.

International monitoring

At the international level, there are two major monitoring efforts of direct relevance for the present set of studies. First, there is the activity of the DPCSD itself which has the responsibility for collecting and collating the country reports being submitted to the Special Session of the General Assembly in June 1997 ('Earth Summit +5'); and, second, there is the large-scale survey conducted by the International Council for Local Environmental Initiatives (ICLEI) in collaboration with the DPCSD. These monitoring activities provide important alternative perspectives for our attempts below to summarise the major comparative results from our own country studies.

Country reports to the CSD

At the time of concluding the present report (May 1997), seven of the eight countries covered by our study had submitted reports to the CSD (the report from the United Kingdom was lacking). As made available over the 'Earth Summit +5' web site, these reports are standardised to reflect the chapters of Agenda 21. They also include brief introductory profiles of each country, lists of acronyms and organisations, some concluding general comments, and a summary rating by each country of 'available data and information suitable for decision-making'.

Though we must be cautious in our interpretation of these reports, they do provide a comparative indication of how the national authorities in question have complied with their reporting responsibilities on Chapter 28 of the Agenda. (The reports on Chapter 28 are reproduced here as Appendix 2.) The following points are of interest for the further discussion:

• Three countries – Finland, the Netherlands, and Norway – rate the availability of data on Ch. 28 as 'very good'. Austria and Germany rate the availability as 'good', while Ireland reports 'some good data, but many gaps'. Sweden has failed to rate for Chapter 28.
• All countries report that their Governments 'support Local Agenda 21 initiatives'.
• With the exception of Ireland – which makes no claim as to LA21 progress – the remaining countries operate with imprecise notions as to what constitutes a 'Local Agenda 21' initiative. Norway and Sweden seem to be particularly 'generous' in granting LA21 status: In the case of Sweden, by implying that any activity for sustainable development qualifies, and, in the case of Norway, by identifying the major pre-Rio municipal reform (the so-called 'MIK-reform') as 'the first phase of Local Agenda 21'.
• Sweden, Finland, Germany, the Netherlands, Norway and Austria make the following substantive judgements as to the number of LA21s initiated in each case: Sweden: 'all Swedish local authorities'; Finland: 'at least 88 Local Agendas 21'; Germany: 'at least 300 local Agendas 21'; the Netherlands: 'at least 140 local Agendas 21'; Norway: '60–70 municipalities and 4–5 counties ... working with the LA21-concept'; and Austria: three cities (as signatories of the Aalborg Charter).
• Sweden is the only country reporting the availability of separate central-government funds made available for LA21 programmes. Sweden is also the only country reporting the appointment of separate LA21 co-ordinators in 'about half of the local authorities'.
• The report from the Netherlands is exceptionally sketchy and incomplete.

The ICLEI/DPCSD survey

The 'Local Agenda 21 Survey' is the result of a decision by the CSD at its fourth session in 1995.4 The survey was conducted along two dimensions: (1) the 'national/regional survey', sent to national governments, National Sustainable Development Councils, and national and regional Local Government Organisations (that is, umbrella associations for municipal and other regional public authorities); and (2) the 'local government survey', sent to 196 local governments which had been previously registered by ICLEI as being particularly committed to Local Agenda 21 work. The first survey has been used by ICLEI to document the quantitative aspects of LA21 implementation, and the second to go into more detail on qualitative aspects of the process.

Focusing here on the quantitative materials, we wish to use the survey results to illustrate the difficulties inherent in the self-reporting procedures employed. The units monitored have been asked to fill out a standardised form, and 24 percent of the units contacted have done so. This is, of course, a relatively low response rate for a mail survey, but, given a general penchant for national organisations to be the bearers of good news, we can assume that the results do not *under-report* the scope of LA21 activity. As we will see, the tendency would appear to be in the opposite direction.

It is important to point out, however, that ICLEI made a clear attempt to 'filter' the results with respect to LA21 criteria. This was done, firstly, by defining the Local Agenda 21 process in a relatively constricted way:

> *Local Agenda 21 is a participatory, multi-sectoral process*
> *to achieve the goals of Agenda 21 at the local level through*
> *the preparation and implementation of a long-term, strate-*
> *gic action plan that addresses priority local sustainable*
> *development concerns. (ICLEI, 1996: 4)*

We see here the same type of distinctions identified in the present study (Introduction and above), whereby a specific reference to Agenda 21 and a commitment to long-term strategic planning are viewed as *efforts in addition to* participatory, multi-sectoral processes aimed at sustainable-development concerns. We are not, in other words, talking about traditional environmental policy initiatives, nor about processes which might be derived from the Brundtland Report alone, but about participatory strategic planning related specifically to Agenda 21.

As a further check on the validity of responses with respect to these criteria, ICLEI followed up the results by contacting the reporting bodies where doubts had arisen. The results were also checked against existing national surveys, and through regional consultation meetings with LGO's and local government officials. As a result of these validity checks, 9 of the 53 national/regional surveys were dropped from the sample. These exclusions were in addition to a non-specified number of cases which were excluded for one or more of the following reasons:

- activities stemming from the delegation of national or state-level Agenda 21 responsibilities to local governments;

- planning that was based on a one-time consultation process rather than an ongoing participatory process of local sustainable development decision making;
- processes that did not engage a diversity of local sectors;
- activities that did not apply the sustainable development concept; that is, an integrated approach to environmental, social and economic issues. (ICLEI, 1996: 4)

Given the relative clarity and restrictive nature of the criteria applied, it is that much more surprising that the quantitative results are as positive as they are. As interpreted by ICLEI, the survey results indicate that there were, at the time of their survey, 11 national LA21 campaigns underway, and that, within the scope of these campaigns, there were 1,487 local authorities which had established LA21 'planning efforts'. In addition, it is reported that there were another nine countries where national campaigns were just getting underway (with an additional 117 local authorities qualifying), and a further 208 units from 44 countries where no national campaign was present. All in all, therefore, the survey documents 1,812 local authorities with LA21 planning processes underway.

This is, of course, an impressive total, and would – if valid according to ICLEI's own criteria – represent significant progress for this aspect of the UNCED program. We must, however, question the validity in light of our own national studies. So as to illustrate the problem, we will focus only on the two countries represented by the authors of this chapter: Sweden and Norway. Our purpose is not to discredit the results of the ICLEI survey, but to focus more clearly on just how difficult the problem of evaluation is. The survey lists Sweden as having 307 local authorities with Local Agenda 21 planning processes in place, and Norway with 415 (ICLEI, Table 1). Together, these two countries account for 40 percent of all cases registered.

The fact that Sweden is recorded with 307 LA21s means that only five political-administrative units at a sub-national level have *not* initiated a Local Agenda 21 planning process. Presumably, this means that all 288 municipalities and 19 of the 24 counties (*län*) have started the process. Though this corresponds roughly with Sweden's country report to the CSD, and is in line with the Swedish self-image reported in our own country study here, we feel a need to repeat what was pointed out in the conclusion to the Swedish chapter: that the type of activity categorised as an LA21 varies greatly. Given the definition used by ICLEI, and making exceptions for the four criteria which should *not* qualify a case for LA21 status, we feel that the over-reporting for Sweden is considerable.

The situation is, however, even more exaggerated for Norway. By registering Norway with 415 LA21s, the ICLEI survey is claiming that only 20 of Norway's 435 municipalities have not initiated the planning process. This figure does not correspond, however, with the Norwegian Ministry of the Environment's own assessment in the country report to the CSD (see above), and *certainly* does not correspond with the country study provided here. To make a long story very short, the only way the Norwegian figure can jibe with the actual situation in Norway, is to accord LA21 status on the basis of the pre-Rio environmental reform ('Environmental Protection in the Municipalities' EPIM, or *MIK-reformen* in Norwegian). As an essential part of this reform, the central Government supported, both financially and through capacity-building, the appointment of 'environmental officers' in any municipality wishing to participate. At the end of 1996, there were 415 officers in place, and it is clearly this figure which has been accepted by ICLEI. There can, however, be no doubt whatsoever that the figure does *not* reflect conditions which correspond with the ICLEI definition and criteria.

There are several reasons why these alternative perspectives are important. The purpose of monitoring the follow-up to the Earth Summit is not to pass out grades and medals, but to improve the process of implementation itself. The problems we raise with respect to the Swedish and Norwegian examples mean, at the least, that the methodology of surveying progress requires closer attention and rigor. Neither ICLEI nor the DPCSD is well served by procedures which appear to favour some national track-records over others. The purpose of the monitoring exercise is to profile and disseminate good-practice for the sake of better implementation everywhere. It is not a contest, but a global challenge of great seriousness.

A second insight from the perspective is the light cast on different central-government strategies for dealing with the LA21 initiative. As we will point out below, there are clear differences in how the responsible Swedish and Norwegian central authorities interpreted the LA21 challenge at the end of the Earth Summit. These differences point toward important lessons for implementation research, and would be quite simply lost if the ICLEI results are accepted at face value.

Finally, there is an issue of great substantive importance as to what actually *does* work in this particular area of implementation. On the one hand, it is easy to see how Norwegian rapporteurs would want to emphasise the MIK reform as a 'first phase' of Local Agenda 21, even though they are obviously aware that neither the symbol nor the broader implications of Chapter 28 have been present in the reform. The reasoning is that the establishment of local environmental officers in nearly every Norwegian municipality is a major step toward environmental protection, and environmental protection is surely a core aspect of Local Agenda 21. What then can be the harm in viewing the reform as an initial step, and in reporting thereby 415 municipalities as qualified for LA21 status?

How one answers this question will, of course, depend on how seriously one takes the LA21 initiative as something *qualitatively different* from environmental protection. On a much more instrumental level, however, one can point out that the harm may lie in a misconceived model of what actually contributes to LA21 progress. The intricacies of policy implementation are so complex that there is no guarantee that an existing reform effort – enacted on its own premises, with a specific set of central guidelines and actors – is a positive foundation for another, more broadly conceived and ambitious, reform effort. In the present case (as pointed out further below), there are clear indications that, in certain cases at least, the existence of the MIK reform creates barriers *against* LA21 activity, rather than the opposite.

It is our hope, therefore, that these perspectives on the international monitoring exercises bring into sharper relief the need for more in-depth analyses of both the methodological and substantive aspects of the evaluation process. Though 'program evaluation' is a well-established discipline within Western scientific communities, the UNCED 'program' for global change is an operation of a very different type from most sector-based administrative reforms. We are only at the beginning of adapting implementation research to this type of problem. The monitoring efforts of ICLEI, the DPCSD and other international and national bodies are vital to the development of more effective procedures for evaluation and change, but they must be complemented by independent research and comparative analysis. In what follows, we make a first effort towards this end by highlighting what we believe to be the most salient cross-national implications of the national case-studies.

AN INITIAL CATEGORISATION: 'PIONEERS', 'ADAPTORS' AND 'LATE-COMERS'

Before trying to summarise and compare the different countries' conditions according to the initial questions for analysis, it might be fruitful to first give an account of the overall status of LA21 in the respective countries. From our assessments, particularly of the total number of local authorities that have embarked on an LA21 process, it is possible to discern three relatively distinct groups. These can be roughly categorised as *pioneers, adaptors* and *late-comers* (Table 1).

While the terms 'pioneers' and 'late-comers' should be relatively intuitive in the present context, the notion of an 'adaptor' is probably less so. We had experimented with terms like 'followers' and 'waiverers' for this category, but found in the end that they did not capture the essence of the profiles in question. For both Finland and Norway, the reaction to

Table I *Profiles of LA2I implementation in eight North European countries*

Pioneers	Adaptors	Late-comers
Sweden	Finland	Germany
United Kingdom	Norway	Ireland
The Netherlands		Austria

LA21 was one of relative initial neglect, to be followed by more conscious attempts to adapt the LA21 idea to existing environmental and sustainable-development policies and activities. Though they did not – as with the 'pioneers' – demonstrate strong initial interest in promoting LA21 campaigns, there gradually emerged a more active and positive attitude to the idea. As for the 'late-comers', all three cases were only beginning to demonstrate an active national interest in LA21 towards the end of 1996.

The implications of the categorisation will be somewhat surprising for any reader familiar with variations in local-government policy for other areas (Lane and Ersson, 1987; Hudson, 1993; Judge, Stoker and Wolman, 1995; Lidström, 1996). For example, the Nordic countries, who in most respects are very similar in their political and administrative traditions, range here from Sweden, with its officially claimed very large number of LA21 initiatives as early as 1994, to Norway and Finland who do not make serious progress in the area before 1996. Similarly, countries with a reputedly well-established environmental policy can be found in all of the three categories: with the Netherlands and Sweden among the pioneers, Norway in between, and Germany considerably lagging behind. Finally, the UK and Ireland appear at the two extremes, despite geographical and linguistic proximity. In the UK, LA21 has been a relative success, while the Irish have barely begun to work with the idea, as is also the case in Austria.

It must be remembered, however, that the positioning of a particular country as a 'pioneer' in this classification refers only to its relative placement, that is, it as a pioneer only in comparison with the other examined countries. Being a 'pioneer' in LA21 implementation does not imply that the majority of municipalities in the country are actually involved in LA21 activity as outlined here. We simply do not have the necessary data to confirm *positive* compliance with the LA21 criteria. We must rely on a combination of self-reporting to the CSD and ICLEI together with our own overall assessments of the information provided by the country studies here. As pointed out above, there is reason to doubt whether, for example, all Swedish local authorities fulfill the LA21 criteria as outlined by both ICLEI and ourselves. There is, however, more than enough evidence to indicate that Sweden is *the* pioneer in this area, regardless of what appears to be an inflated reporting situation.[5] As a general conclusion, it can be stated that the pioneers have a larger share of municipalities embarked on specific LA21 activities as compared with the adaptors and late-comers, who are mostly involved in traditional environmental activities and, to some extent, 'sustainable-development' projects, with a much lower profile for Chapter 28 itself.

So how can these differences be explained? In this book, we have aimed primarily at giving a descriptive account of the national situations, and have not set the task of systematically comparing explanatory factors. For such an enterprise, a more developed analytical framework would be necessary, as well as a more standardised methodology for the research. We have been more modest. Our goal has been to lay a foundation for further conceptual and theoretical work, as well as to provide as much documentation of the existing situation as time and resources allowed. So as to derive as much as possible from the latter in the direction of realising the former, we will here attempt to summarise and systematise the results according to the categories outlined in the Introduction. We would hasten to remind the reader, however, that the country studies have only been guided by, not disciplined by, these categories. Much of the 'story' of national implementation lies in the particularities of each case, so that our attempts at systematisation must not be seen as a replacement for the country studies themselves, but merely as a supplement.

THE SEARCH FOR CROSS-NATIONAL PATTERNS

Environmental policy traditions and local-government autonomy: Baseline characteristics prior to UNCED

The baseline conditions for integrating environmental concerns at the local level of government (that is prior to Agenda 21) vary considerably among the countries. At least two factors which may influence the local capacity for implementing LA21 can be extracted from the case studies: first, the timing and establishment of a national environmental policy in general, and second, the degree of local autonomy for LA21 action in particular. One may hypothesise that an early and well established environmental policy should contribute to speeding up the implementation process for LA21, while a late and less established environmental policy would impede the process. This would be true to the extent that LA21 processes build largely on a widening of the traditional tasks for the environmental administration.

But it is also relevant to analyse the degree of local autonomy for LA21 action. The concept of local autonomy has been much discussed among political scientists. One must distinguish between local autonomy in general, and the specific autonomy that concerns a particular policy area, such as LA21. Both of these aspects are relevant, since the general autonomy sets the overall limits for municipal action. With regard to specific autonomy, Page and Goldsmith (1987: 158) have pointed out that the discretion of local government varies greatly from service to service. Two aspects of local autonomy are relevant: first, limitations at the local level with regard to social and economic factors (what Gurr and King (1987) call 'Type I autonomy'); and, second, central and local government relations ('Type II autonomy'). This distinction has also been referred to as vertical (central-local) autonomy, and horizontal (within the local level) autonomy (Hudson, 1993). Furthermore, the degree of LA21 autonomy is dependent on both the 'freedom of action' and the 'capacity for action' (Lundqvist, 1987). Whereas the freedom of action refers to the limits for political and legal autonomy, the capacity for action concerns the availability of resources, ability and competence. To speak of a high degree of local autonomy in policy-making, there should be a high score on both of these factors.

The comparison of local autonomy for LA21 action in the eight country-studies thus concerns a combination of several aspects that include both vertical and horizontal autonomy: (1) the general autonomy in central-local relations; (2) the specific autonomy with regard to the LA21 policy area in political and legal terms; and (3) the local capacity for action as measured by resources and competence. These are dimensions we will want to pursue in our future analyses, but already at this stage we are willing to venture an initial categorisation (Table 2).

The higher the autonomy, and the more recently established environmental policy tradition, would thus favour the development of LA21, whereas low autonomy, paired with late establishment of environmental policy, would impede the process. With the exception of the UK and Germany, it appears that this hypothesis applies to the present case-studies. The countries with high 'scores' on established environmental policy and local autonomy are indeed further ahead in their implementation of LA21 compared to those with lower 'scores', namely Ireland and Austria. However, Germany is lagging behind on LA21 despite its favourable conditions according to these two dimensions, and Finland cannot easily be fitted into the picture either. Furthermore, as already indicated, the UK example is rather surprising. There are clearly additional reasons for local authorities to engage (or not) in LA21 activities.

First, it should be noted that a 'local authority' means different things in the different countries. Germany and Austria are the only states among

Table 2 *Comparison of eight European countries with respect to the establishment of environmental policy and the degree of local-government autonomy in relation to LA2 1*

Municipal autonomy, especially in relation to LA2 1 tasks	Environmental policy tradition	
	Early establishment	*More recent establishment*
High	Sweden Norway Germany The Netherlands	Finland Austria
Low		United Kingdom Ireland

the eight that have a federal structure, which means that the regional (*Länder*) and municipal governments together exercise considerable influence and autonomy over affairs (Lane and Ersson, 1987: 207). Second, the countries vary considerably with regard to their number of municipalities. The largest figure is found in the two federalist states, with 16,121 local authorities for Germany and 2,353 for Austria. By comparison, the Netherlands has only 600 units; the United Kingdom 478; Finland 452; Norway 435; Sweden 288; and Ireland 34 with major environmental tasks and another 54 with limited tasks.[6]

By implication, the greater the number of local authorities subject to LA21 expectations, the more difficult it is to disseminate the relevant information and resources. Additionally, the variation in how local units interpret and respond to LA21 should surely increase proportional to the number of units. On the other hand, however, the dissemination of standard solutions and the diffusion of innovative ideas might imply a standardisation of policy even in those countries with large numbers of local authorities. Indeed, the nature of communication channels between local authorities and various organisations that are involved in LA21 is probably a more important factor than the number of municipalities to be reached. Moreover, the professional networks between LA21 administrators at the local level and between central and local levels are likely to play a crucial role in how the LA21 message becomes adopted.

In Germany, the local authorities have traditionally exerted rather great powers in tasks relating to LA21, but this situation has apparently changed recently with the merging of East and West Germany. Increased centralisation has occurred as a means for redistribution of welfare and as a response to the rapidly growing numbers of unemployed. The two countries in the bottom right category in Table 2, which combine a low degree of local autonomy with comparably weak environmental policies (or perhaps more accurately, late national responses to international environmental policy) are the UK and Ireland. As reported in the country studies, ecological modernisation processes occurred between the years 1987 and 1992 in the UK, and from 1990 in Ireland with its first Environmental Action Programme. Local government in Ireland is weak as to both power and resources, yet they are entrusted with tasks of environmental protection and planning. Environmental policy matters have, therefore, become highly politicised as a local democratic issue. In order to use the EU structural funds for implementation of local policy goals, local partnerships have been created which have become viewed as a threat to local democracy due to the feeble political power of local government.

In contrast, the Nordic countries have a long tradition of local government autonomy (in practice, though not constitutionally) which includes the right to levy local taxes and the provision of most basic welfare services. Since the mid 1980s, environmental policy tasks have been largely decentralised from national to local administration. There remain in place, however, a number of central-government support mechanisms which still serve to guide the local implementation of environmental policy. In Norway, for example, until very recently the local environmental officers have been paid from the national budget through earmarked funding, and in Sweden several national funds are available to subsidise local investment for sustainable-development projects and 'green jobs'. The Finnish environmental protection administration was established some years later than in Norway and Sweden, but has caught up in the late 1990's after a recession in the early 1990's affected the economy more strongly than its neighbours. The concept of sustainable development has also gradually come to penetrate various Nordic environmental and planning acts from around 1990, but, as the changes were largely instituted as environmental reforms, they have in general failed to stress the participatory, North-South, and more deep-going socio-economic dimensions of the Agenda 21 perspective.

The Netherlands is probably the most advanced country among the eight in having developed a comprehensive approach to environmental planning, which allows for target-group involvement and participatory methods. Their National Environmental Policy Plan from 1989 includes the notion of sustainable development and is often referred to as a 'blueprint for sustainable-development planning'. The municipalities were already experimenting with local democracy in their well-developed local environmental policy prior to UNCED. The Dutch local governments are, however, heavily dependent on national funding for carrying out environmental projects and for financing the local environmental inspectorates.

The antecedent role of national and local governments in UNCED

The most active countries in developing the Local Agenda 21 initiative within UNCED were Norway and Sweden together with the Netherlands and the UK. Hence, the preparations for implementing LA21 were already underway in these countries, particularly at the local level. In the Netherlands, there was a large NGO involvement in the UNCED preparations. In the UK, the Local Government Management Board (LGMB) was given the task by national government to promote LA21, and a Central and Local Government Environmental Forum was set up in 1991 to co-ordinate these efforts. From both Norway and Sweden, representatives from pioneer municipalities played a prominent role in promoting the LA21 idea within UNCED. Some Norwegian municipalities formed, for example, special commissions together with other partners from business, NGOs and labour unions, and, in Sweden, a special youth NGO network (q2000) was formed to prepare for UNCED and its implementation.

The Finnish government, however, was not as active as the other Nordic countries at the time of UNCED because of the economic depression that pushed environmental issues into the background. Similarly, the German Federal Government was little involved in supporting the LA21 idea, although it did play a major role in the work towards the Convention on Climate Change. Ireland and Austria had apparently relatively little input into the UNCED preparations for this area. Not surprisingly, those countries which were most interested in LA21 at the time of UNCED are also those which were most forceful in following up on LA21, with the very obvious (and unexpected) exception of Norway.

Reaction of national government to the LA21 idea

As pointed out most particularly in the Swedish and Dutch chapters, local initiatives for sustainable development are unlikely to succeed without the support of national policies. The strength of national government support for LA21 can thus be seen as a vital factor for influencing the success of local authorities in instigating and developing LA21 activity (though the UK is a clear exception here). Two questions might be used in this context to indicate how much interest national governments pay to LA21: First, whether some kind of a national committee has been established for the purpose of co-ordinating and spurring LA21 implementation; and second, whether special national funding has been allocated to this end. Table 3 portrays the eight cases along these dimensions.

The cross-classification clearly shows that the combination of both a national committee and national financial support is conducive to 'pioneer' status. The United Kingdom proves to be somewhat of an exception, however, as pioneer status has here been achieved mainly through other means. Admittedly, the Central and Local Government Environmental Forum, set up in 1992, played an important role in bringing local government representatives to the Rio Conference, and continued to work thereafter with LA21 implementation, but the key factor would seem to be the strong involvement from the Local Government Management Board supported by leading NGOs. (It must also be pointed out, that the situation in Great Britain was also apparently affected by the political situation itself, with both Labour and the Liberal Democrats taking an active part in LA21 for party-political and electoral reasons.)

The lack of national government support for LA21 in some countries does not necessarily mean that there are no means of assistance to relevant areas from central units of government. In addition to the UK situation, we have seen that, in Germany, the state government of North-Rhine/Westphalia supported a LA21 co-ordination agency in 1996, and, in Ireland, the Local Government Reform currently underway implies a strengthening of local community power for a more active and systematic implementation of LA21 than has thus far been the case. It has also been shown that the Norwegian Ministry of Environment has supplied funding to municipal environmental officers from 1992 and onwards, and that this *can be* interpreted as direct support for LA21 goals. More recently (1997), the Norwegian MoE has established an internal secretariat for more active follow-up of the LA21 initiative, and in Austria the Federal Ministry for Environment, Youth and Family Affairs has commissioned a research project to analyse the Agenda 21 process with the goal of encouraging LA21 activities in the future.

The national support for sustainable development initiatives in a more general sense (that is, not particularly emphasising LA21) displays a more coherent picture among the different countries, at least on the surface. In all of the eight countries, some form of national plan for sustainable development has been adopted, and various committees have been formed to co-ordinate and integrate policies between sectors, and to enhance collaboration between public and private organisations. Examples of such efforts are manifold in the preceding chapters, and do not have to be repeated here. We would again point out, however, that the notion of 'sustainable development' tends, in all countries, to be followed up primarily as traditional 'environmental policy', with few instances of deeper-going or more global policy integration. The German, Norwegian, Finnish and Swedish chapters are quite specific on this point, and several country reports show that the introduction of new participatory approaches as a basis for sustainable-development planning is particularly poorly developed.

Table 3 *Central government support for LA21 implementation*

National financial support is provided for LA21 initiatives?	National committee exists for LA21?	
	Yes	*No*
Yes	The Netherlands (from 1994) Sweden (from 1995)	Norway
No	United Kingdom (from 1992) Finland (from 1996)	Germany Ireland Austria

The level of national support for co-ordination and implementation of LA21 proves also to be important for the production and promulgation of information about Agenda 21. The Swedish and Dutch national authorities seem to have been the most active among the eight countries in producing and disseminating reports, handbooks, and 'best-practice' guides. In the United Kingdom, the initiative has again been taken largely by the umbrella associations for local-government authorities, but individual local councils have also been front-runners in disseminating information and guidelines. In Norway, on the other hand, it is particularly notable that neither the central government any other organisation, public or private, has yet managed to translate Agenda 21 into Norwegian.

Local-community networks and associations

In all three of the 'pioneer' countries, municipal networks have played an important role in co-ordinating LA21 efforts. In addition, such networks have been a major inspiration for starting up new activities. In the Netherlands, local 'platforms' for development co-operation and for Green Housekeeping are frequent at the municipal level, and collaboration with NGOs (including the Inter Church Peace Platform and other development aid organisations) has stimulated Dutch municipalities to work with the North-South and peace dimensions of LA21. After Rio, the Local Government Management Board in the UK launched the LA21 Initiative to promote implementation and help define sustainable development at the local level. Despite its limited resources, it has carried out a very energetic programme that includes monthly mailings to its member municipalities. Undisputedly, the relative LA21 success in the UK can largely be explained by this initiative. The Swedish Association of Local Authorities has also been very active in spreading information about LA21, and, in Norway, the association (KS) produced guidelines for local environmental activity where Local Agenda 21 was, for the first time, presented to municipal representatives.

In the Nordic countries, the Eco-Municipality Network dating from 1980 represents a similar approach to local environment-and-development policy as that expressed in LA21, long before these issues were on the international agenda. In both Finland, Norway and Sweden, there has been an interchange between this network and LA21 development in general. To date, ten Norwegian and 40 Swedish municipalities are members of the Eco-Municipality Network, while about half of the 20 Finnish eco-municipalities that existed in 1992 have now become active in LA21.

International networks which relate directly to LA21 include the Aalborg Charter and the Climate Alliance. Whereas the signatories of the Aalborg Charter seem to predominate among the Nordic group (especially in Finland), the Climate Alliance has been most influential in the Netherlands, Germany and Austria. In the latter two countries, the membership in the Alliance has indeed been referred to by the respective governments as an LA21 indicator, that is, they have reported efforts within the Climate Alliance as equivalent to LA21 status. Though this is probably stretching the ICLEI criteria, it is clear that the goals and prescriptions of the Aalborg Charter and Climate Alliance are in many ways similar to LA21. For example, participatory methods for developing renewable energy and reducing transport emissions are essential to local sustainable development and well in line with LA21.

In Germany, the focal point for LA21 co-ordination has been located within the established environmental organisation. The German Association of Cities has promoted LA21 by developing a guideline in 1995 and by urging its 6,400 member cities to implement it. Likewise, the Association of Finnish Local Authorities has established a Section for Sustainable Development in 1997 to co-ordinate municipal activities and recently launched a LA21 project involving 60 municipalities. The Norwegian Association for Local and Regional Authorities (KS) has been even more active in this respect, although LA21 was only officially put on the programme in the Spring of 1996. In a resolution by KS from its annual congress in 1992, it introduced the need to concentrate on reducing the total level of consumption in Norway – an appeal which is still very radical compared to most LA21 initiatives which seldom challenge the roots of high-consumption societies.

The Irish case differs from the other countries in that there are no significant local networks within Irish municipalities. Instead, the NGOs in Ireland, together with local businesses, are the most active in local sustainable-development work, as will be further discussed below. A general impression from the eight country-studies is that those countries with less developed LA21 processes are comparatively more engaged in other international networks connected to local sustainable development, whereas the pioneer countries in LA21 seem to have concentrated their efforts on national networking and to a somewhat lesser extent become involved in the international initiatives.

NGOs and the social partners

The role of NGOs in promoting LA21 appears to follow a similar pattern as the national municipal networking described above. In the pioneer countries, various NGOs have taken on the Agenda 21 message and formed partnerships with the associations for local authorities to spread the ideas and produce guidelines and collections of 'best practice'. The most active NGOs in the pioneer countries include WWF and Friends of the Earth in the UK; development-aid NGOs and the Inter-Church Peace Platform in the Netherlands; and the Swedish Society for the Conservation of Nature and q2000 in Sweden. However, in all these three countries, the NGO involvement in LA21 has been most significant at the national level, and much less so at the level of implementation within the municipalities themselves. Many of these NGOs concentrate their efforts on influencing national policy for sustainable development, while local initiatives tend to come from a range of other types of local organisations on a case-to-case basis.

The most varied and advanced participatory methods at the local level seems to be found in the United Kingdom, most probably because of the limited power and resources available to local authorities, making co-ordination and partnerships essential for achieving local change. The dominance of Thatcherism in the UK during the last decades has fostered a range of private solutions to traditional welfare-state tasks, a deeply penetrating change which seems to have inspired local communities to take actions for sustainable development in their own hands. In the Dutch and Swedish cases, with considerably greater resources at the local level of government, local authorities have the possibility of achieving more without having to liaise with NGOs or business and industry. Yet the Swedish and Dutch reports also show that LA21 processes at the local level strive to achieve greater involvement of citizens, local groups and business, and that this factor constitutes a vital difference between LA21 and more 'traditional' local environmental policy. Both in the Netherlands and Sweden, it seems, nonetheless, that it has been most difficult for local authorities to obtain close collaboration with local business as compared with, in particular, various educational organisations such as schools and day-care centres.

A tendency to leave business outside of the process is also apparent in the other countries (with the possible exception of Ireland). In Germany, local NGOs and churches are often partners in sustainable development initiatives, while representatives from business and industry are largely absent. The Finnish situation is somewhat exceptional in that the role of NGOs to date has been quite marginal, and co-operation between NGOs in LA21 matters has not focused on the municipal level. In Austria, international (European) networks have made the greatest impact in spurring local initiatives, while national NGOs have been relatively passive. In Norway, the role of NGOs and business is also of little significance to the LA21 process so far, though there has been a growing active involvement on the part of the highly influential 'Environmental Home Guard' (*Miljøheimevernet*). In general, the Norwegian case reveals a continued proclivity for administrative approaches, with very few initiatives for new forms of public involvement in overall municipal environmental policy and planning.

Finally, the Irish case shows that the role of the EU structural funds appears to have played a significant role in social innovation. In particular, it has provided a precedent for the participative 'bottom-up' ideal embedded in LA21. New partnerships have been formed at the local level which, in practice, act as both complements and competitors to local government. The problem, as pointed out in the Irish chapter, is that these entities lack the fundamental legitimacy and accountability that would allow for further acceptance within the Irish society. As a result, these partnerships are, for the most part, seen as a threat rather than as a complement to local democracy. Although this situation is particularly expressed in the Irish case, with its extremely weak local-government autonomy, it might become a growing political issue also in the other countries if and when the power and influence of local partnerships takes hold.

Irish NGOs have been little active in promoting LA21 thus far, but have nonetheless contributed to spreading ideas about sustainable development. At the national level, the Network of Irish Environment and Development Organisations was formed already at the time of Rio, and An Taisce (the National Trust for Ireland) has brought together local authorities, business, environmental organisations and academics to discuss strategies for sustainable development from 1994 on. With the upcoming local government reform in Ireland, the role of partnerships and NGO involvement may well become a significant force for change in the future.

POLITICAL IMPACT AND FUTURE PROSPECTS

Needless to say, the greatest apparent impact of LA21 is found among the 'pioneers' (Sweden, UK and the Netherlands), where relatively large numbers of local authorities have embarked on the process of developing their own LA21 plans. Finland and Norway have more recently become engaged in the adaptation processes mentioned, and with the relatively strong position of local authorities in these countries, there is reason to believe that they will soon catch up to the front-runners. Also the three 'late-comers' (Germany, Ireland and Austria) report a growing interest in LA21. There is, according to the eight country-studies contained in this book, apparently a current momentum for further LA21 development in the near future.

It remains to be seen, however, to what extent the present interest in LA21 is a mere reflection of the five-year assessment coming up in June 1997. Naturally, the approach of the special session of the General Assembly has spurred governments to evaluate their progress so far, and heighten initiatives vis à vis Agenda 21 in most areas. In both Norway and Finland, the late impetus for national efforts of this kind shows that the central governments at least have now better understood that LA21 implies a very different approach from more traditional local environmental policy formulation and implementation. Moreover, as pointed out above, it is difficult to assess just where the line should be drawn as to the symbolic effect of *calling existing activities 'Local Agenda 21'* and documenting *actual compliance* with the relatively strong criteria laid down by ICLEI. Indeed, the actual content of LA21 processes varies immensely both among countries and within them. While a rather small number of municipalities in the 'pioneer' countries can be regarded as setting the pace for innovative LA21 initiatives, the majority most probably have not initiated activities which aim towards deep-seated change of production and consumption patterns.

In three of the countries, the years 1997-98 loom as particularly decisive in terms of future prospectives for LA21. In Ireland, the Local Government Reform coming up in 1998 will undoubtedly have an impact on the politics of local democracy; in Norway, the earmarking of national funding for municipal environmental officers has already ceased, leaving the future status of the reform uncertain; and, in the Netherlands, the Government will apparently cut back the special VOGM support available for LA21 in 1998. But there are also upcoming changes in the other two 'pioneer' countries which may slow down LA21 considerably and diminish the distance to the 'adaptors' and 'late-comers'. The Swedish Social Democrats are currently facing record low support in the opinion polls, and, with an election scheduled for 1998, the level of public spending for environmental concerns can become a major issue. And in the UK, with Labour now firmly in control of central government, there may be less interest in pursuing Agenda 21 at the local level.

At the same time, however, there are clearly a number of front-running municipalities in the pioneer countries which may try to pursue global sustainable-development goals which are more far-reaching than those of their national governments. Prospects here point in two possible directions: either, it will put pressure on national authorities to increase their efforts towards the realisation of such goals and to further enhance the implementation of the UNCED agreements; or it will create irresolvable conflicts between competing policy goals at the national and local levels of government. In the latter case, local authorities might be faced with having to revise downwards their ambitions, which would in turn threaten the political legitimacy of LA21 and diminish the potential of future development towards local sustainability strategies.

As a final word at this stage of the research process, we would like to conclude by identifying what we believe to be the most significant factors affecting the implementation of Local Agenda 21. Each of these factors appears to have had positive effects in one or more of our countries, and any combination of factors should have a cumulative positive effect.

- A previous involvement on the part of representatives of local authorities in the UNCED process.
- An active positive attitude on the part of responsible central-government officials to the LA21 idea.
- Central-government initiatives and campaigns to disseminate information on Local Agenda 21.
- The availability of central-government financial resources to subsidise LA21 initiatives.
- Enough local-government autonomy to render the LA21 idea interesting and possible.
- Membership in cross-national environment-and-development alliances, charters, etc.
- A previous history of international 'solidarity' orientations and activities at the local level.
- Previous municipal involvement in environmental and sustainable-development pilot projects.
- Previous experience with 'co-operative management regimes' (among social partners and stakeholders).
- Active individual 'firebrands' for LA21 at the local level.
- Perceived possibilities for coupling LA21 with the creation of new jobs
- Perceived conditions of 'threat' to local environment-and-development conditions from external sources.

As for negative factors, we choose to be more circumspect since it is always more difficult to explain why a phenomenon *doesn't* exist, than it is to identify the positive correlates of actual events. On the one hand, we can be very general and say that an absence of any of the factors mentioned above obviously seems to hinder a more active and effective implementation of Chapter 28. For practitioners, this in itself should provide an adequate empirical basis for promoting LA21 activity.

From the point of view of the transition from descriptive evaluation to explanation, however, we would like to conclude with a more focused summary perspective. Our reading of the eight country-studies indicates a relatively simplistic, but integrated, four-point framework for a better understanding of how and why the call for LA21 activity has, or has not, been heeded in Northern Europe. For each of these points, we identify what we believe to be key questions and dimensions for future model-building and analysis.

Interpretation of the implementation task

• A question of 'defining the situation', with a need for documenting both the 'history of meaning' related to the task and the current power structure for implementation. Which national 'agent' has responsibility for bringing the particular aspect of the global program 'home'? How is the particular task integrated into the overall national strategy for following up and implementing the global program for sustainable development, and what is the relationship between the responsible agent and the broader constellation of forces affecting policy priorities and the distribution of implementation resources?

Domains and levels of implementation responsibility

• How is the implementation task viewed with respect to central-local government? What is the current mix of constitutional authority, policy responsibility, and resource allocations among national, regional and local authorities? Is the 'facilitator' role of national authorities accepted and acted upon, and how are non-governmental organisations – particularly umbrella organisations for local and regional authorities – integrated into the implementation process?

The availability of resources and the inertia of reforms

- Are resources – in the form of information, guidelines and earmarked funding – made available for specific acts of implementation directed towards change? What is the current economic and fiscal situation of local communities, and what is the status of existing local environmental policy responsibility. Is there compatibility between the general characteristics of the LA21 idea and existing official environmental policy, or does the history, priorities and institutionalisation of current policy create barriers against new initiatives?

Mobilisation of local citizens and stakeholders

- To what degree have individual citizens and representatives of the major groups previously been involved in environment-and-development activities at the local level? Are there legal provisions in place for involving 'affected parties' in planning and implementation, and have NGOs (including business and labour) been active or passive in the specific policy area? How do local politicians and personnel within the responsible local administration view the prospect of increased popular involvement: As a welcome and constructive supplement – or as a threat to established positions and hard-won sectoral achievements?

NOTES

1 Leading representative examples here are the International Institute for Sustainable Development (IISD) in Canada , the Wuppertal Institute in Germany, the World Bank, the World Health Organisation, the New Economics Foundation in London and the consultative services of Maureen Hart in the United States. A comprehensive program for cataloging indicator projects is underway at the International Institute for Sustainable Development (IISD) in Winnipeg, Canada. Under the direction of Peter Hardi and Laszlo Pinter, the program has already published the most thorough overview of sustainable-development indicator-projects available (IISD, 1995), and the data-bank is under continual renewal and up-dating. Internet-users should visit: http://iisd1.iisd.ca/.

2 Developments on indicator policy and reporting within the CSD system can be monitored at the 'Delegate's work station' of the DPCSD: http://www.un.org/dpcsd/index.html. An overview of SCOPE activities on indicators is available in SCOPE (1995).

3   The compilation of 'methodology sheets' is available at the UN gopher site (gopher://gohper.un.org:70/00/ esc/cn17/1996-97/indicators), or as a hard-copy publication from the DPCSD.
4   The results of the survey, with background and methodology, are available at the ICLEI website: http://www.iclei.org/la21/la21rep.htm. It should be pointed out that the drafts of the country studies in the present report were completed prior to the availability of the ICLEI survey.
5   One simple indication of this is the excellent official web site for Agenda 21 activities. In addition to comprehensive overviews of best-cases and the ability to play the game 'Agent 21', the site now lists 288 names and addresses of 'Local Agenda 21 co-ordinators'. This means, of course, a co-ordinator for every muncipality in Sweden. Visit: http://www.agenda21.se/Kommunerna/index.htm.
6   The figures do not include regional and/or county units.

REFERENCES

Goldsmith, Michael (1995) 'Autonomy and City Limits', In D. Judge, G. Stoker and H. Wolman (eds) *Theories of Urban Politics*, London: Sage Publications.
Gurr, T. and T. King (1987) *The State and the City*, Chicago: Chicago University Press.
Hudson, Christine (1993) *Against All Odds: Local Economic Development Policies and Local Government Autonomy in Sweden and Britain*, Umeå: Department of Political Science, Umeå University.
ICLEI (International Council for Local Environmental Initiatives) (1996) *Local Agenda 21 Survey: A Study of Responses by Local Authorities and Their National and Intenational Associations to Agenda 21*, Toronto: ICLEI Web Site (http://www.iclei.org).
IISD (International Institute for Sustainable Development) (1995) *Performance Measurement for Sustainable Development: A Compendium of Experts, Initiatives and Publications*, (Compiled by Laszlo Pinter, Peter Hardi and Lisa McRorie-Harvey) Winnipeg, Manitoba: IISD.
Judge, D., Stoker, G. & Wolman, H. (eds.) (1995) *Theories of Urban Politics*, London: Sage Publications.
Lafferty, William M. and J. Meadowcroft (1996) 'Implementing Sustainable Development in High-Consumption Societies.' A Comparative Assessment of National Strategies and Institutions, Paper presented to the Oxford Workshop of the COMPSUS Research Network, Mansfield College, Oxford, September 5–8, 1996.
Lane, Jan-Erik and Svante O. Ersson (1987) *Politics and Society in Western Europe*, London: Sage.
Lidström, Anders (1996) *Kommunsystem i Europa* ('Municipal Systems in Europe') Stockholm: Norstedts Juridik AB.
Lundquist, Lennart (1987) *Implementation Steering. An Actor-Structure Approach*, Lund: Studentlitteratur.

Page, E. C. and M. J. Goldsmith (eds) (1987) *Central and Local Government Relations*, London: Sage Publications.

SCOPE (Scientific Committee on Problems of the Environment) (1995) *Scientific Workshop on Indicators of Sustainable Development*, Wuppertal, Germany, November 15–17, 1995. Edited by Suzanne Billharz and Bedrich Modan, Prague: Charles University Environement Center.

Appendix 1:

Agenda 21, Chapter 28:
Local Authorities Initiatives in Support of Agenda 21

PROGRAMME AREA

Basis for action

28.1. Because so many of the problems and solutions being addressed by Agenda 21 have their roots in local activities, the participation and cooperation of local authorities will be a determining factor in fulfilling its objectives. Local authorities construct, operate and maintain economic, social and environmental infrastructure, oversee planning processes, establish local environmental policies and regulations, and assist in implementing national and subnational environmental policies. As the level of governance closest to the people, they play a vital role in educating, mobilizing and responding to the public to promote sustainable development.

OBJECTIVES

28.2. The following objectives are proposed for this programme area:

(a) By 1996, most local authorities in each country should have undertaken a consultative process with their populations and achieved a consensus on 'a Local Agenda 21' for the community;

(b) By 1993, the international community should have initiated a consultative process aimed at increasing cooperation between local authorities;

(c) By 1994, representatives of associations of cities and other local authorities should have increased levels of cooperation and coordination with the goal of enhancing the exchange of information and experience among local authorities;

(d) All local authorities in each country should be encouraged to implement and monitor programmes which aim at ensuring that women and youth are represented in decision-making, planning and implementation processes.

ACTIVITIES

28.3. Each local authority should enter into a dialogue with its citizens, local organizations and private enterprises and adopt 'a Local Agenda 21'. Through consultation and consensus-building, local authorities would learn from citizens and from local, civic, community, business and industrial organizations and acquire the information needed for formulating the best strategies. The process of consultation would increase household awareness of sustainable development issues. Local authority programmes, policies, laws and regulations to achieve Agenda 21 objectives would be assessed and modified, based on local programmes adopted. Strategies could also be used in supporting proposals for local, national, regional and international funding.

28.4. Partnerships should be fostered among relevant organs and organizations such as UNDP, the United Nations Centre for Human Settlements (Habitat) and UNEP, the World Bank, regional banks, the International Union of Local Authorities, the World Association of the Major Metropolises, Summit of Great Cities of the World, the United Towns Organization and other relevant partners, with a view to mobilizing increased international support for local authority programmes. An important goal would be to support, extend and improve existing institutions working in the field of local authority capacity-building and local environment management. For this purpose:

(a) Habitat and other relevant organs and organizations of the United Nations system are called upon to strengthen services in collecting information on strategies of local authorities, in particular for those that need international support;

(b) Periodic consultations involving both international partners and developing countries could review strategies and consider how such international support could best be mobilized. Such a sectoral consultation would complement concurrent country-focused consultations, such as those taking place in consultative groups and round tables.

28.5. Representatives of associations of local authorities are encouraged to establish processes to increase the exchange of information, experience and mutual technical assistance among local authorities.

MEANS OF IMPLEMENTATION

(a) Financing and cost evaluation

28.6. It is recommended that all parties reassess funding needs in this area. The UNCED Secretariat has estimated the average total annual cost (1993-2000) for strengthening international secretariat services for implementing the activities in this chapter to be about $1 million on grant or concessional terms. These are indicative and order of magnitude estimates only and have not been reviewed by governments.

(b) Human resource development and capacity-building

28.7. This programme should facilitate the capacity-building and training activities already contained in other chapters of Agenda 21.

Source: United Nations (1992), Report of the United Nations Conference on Environment and Development, Rio de Janeiro, 3-14 June 1992, Vol. I: Resolutions Adopted by the Conference. New York: United Nations. (As later edited by the UNCED/CSD Secretariat.)

Appendix 2:

Country Reports on Chapter 28 of Agenda 21,
Submitted to DPCSD/'Earth Summit +5': Special
Session of the United Nations General Assembly,
New York, June 23–27 1997

AUSTRIA:

Three Austrian cities (Vienna, Graz, Linz) signed the Charter of Ålborg to draw up a Local Agenda 21, Vienna has also signed the Charta of the European Regions for the Environment (Valencia).

The Government supports Local Agenda 21 initiatives.

In accordance with the principle of federalism, as laid down in the Austrian Constitution, municipal and local authorities play an essential role in public administration and policy formulation in Austria. Many local authorities have entered into partnerships with local authorities of other Austrian provinces or even beyond national borders. The increasing number of partnerships with local authorities of Hungary and the involvement of Austrian territorial administrative bodies in the field of climate control are particularly noteworthy.

Some 101 municipalities and communities as well as eight Austrian Laender together with municipalities from the neighbouring countries have formed a 'Climate Alliance'. They have committed themselves to reducing their carbon dioxide emissions by the year 2010 through concrete measures in the field of traffic, energy, procurement etc. and to supporting their partners in the Amazon region in the active preservation of rainforests.

Initiatives taken by the Provinces and aimed at the rehabilitation and revival of rural communities are of special importance. The village renewal strategies focus on the social, economic and cultural revival of village life.

The Federal Laender, Federation of Austrian Towns and Federation of Austrian municipalities are members of the Austrian UNCED Commission.

FINLAND:

There are at least 88 Local Agendas 21. They involve 50% of population. Government supports Local Agenda 21 initiatives.

The Association of Finnish Local Authorities started a pilot project, the Municipal Project for Sustainable Development, in 1992. The project ran through 1993, and although concrete changes in municipalities were minor, the project significantly prepared municipalities to develop Local Agenda 21 programmes.

The Association of Finnish Local Authorities has promoted the implementation of the objectives of Agenda 21, and increased awareness and responsibility on sustainable development among office-holders by defining sustainable development in municipalities, organizing training courses, publishing articles, and creating tools for the promotion of sustainable development.

According to the mapping of the Association of Finnish Local Authorities, there were 41 municipalities working on Local Agendas 21 in autumn 1995. Although these municipalities comprised less than 10% of Finland's municipalities, some 38% of the Finnish population lived in them. In autumn 1996, the number of municipalities preparing Local Agendas 21 had increased to 88. Half of the Finnish population lives in these municipalities. Almost all larger municipalities are preparing them. Only about 10% of municipalities with a population of 2,000-6,000 are involved, but, among the smalles towns (fewer than 2,000 people), nearly 25% are working on Local Agendas 21.

Many municipalities have also actively participated in international cooperation to promote sustainable development in municipalities. By signing the so called Ålborg document, 22 municipalities have joined in the Sustainable Cities in Europe campaign.

In the near future, the Association of Finnish Local Authorities will support the participating municipalities by publishing a Local Agenda 21 guidebook, by helping them in developing local agenda programmes, by organizing a conference on climate change issues for the senior management of municipalities, and by arranging other seminars together with provincinal associations and regional environment centres.

GERMANY:

There are at least 300 Local Agendas 21. They involve 25% of population and 90% involve representation of women and/or youth. All local authorities in Germany (18,000) work for actions for 'Sustainable Development'.

The Government supports Local Agenda 21 initiatives.

The Association of German Cities and Towns (Deutscher Städtetag – DSt) carried out an action rogramme on Local Agenda 21. The DSt has produced a guideline for all German cities and towns to implement a 'Local Agenda 21'. Over 90% of the local authorities deal with the task 'sustainable development' in their areas.

IRELAND:

The Government supports Local Agenda 21 initiatives.

In Ireland, the local authorities are empowered by the Local Government Act, 1991. It was recommended that the National Sustainable Development Strategy for 1997 should be accompanied by a complementary strategy for the local levels. The strategy should involve the whole community, its local elected members, and other community and representative groups.

Given the structure of governance in Ireland, the pivotal role for the purposes of Local Agenda 21 should be at county and borough level. Guidelines were issued by the Department of the Environment in mid-1995 to assist local authorities in developing Local Agendas 21.

THE NETHERLANDS:

There are at least 140 Local Agenda 21s.

Government support of Local Agenda 21 initiatives: No information
Brief comments on this chapter (maximum 100 words) (please, do not exceed this page): No information

NORWAY:

The Government supports local agenda 21 initiatives.

Local Agenda 21 in Norway is based on and associated with the 'Reform of Environment Protection in the Municipalities' project, abbreviated to the 'MIK-reform'. The project was initiated in 1988, and from

1997 it will be an integral part of the local municipality system. The MIK-reform is based on holistic and long-term planning and policy at municipality level. The Ministry of Environment for its part runs different LA21 related programmes which will provide important experiences in the implementation of LA21 in Norway. In addition there are other initiatives from 'The Norwegian Network of Health-and Environmental Municipalities', FRISAM (The Norwegian Centre for Voluntary Work), The programme for Eco-Municipalities and other organizations. The experience and results of these programmes and projects will be used as a foundation for the further development of the MIK-reform into LA21 in Norway. All the Norwegian municipalities have implemented the MIK-reform, regarded as the first phase of Local Agenda 21.

The Government plans to support LA21 initiatives in 1997. The Ministry of Environment is working out a strategy on how to implement LA21 in Norway, based on the above mentioned reform, projects and programmes, and in close co-operation with the Confederation of Norwegian Business and Industry (NHO), the National Labour Organisation (LO), the Norwegian Association of Local and Regional Authorities (KS) and other relevant organizations.

The MIK-reform can be seen as the first generation of LA21. In addition to the traditional environmental problems, the following aspects will be emphasized in the recently initiated phase two of the Local Agenda 21 work:

1. Local participation in both planning and action programmes.
2. The global aspect in LA21 will have to be strengthened and developed further and integrated into the processes of local planning.
3. The social and economical aspects of Agenda 21.

Some municipalities, counties and NGOs have already started LA21 processes, often in combination with or based on other related projects and programmes. The cities of Fredrikstad and Bergen have started LA21 processes and made resolutions about making a LA21 programme. The two municipalities Sund and Giske are implementing and monitoring LA21 programmes. At the county level, Akershus county has among others introduced the term 'Regional Agenda 21' and is working on the implementation of LA21 at the regional level. We estimate that 60-70 municipalities and 4-5 counties are working with the LA21-concept today.

SWEDEN:

The Government supports local agenda 21 initiatives.

Sweden's 288 local authorities play a very important role in environmental protection work and in the work towards longterm sustainable development. Each municipal governement must see to it that industry, traffic, waste management and energy use take health and environmental consideration in account. Their environment and public health committees as well as their building committees bear the the main responsibility for local environmental matters.

The Environmental Protection Agency, in cooperation with the National Board of Housing, Building and Planning, the Swedish Association of Local Authorities and representatives of the country administrations, among others, recently (1996) embarked on an evaluation of work by the county administrations on their environmental strategies.

All Swedish local authorities have begun work on developing and implementing Local Agenda 21 initiatives. About half of the local authorities have Agenda 21 coordinators, and are organizing seminars, courses and practical counselling activities for the general public. The local authorities are also working with businesses and NGOs, as well as with various projects such as public awareness campaigns, environmental audits and green accounting. Main issues have so far concentrated on waste management, water and sewage treatment and consumption. Traffic, energy, nature conservation, construction and toxic chemicals are also beeing adressed. 2/3 of the local authorities have environmental criterias for municipal purchasing. 90 percent of the local authorities have in one way or another went in for information to the public, 40 percent have given information designed for women and youth.

Sweden has allocated approx. US$ 1.5 million to support Local Agenda 21 activities through the Environmental Protection Agency in the form of grants to local authorities and NGOs.

UNITED KINGDOM:

Country report not submitted to CSD at time of publication.

Source: 'Earth Summit +5' web site: http://www.un.org/dpcsd/earthsummit/weuro-cp.htm.

Appendix 3:

The Ballagio Principles:
Guidelines for Practical Assessment of Progress
Toward Sustainable Development

BACKGROUND

In 1987, the World Commission on Environment and Development (Brundtland Commission) called for the development of new ways to measure and assess progress toward sustainable development. This call has been subsequently echoed in Agenda 21 of the 1992 Earth Summit and through activities that range from local to global in scale. In response, significant efforts to assess performance have been made by corporations, non-government organizations, academics, communities, nations, and international organizations.

WHO DEVELOPED THE PRINCIPLES?

In November 1996, an international group of measurement practitioners and researchers from five continents came together at the Rockefeller Foundation's Study and Conference Center in Bellagio, Italy to review progress to date and to synthesize insights from practical ongoing efforts. The attached principles resulted and were unanimously endorsed.

WHAT IS THEIR USE AND WHO ARE THE USERS?

These principles serve as guidelines for the whole of the assessment process including the choice and design of indicators, their interpretation and communication of the result. They are interrelated and should be applied as a complete set. They are intended for use in starting and improving assessment activities of community groups, non-government organizations, corporations, national governments, and international institutions.

OVERVIEW

These principles deal with four aspects of assessing progress toward sustainable development. Principle 1 deals with the starting point of any assessment – establishing a vision of sustainable development and clear goals that provide a practical definition of that vision in terms that are meaningful for the decision-making unit in question. Principles 2 through 5 deal with the content of any assessment and the need to merge a sense of the overall system with a practical focus on current priority issues. Principles 6 through 8 deal with key issues of the process of assessment, while Principles 9 and 10 deal with the necessity for establishing a continuing capacity for assessment.

1. Guiding Vision and Goals

Assessment of progress toward sustainable development should be guided by a clear vision of sustainable development and goals that define that vision.

2. Holistic Perspective

Assessment of progress toward sustainable development should:

- include review of the whole system as well as its parts
- consider the well-being of social, ecological, and economic subsystems, their state as well as the direction and rate of change of that state, of their component parts, and the interaction between parts
- consider both positive and negative consequences of human activity, in a way that reflects the costs and benefits for human and ecological systems, in monetary and non-monetary terms

3. Essential Elements

Assessment of progress toward sustainable development should:

- consider equity and disparity within the current population and between present and future generations, dealing with such concerns as resource use, over-consumption and poverty, human rights, and access to services, as appropriate
- consider the ecological conditions on which life depends
- consider economic development and other, non-market activities that contribute to human/social well-being

4. Adequate Scope

Assessment of progress toward sustainable development should:

- adopt a time horizon long enough to capture both human and ecosystem time scales thus responding to needs of future generations as well as those current to short term decision-making
- define the space of study large enough to include not only local but also long distance impacts on people and ecosystems
- build on historic and current conditions to anticipate future conditions – where we want to go, where we could go

5. Practical Focus

Assessment of progress toward sustainable development should be based on:

- an explicit set of categories or an organizing framework that links vision and goals to indicators and assessment criteria
- a limited number of key issues for analysis
- a limited number of indicators or indicator combinations to provide a clearer signal of progress
- standardizing measurement wherever possible to permit comparison
- comparing indicator values to targets, reference values, ranges, thresholds, or direction of trends, as appropriate

6. Openness

Assessment of progress toward sustainable development should:

- make the methods and data that are used accessible to all
- make explicit all judgments, assumptions, and uncertainties in data and interpretations

7. Effective Communication

Assessment of progress toward sustainable development should:

- be designed to address the needs of the audience and set of users
- draw from indicators and other tools that are stimulating and serve to engage decision-makers
- aim, from the outset, for simplicity in structure and use of clear and plain language

8. Broad Participation

Assessment of progress toward sustainable development should:

- obtain broad representation of key grass-roots, professional, technical and social groups , including youth, women, and indigenous people – to ensure recognition of diverse and changing values
- ensure the participation of decision-makers to secure a firm link to adopted policies and resulting action

9. Ongoing Assessment

Assessment of progress toward sustainable development should:

- develop a capacity for repeated measurement to determine trends
- be iterative, adaptive, and responsive to change and uncertainty because systems are complex and change frequently
- adjust goals, frameworks, and indicators as new insights are gained
- promote development of collective learning and feedback to decision-making

10. Institutional Capacity

Continuity of assessing progress toward sustainable development should be assured by:

- clearly assigning responsibility and providing ongoing support in the decision-making process
- providing institutional capacity for data collection, maintenance, and documentation
- supporting development of local assessment capacity

Source: International Institute for Sustainable Development (IISD), Winnepeg, Manitoba, Canada. Web site: http://iisd1.iisd.ca/measure/bellagio1.htm.

Index

Page numbers in **bold** refer to boxes, tables and figures